PLAYS FOR TODAY
WITH CSEC® STUDY GUIDE
Ti-Jean and His Brothers
An Echo in the Bone
Man Better Man

Derek Walcott
Dennis Scott
Errol Hill

CSEC® STUDY GUIDE FOR *TI-JEAN AND HIS BROTHERS* BY
Kenneth Jaikaransingh

HODDER
EDUCATION
AN HACHETTE UK COMPANY

Hachette UK's policy is to use papers that are natural, renewable and recyclable products and made from wood grown in sustainable forests. The logging and manufacturing processes are expected to conform to the environmental regulations of the country of origin.

Orders: please contact Bookpoint Ltd, 130 Park Drive, Milton Park, Abingdon, Oxon OX14 4SE. Telephone: (44) 01235 827720. Fax: (44) 01235 400454. Email education@bookpoint.co.uk.Lines are open from 9 a.m. to 5 p.m., Monday to Saturday, with a 24-hour message answering service. You can also order through our website: www.hoddereducation.com

Ti-Jean and His Brothers © Derek Walcott 1970

An Echo in the Bone © Dennis Scott 1985

Man Better Man © Errol Hill 1985

Study Guide © Hodder & Stoughton Ltd 2017

First published in 1985 by Pearson Education Limited
This edition published in 2017 by Hodder Education,
An Hachette UK Company
Carmelite House
50 Victoria Embankment
London EC4Y 0DZ

www.hoddereducation.com

Impression number   10 9 8 7 6 5 4 3 2 1

Year   2021 2020 2019 2018 2017

Cover artwork © Tony Randell

Typeset in India by Aptara Inc.

Printed in Great Britain by CPI Group (UK) Ltd, Croydon, CR0 4YY

ISBN 978 1510 414 303

A catalogue record for this title is available from the British Library.

Contents

Introduction

The three plays included in this volume have several qualities in common. Not only are the authors all West Indian; the plays themselves emerge from the substratum of Afro-Caribbean life which is reflected in their mythos, their pulse, their speech and song. Although they were written at different times in the recent past by authors hailing from Trinidad, Jamaica and St Lucia, all three dramas deal with the supernatural, are essentially about the folk experience, and speak with the rhythms of vernacular idiom. The individual playwrights may have different ends in view and may employ varying dramatic means to reach those ends, but the source of their inspiration is the uniquely Caribbean experience that runs like a subterranean stream through the method and meaning of all three plays.

On the surface, Errol Hill's *Man Better Man* is a comedic folk story about stick-fighters, their courage, desires and fears, set in a colourful carnivalesque environment. These once socially despised *batoniers* are the legendary heroes of folk history. At a time when public freedom, made manifest in the annual carnival celebration, was in danger of being suppressed, the stick-fighters were in the vanguard of the struggle to preserve the festival intact. Thus when Hill opens his play with a Prologue that calls on the old warriors to 'come out in the road' and do battle, he is invoking the spirits of ancestral guardians to preside at the performance of his play and reminding audiences of the recurrent need to protect hardwon freedoms.

Dennis Scott's *An Echo in the Bone* shatters sequential time in a series of dreamlike episodes. Characters effortlessly adopt other personas as racial memory is evoked to flash sequences of black slavery, peonage, and attendant evils before our eyes. Yet the entire action is subsumed in a single evening's performance of the traditional Nine-Night Ceremony which is held to honour the spirit of a departed loved one. By re-enacting, with the aid of ritual possession, the central events that led to the murder of a white estate owner by a black peasant farmer who then drowns in a river while attempting to escape, understanding is shared and atonement made.

In *Ti-Jean and His Brothers*, playwright Derek Walcott draws on St Lucian folklore for his story of a poor mother and her three sons who dwell on the edge of a forest. But this forest is magical; it is inhabited by creatures that talk and by the devil and his minions, among them an aborted infant who wishes to be born so that he may taste life. The devil takes other forms. At one time he is Papa Bois, the Old Man of the Forest but wearing now a forked tail, and at another he is the white Planter whose principal aim in life is to enslave the minds and spirits of his black workers. Once again we are in the realm of fantasy where the actual and the miraculous collide and where man is thrown back on his own resourcefulness for self-preservation.

There are similar resonances, too, in the structure of the plays, although this similarity may not be immediately apparent to the casual reader. At one level, *Man Better Man* and *Ti-Jean* both follow a linear pattern of plot development while *An Echo in the Bone* is layered with swiftly moving temporal changes, back and forth between present and past. More important is the fact that each author seems to be consciously seeking a format that will permit him to encompass the expressive elements that typify life as he has experienced it in the Caribbean. Oratorical speech, chant, song, choruses, drumming, music and dancing, and the underlying tensions that inhabit relations between peoples of different racial ancestry are woven into the fabric of the plays.

For his milieu, Hill takes the giddy atmosphere of carnival, with its wild abandon of caution and propriety, in order to celebrate the exploits of the battling troubadours. Likewise, he adopts the spicy rhymed language of the calypsonian for his dialogue, thus easing the transition from speech to song. Walcott, a renowned poet and weaver of words, takes the versatile Anancy storyteller for his model and unfolds his folktale with the careful formality of a practised craftsman. Like the traditional spinner of stories, he too can speak in many tongues using choral speech, singing and dancing to enhance his presentation. As noted above, the format of Scott's play is patterned on a death ritual during which the past is made manifest through communal submission to the power that resides in drum, word, song and gesture. The search for a West Indian theatrical idiom is then implicit in the plays presented here.

Nor do the authors mine Caribbean lore merely for the sake of enriching their art. The plays may summon the past but they are not fixed in distant time. Each in its own way carries a message of urgency for Caribbean peoples and, by extension, to all those who must shed the burden of past oppression and take command of their lives in the present. The message is one of courage, endurance and self-reliance, with due reverence for those who went before, in facing up to the challenging times of today's world.

Ti -Jean and His Brothers
The author

Derek Walcott published his first collection of *25 Poems* when he was nineteen years old and his first full-length play, *Henri Christophe*, a drama on the Haitian revolutionary leader, a year later. Walcott has to his credit over a dozen books of poetry and his verse was published regularly in the leading literary journals on both sides of the Atlantic. He also wrote some three dozen plays, fifteen of which have appeared in print.

Walcott was born on the West Indian island of St Lucia and attended the West Indies University of Jamaica where he gained a degree in English and a diploma in Education. Before entering the university, he had already produced several of his short plays in St Lucia and he continued to write and stage his plays while at college. Upon graduation he taught in school for some years until 1957 when he was commissioned to write an epic drama to mark the inauguration of the West Indies Federation in Trinidad. From this time on, Walcott devoted himself primarily to writing and play directing. In addition to his creative writing, he was a feature writer and critic for newspapers in Jamaica and Trinidad.

In 1958 Walcott moved to Trinidad and the following year, in order to produce his plays, he formed the Trinidad Theatre Workshop company which he directed for two decades. He began touring with this company in 1967 and visited several Caribbean lands, the United States and Canada. His plays have also been produced professionally in North America and in Britain.

Walcott received numerous honours for his writing, among them being the Guinness Award for Poetry, the Heinemann Award for Verse, the Royal Society of Literature Award, the Cholmondeley Award, and an Honorary Doctor of Letters Degree from the University of the West Indies. He was the recipient of an Obie Award for his play, *Dream on Monkey Mountain*, which was presented by the Negro Ensemble Company in New York in 1971. In 1981 the prestigious 'genius-award' was bestowed on him by the MacArthur Foundation which amounted to a grant of $250,000 with no stipulations attached. He held the position of Visiting Professor of Poetry and Theatre at Boston University in Massachusetts, USA for over two decades, and was scholar-in-residence at the University of Alberta and Professor of Poetry at the University of Essex.

Derek Walcott died in March 2017.

The play

Derek Walcott, premier Caribbean dramatist and a major poet of our time, called *Ti-Jean and His Brothers* his most West Indian play: 'the least forced, the most spontaneous, the least laboured of my plays so far, both in rhythm and concept.'[1] Walcott wrote it in 1957 during a five-day stay in New York on his first visit to the metropolis, 'out of sheer terror of the place and a fierce but illuminating nostalgia for the untheatrical simplicities of St Lucia, the island where I was born ... It was created under the pressure of sudden loneliness and exile.'

When the play, in a revised version with additional music and songs, was being prepared for a 1970 presentation at the Town Hall in Port of Spain, Trinidad, Walcott elaborated on its genesis and his search for an appropriate form in which to couch his folk-fable. He wished, he said, to write 'a softly measured metre whose breathing was formally articulated yet held the lyrical stresses of dialect speech', and he found it in breaking the iambic line in half, into something more lilting, something that had the innocence of a child's recitation:

> Well, one time it had a mother,
>
> That mother had three sons.
>
> The first son was Gros Jean.
>
> That son he was the biggest,
>
> His arm was hard as iron,
>
> But he was very stupid.

Walcott admitted that the lilt might seem 'almost moronic', but he felt that if, in delivering such a metre, one could hear simultaneously the sound of the flute, the cuatro, and the drum; and if, in addition, one could imagine 'the care and arrest of those old country-firelight storytellers who frightened us all as children', such a rhythm would be more instinctual yet more formal than prose.

Looking back on the work objectively, Walcott sensed the influence of Garcia Lorca, 'particularly in the swift but self-arresting metre', and Brecht in the distancing of characters, and through Brecht, the Noh Theatre with its use of masks, musicians, and the mimetic indication of scenery. Beyond all this and at the very core of the play, there was:

> What was there too, but was too deep to be acknowledged, was the African art of the storyteller, a tradition which survived in my childhood through the figure of a magical, child enchanting aunt, and the memories of firefly-pricked rain forests at dusk, the sound of rain and wind in the leaves (one could never tell which), and those skin-prickling chants whose words may change, but whose mode goes as far back and even past the tribal memory.

Other St Lucian rituals contributing to the play were the Christmas black mass dances of Papa Diable and his Imps, the Bolom or Foetus, and the melodies which they used. Walcott concludes: 'these figures out of the tapestry of world peasant mythology may take varying shapes, but their source is Protean and universal.'

To introduce his folktale, Walcott employs a group of forest creatures – Cricket, Frog, Firefly and Bird – reaching back to the ancient choric device which formed the mainstay of classical Greek drama. Aristophanes had used a chorus of frogs in one of his comedies and Walcott acknowledges his debt with a parodic tilt in his opening scene:

FROG: Greek-croak, Greek-croak.

CRICKET: Greek-croak, Greek-croak.

FROG: (*Sneezing*) Aeschylus me!

The mood is playful and festive. We are being prepared for the magical world of play, a world in which creatures talk, devils appear in different shapes, and an unborn foetus becomes an unwilling messenger of doom. It is a world, too, of poor people who live a marginal existence, but whose faith is strong and who do not despair until they are overcome by the forces of evil. Finally, it is a world in which instinct and innocence triumph over unfeeling malevolence.

The story of the play is quickly told. A poor mother lives on the edge of the forest with her three sons, Gros Jean, the muscle-man; Mi-Jean, the would-be intellectual; and Ti-Jean, the intuitive hero. Each son goes forth into the world to seek his fortune and each encounters the devil who offers a contest: whoever makes the other one angry wins. If the Devil wins, he devours the loser; if man wins, he gets the Devil's gold and a wish fulfilled. The two older brothers lose the contest when they try to perform tasks set by the Devil and which cannot possibly be accomplished. In frustration they become angry and are eaten. Ti-Jean's strategy, with which he overcomes the Devil, is simple and effective. Instead of wrestling with impossible jobs, he eliminates them. He castrates the Devil's goat that would not be tied, then he kills it and makes a meal of goat curry. Rather than count all the leaves of cane in the fields, he sets fire to the canes; finally, he burns down the Devil's house. Told of these rebellious acts, the Devil becomes furious and loses the battle of wits. Ti-Jean emerges the victor; he receives a shower of gold and, for his fulfilled wish, he gives life to the Bolom.

As viewed by the critic John Simon, the play exists on several levels.[2] It is first a simple folktale recounted in the distilled dialect that Walcott has fashioned. At another level, it is a metaphysical verse play with music. At a third level, it is a relevant black parable inciting to anti-white revolution. While one might not agree wholly with this analysis, it is interesting to note that the characters assumed by the Devil in his resolve to destroy the family correspond to the three phases mentioned above. He appears first as Papa Bois, wrinkled guardian of the forest with cloven, hairy hoof and forked tail hidden under his long, sackcloth skirt. This is the creature of folklore. Next he is revealed as the Devil himself, 'the prince of obscurity' who, weary of immortality, is longing to experience human emotion, to be in love, to have children and, yes, even worries of his own. This is metaphysical speculation. Third, the Devil takes the persona of a white Planter who lives in the Great House on his cane and cotton estates where he keeps 'poor damned souls' of black labourers in bondage. When Ti-Jean calls on the sweating workers to burn the fields and they do so, this is equated with the Black Power Revolution which was sweeping the United States at the time of the play's performance in New York in 1972.

Other interpretations are possible, however. Writing on the Trinidad production in 1970, Eric Roach sees the three brothers as symbolic of the movement of generations through West Indian history.[3] In his view, Gros Jean typifies:

the brawny post-slave generation who succumbs to everything that his 'iron-arm' cannot master ... Mi-Jean, the self-taught moron, already infused with middleclass snob values, is proudly running off to be a lawyer or doctor in the wilderness beyond, ignorant of what is going on in his own backyard. Ti-Jean, however, is of today's generation. He divines what the evil about him is in any form it appears.

Roach goes further. He believes it is possible for the socio-politically involved man to interpret the Bolom's cry for life as 'Save your country, Ti-Jean. Without me you cannot exist.' Thus, when Ti-Jean begs the Devil for the Bolom's life, everyone in the audience breathes a sigh of relief.

Another variant on the theme of the overthrow of colonialism was voiced by the Jamaican reviewer when the play was presented on the University campus in that country in 1973.[4] In this account, the drama was interpreted as a retelling of the struggle against colonialism and the final victory of the formerly colonized. The three brothers represented those who tried to challenge the colonizers. The colonial system was the Devil in his various guises (it is often difficult to distinguish him from God), while the Bolom, 'a curled-up, disfigured mass which claims to be a child strangled at birth by its mother', represented the West Indian people kept down by the tyranny of colonialism. When Ti-Jean outwits the Planter and brings the Bolom to life, it becomes a brother to Ti-Jean and there is established a unity in strength.

Walcott has had most of his major plays performed in North America. *Ti-Jean and His Brothers* was first presented in St Lucia in 1957 in a 'ballet version' which was directed by Walcott's twin brother, Roderick. The play received its first full production as a straight drama with incidental folk music at the Little Carib Theatre in Port of Spain, Trinidad, in 1958, when it was directed by the author. Thereafter, it was twice revised, with new music composed by Andre Tanker, and produced by Walcott's own company, the Trinidad Theatre Workshop, in 1970 and performed in Trinidad, in Jamaica in 1971, and for Joseph Papp's New York Shakespeare Festival at the Delacorte Theatre, Central Park, in the summer of 1972. The play has also been produced in Canada and on television.

In New York, the production enjoyed a mixed press. While some critics praised the language and music of the play, others accused the author of too much philosophizing or of presenting too sentimental an affirmation of life. West Indian productions, on the other hand, have been almost uniformly praised, not merely for the socio-political meanings implicit in the text, but also for Walcott's renowned power with language, his conception of character, and his cunning artistic use of the folk culture. He himself has written:

> Our culture needs both preservation and resurgence, our cries need an epiphany, a spiritual definition, and an art can emerge from our poverty, creating its own elation. Our resilience is in our tragic joy, in the catharsis of folk humour. Our art, for the time being, because it emerges from and speaks to the poor, will find its antean renewal in folktale and parable. We present to others a deceptive simplicity that they may dismiss as provincial, primitive, childish, but which is in truth a radical innocence. That is what our fable is about.[5]

An Echo in the Bone
The author

Dennis Scott of Jamaica taught at the Yale School of Drama in New Haven, Connecticut, and was Head of the Directing Programme from 1986 until his death in 1991. He received his Bachelor of Arts in English with First Class Honours at the University of the West Indies and later took a diploma in Drama in Education at the University of Newcastle-upon-Tyne, England. He taught at Jamaica College and at Presentation College in Trinidad and Tobago for several years before becoming Director of the Jamaica School of Drama in 1977, a post he relinquished after six years.

Professor Scott was a published poet, a playwright and play director. He conducted theatre workshops in the West Indies and with the National Theatre of the Deaf in the United States. He was regularly on the roster of directors at the Playwrights Conference conducted by the Eugene O'Neill Theater Center in Waterford, Connecticut. His plays have been produced in the Caribbean, at the Kennedy Center in Washington, D.C., and at the Festival of Black Arts, Lagos, in 1977.

Among his many honours are the Shubert Playwriting Fellowship (1970), the International Poetry Forum Award (1973), the Commonwealth Poetry Award (1974), the Prime Minister's Medal for Service to the Arts in Jamaica (1983), and other gold and silver medals for playwriting and directing at Jamaica festivals.

The play

Because the storyline of this play is revealed in fragments which are scattered through the fabric of the work, it may be useful to begin an analysis by summarizing the basic plot. Nine days prior to the start of the play, Mr Charles, a white estate owner, has been killed and his presumed murderer is a black peasant farmer called Crew. After the killing, Crew has disappeared, leaving his bloodied shirt and machete on the river bank. Crew's wife, Rachel, is certain that her husband has died and that his body lies at the bottom of the river. Thus, in keeping with her religious belief, she holds an all-night 'wake' which her family and close friends attend. This is where the play's action begins. As the gathering comes together to extoll the dead man's virtues, to sing, dance, drink rum and smoke ganja, several queries hang in the air unresolved. Did Crew kill Mr Charles? If he did, why? Where is Crew now? If he has died, how did it happen?

Despite the murder and the mystery, it would be foolish to assume that this is simply another 'whodunnit' thriller. The author has more important ends in view. No character other than Crew is suspected of the murder and, quite early in the opening scene, Crew's spirit manifests itself by possessing one of the young men attending the wake. So Crew did kill the estate owner after all and subsequently died himself. But why and how?

Verbal explanations will not suffice. Because the answers lie deep in racial memory, because they 'echo in the bone', it will be necessary to relive the past, not just the immediate past but the history of an oppressed people in order to find meaning in madness. To make this journey back into the communal psyche, author Scott has summoned a traditional death ritual, the Nine-Night Ceremony, in whose observance is compressed the actual and supernatural, the past and present, the living and dead. They come together in a single consecrated space during a single night's watch. As Carroll Dawes, director of the premier production of the play, wrote in a programme note:

> The play asks a question about the experience of violence and attempts not to explain its constituents but to recreate the complex organism. We may puncture it at any point in time, space, place, or race. The same tissues pulse, the same blood spurts, the same heart must be healed.[6]

The Nine-Night Ceremony is a standard death ritual that is practised in Afro-Caribbean religions. In Jamaica it is observed by the followers of Pocomania and certain other Revivalist Cults. The ritual is based on the belief that the spirit of a dead person will return to its home on the ninth night after death. The ceremony is held in order to persuade the soul of the deceased that all is well and to send it away from the house with cheers and rejoicing.

11

To accomplish this end, an aura of festivity is created. Hymns are sung, speeches made, games played, liquor served, drums beaten, and dances danced.

A table (which serves as an altar) is dressed with lighted candles, a glass of water, a vase of flowers and, leaning against the vase, a photograph of the dead person. At midnight, after libations have been poured to consecrate the ground, the spirit appears by possessing the Leader or other dignitary. The possessed individual receives oracular powers and can divulge hidden truths. Orders may be given as to the disposal of the dead man's property. During the night, others may also 'catch the spirit'. At daybreak, water from the glass is thrown into the street, ceremonial vessels are put outside, belongings of the dead are given away, and the spirit is freed from its former home.[7]

The author's decision to structure his play upon the format of the ritual has distinct advantages. Theatrically, he is able to present what is essentially an episodic and panoramic view of history in the most economical way imaginable. The entire action of the play takes place within a fairly circumscribed area of a dilapidated barn containing rusted metals, a huge linked chain, and a couple of different levels for acting. A table, a few kitchen utensils and tools complete the stage properties. Yet, by the transforming power of the ritual ceremony, this mundane stage picture becomes a slave ship moored off the African coast, an auctioneer's office, a grocer's shop, a wooded hillside, a Great House, a field, and a room in Rachel's cottage. The smoothness with which these transitions occur does more than save time and money; it enables the tensity in the drama to be maintained without the inevitable release that occurs when scenery is shifted to bring on a new locale.

Not only are the physical dimensions expanded, the characters too multiply in number without the need for more bodies than the original group of ten (six men and four women) who gather for the ceremony. Here the act of possession, which is the central objective of the ritual, induces a change of persona in the possessed individual without any obvious change in facial makeup or dress. By extending this phenomenon to the enactment of distant historical events, any character can assume another personality with which he or she has an affinity. Since, however, the basic conflict of the play is sharply focused on the symbolic figures of white landlord and black peasant, and since the core characters are all black, it was thought wise in at least one production of the play to use facial masks when white characters were portrayed: 'the use of the mask enables the actor to explore the echo in the well of his unconscious. Its use also allows for a tightness of presentation that is remarkable.'[8]

In a production that is sparingly mounted, symbols acquire great significance. They pervade the play and a sensitive director will use them effectively to enhance the action by striking visualizations. A principal element in the performed ritual is the drum. Beating, it starts the ceremony, it is used in scenic transitions, it evokes the spirit possession. It is one of the obvious links with an African past and it speaks with an insistent authority that cannot be denied. Little wonder, then, that the drummer, Rattler, is a mute. He has no need of verbal expression when he can talk so effectively through his instrument.

Another symbolic image is the huge rusted chain that hangs down from the roof and dominates the stage. An obvious reference to the shackles of slavery, the chain bears silent testimony to the continuing economic enslavement of the black worker. Hence Sonson angrily denounces Mr Charles to his mother:

> That is how they go on, eh? Like the Lord put them on the earth to walk all over the rest of us. Ma, from slavery days them don't change, they still think they better than the rest. Why the hell he don't stay in town and leave us alone?

And later, as Crew, having committed the murder and before he climbs up the chain to make his escape: 'I not going to jail for this, you hear me! I suffer too long – three hundred years! Three hundred!'

The ostensible cause of the murder is Mr Charles's rejection of Crew's request for water for his farm. The course of the river has been diverted from Crew's farmland. As a result, the earth has dried up and nothing will grow. Crew and his family are destitute. However, the river flows through the neighbouring property owned by Mr Charles, and Crew is seeking permission to channel some of the water into his ground. Instead of giving a sympathetic ear to the plight of the peasant farmer, Mr Charles arrogantly upbraids him for bringing his problems to the front door of the Great House and turns away. Crew tries to restrain him but Mr Charles pushes Crew down and makes to kick him. It is at this point that Crew reaches for his machete.

So far the quarrel is minor to provoke a savage act of murder. Were this a real-life drama instead of an imagined play, one would expect that Crew would be branded a drunken, brutal murderer and sent to the gallows with dispatch. In the play, however, the author is careful to account for Crew's ungovernable rage by reference to history. He selects incidents from the near and distant past to show that violence has been inherent in the relations between the two races – with Blacks being invariably the victims – from the day the first slaving vessel arrived off the coast of Africa.

Thus there is the scene aboard a slave ship where Africans are barbarously mutilated without a moment's reflection by those in authority. Another scene occurs in the office of a slave auctioneer, where young black women suffer the indignity of having their bodies publicly inspected by potential buyers as if they were so many animals. In a third scene two Maroons (Blacks who have escaped slavery and live in the Jamaican mountains) come across a wounded slave-owner who has been out hunting runaways with dogs. They spare his life. In the Great House, a dying proprietor is cared for by his black maidservant whom he despises, although he has bedded her often. Then there is the scene in which we learn that Mr Charles has seduced Crew's wife, Rachel, and is now urging her to come back to the Great House as his housekeeper. In fact, there is a suggestion that Crew's present predicament has been deliberately manufactured to force Rachel to accept Mr Charles's offer.

The fact that all the characters in these historical episodes are played by the same group of actors reinforces the theme that the suffering experienced by the Blacks is not only individual but communal and racial. Crew's murderous act thus becomes a logical if desperate response to centuries of oppression. When Sonson, whose own fierce pride equals his father's and who is therefore chosen to carry his father's spirit, as Crew raises his machete over Mr Charles and the action freezes, it is the climactic moment in the play. It is marked by 'a long building scream from the chorus' followed by blackness.

The act of murder is symbolic too. It is also an act of purification. It absolves the past record and looks hopefully towards the future. It typifies a cleavage between two dispensations: the old one of master–slave relationship and the new one of multiracial brotherhood. As Rachel says in the final speech of the play: 'No matter what is past, you can't stop the blood from drumming, and you can't stop the heart from hoping. We have to hold on to one another. That is all we can do.'

In this respect, the death of Crew (or was it suicide?) is more than mere poetic justice to give the play a tidy ending. As recounted in the last scene, after Mr Charles's murder, Crew made his escape by climbing a tree onto the roof of the Great House. Then he managed to get down to the river where he tried to wash the blood off his body. What happened next the author leaves unclear. Was Crew being pursued and did he drown while trying to swim across the river? Or was his drowning a deliberate act of self-sacrifice performed to save his family the humiliation of his trial, sentencing and hanging? If the latter were true, would he not have left on the river's bank evidence of his crime so that none other should be held responsible?

However Crew died, it is important to remember that he belonged to the old order, and although the means whereby a new order is ushered in, he cannot survive into the new. Yet his place will be taken by another. Sonson survives, and Jacko, and Brigit, especially Brigit who carries a child in her womb and who persuades her husband, Jacko, to help Sonson down from his dangerous perch on the roof of the barn, thus reconciling the enmity that existed between the two brothers.

An Echo in the Bone was first produced in 1974 by the University Drama Society, Jamaica, to mark the University's twenty-fifth anniversary of its founding. The production was recast and revived for entry in the Festival of Black Arts held in Lagos, Nigeria, in 1977. The play received a highly acclaimed performance by Group 15 in Trinidad in 1976, under the direction of Rawle Gibbons, and it was also produced in Barbados by Stage One in June, 1982.

Available reviews of these productions stress the experimental nature of the work and its challenging premise. In his generally favourable critique of the Trinidad production, Victor Questel concluded that 'Scott has written a play that has pushed Caribbean theatre forward into areas it must explore.'[9]

Man Better Man

The author

Trinidad-born Errol Hill was the John D. Willard Professor of Drama and Oratory at Dartmouth College, Hanover, New Hampshire, where he taught drama and theatre for many years. Before going to Dartmouth, Professor Hill held academic appointments at the City University of New York, the University of Ibadan in Nigeria, and the University of the West Indies. He had also worked as an actor and announcer with the British Broadcasting Corporation.

Professor Hill was a graduate of the Royal Academy of Dramatic Art in London, England, and of Yale College and the Yale School of Drama. He published eight plays and was a play director and actor as well as a teacher and scholar. His books include *The Trinidad Carnival, The Theater of Black Americans, The Cambridge Guide to African and Caribbean Theatre* and *Shakespeare in Sable: A History of Black Shakespearean Actors.* He was a founder-member of the Whitehall Players in Trinidad and of the Federal Theatre Company in Jamaica.

Among his awards are a British Council Scholarship, Fellowships from the Rockefeller Foundation, the Theatre Guild of America, the Guggenheim Memorial Foundation, a Regional Citation from the New England Theatre Conference, and a Gold Medal in Drama from the Government of Trinidad and Tobago. Errol Hill died in 2003 at the age of 82.

The play

When he first came to write *Man Better Man* in 1956, Errol Hill had already written and produced half a dozen short plays about island life of which *The Ping Pong* (1950), a play on the steel band, is best known. After attending the Royal Academy of Dramatic Art, London, on a British Council Sponsorship,

Hill returned to the West Indies in 1952 and was appointed the following year as Drama Tutor at the then University College in Jamaica. Energetically he began to promote indigenous theatre throughout the West Indies by encouraging the writing and staging of native plays. He started a collection of Caribbean plays and, in 1955, began their publication under the imprint of the University of the West Indies.

The first version of *Man Better Man*, written in vernacular prose and devoid of music, was produced by the University Players in Jamaica in 1957. The play then underwent considerable revision. It was wholly rewritten in calypso verse, music and song lyrics were added, and the role of the calypsonian was enlarged. From a melodramatic revenge play, the plot was transformed into an ingenuous comedy with music and dancing.

The sport of stick-fighting is known around the Caribbean. It was practised by slaves and may have originated in West Africa. Known as the 'calinda', it was described in 1838 as 'an agile, dexterous dance performed to Negro drums, while the dancers engaged in mock combat with their "beau-sticks" which were about thirty inches in length'.[10] Following the abolition of slavery, the sport became associated with the Trinidad Carnival. Dexterity was still admired as the stickmen danced and chanted to the drums, but the combat was no longer make-believe; blows were hammered at an opponent and parried by him in earnest, and many a dueller was forced to retire with a broken head.

The incidents related to the play are based on historical events. During the second half of the nineteenth century, stick-fighting in Trinidad was in its heyday. Well organized bands of stick-men in the city and in many small rural towns vied for supremacy. Their exploits and the prowess displayed by their champions are vividly recalled by devotees of the sport and have survived as oral history. It was the practice for these bands to roam the streets in the early morning hours of the carnival and to shout their challenges to rival groups. When they encountered each other, a great fracas would ensue. Oftentimes, too, competitive duels were fought in backyard arenas before invited and partisan spectators. In 1881 when the police tried to intercept the stick-fighters' parade during carnival, a riot broke out that eventually led to the dissolution of the bands.

In his analysis of the play, Louis D. Mitchell notes several parallels with medieval courtly life.[11] The calypsonian, for instance, enjoys a position roughly analogous to the Anglo-Saxon court *scop*.

> He immortalizes the Island's heroes in song, and his repertoire constitutes a veritable oral chronicle. Pogo's Homeric cataloguing of famous stick-fighters displays a continuity of an heroic tradition. Villagers manifest an awareness that they see tradition-in-the-making: 'Excitement for so/More trouble and woe/A day to recall/When you grow old.'

For Professor Mitchell the stick-fight between Tim Briscoe and Tiny Satan is reminiscent of a medieval tournament whose proceedings are governed by rigid ritualistic customs:

> Aspects of trial-by-combat are ever present, along with the strong emphasis on personal honor and its defence. Indeed, stick-fighting is envisioned among these Island dwellers as a folk-institution. The fighter is a true folk-hero, like Beowulf or Achilles, who embodies not only the primitive drive of the Islanders, but also the qualities which they esteem most highly – physical courage, prowess in battle, personal honor. The reigning champion becomes a personification of the communal ideal.

The obeahman is a well-known character in the gallery of Caribbean originals. Belief in his proverbial powers to foretell the future and avert disaster still finds adherents among the populace. He is not, of course, always fraudulent and Diable Papa must surely be credibly successful to survive for long in the village and be so much feared. However, he is not above exploiting a foolhardy customer who insists on receiving treatment when the obeahman knows his case to be hopeless, particularly when the risk of exposure is minimal.

The medium, Minnie Woopsa, was brought up by the obeahman who keeps to himself, surrounded by books and his magical paraphernalia. Timid in crowds, she has studied the magical arts and acquired the knowledge of herbs and their reputed efficacies. Minnie is the only character in the play through whom communication is established with the supernatural. She receives signs and omens of the future which Diable Papa has learnt to respect. Fearing she might otherwise displease her controlling spirit, she opposes the obeahman only when she believes his scheming will cause serious harm or death to the innocent Briscoe.

The Portuguese shopkeeper is another of the staple characters of village life. An outsider who has adopted native customs, he is yet cynical of local superstitions and becomes the focal point of opposition to the obeahman. His presence in the play attests the multiracial nature of Trinidad society. When the play was produced in New York in 1969, a few reviewers dismissed it as irrelevant to the pressing social issues of the day, whereupon Antoinette Camacho Jackson wrote an unpublished letter to the *New York Times*.[12] Claiming to be the daughter of a Portuguese rum shopkeeper and granddaughter of a City Councillor of Port of Spain, Trinidad, at the turn of the century, Mrs Jackson pointed out that, for her, 'the social significance of the play lies in the relationship between Portagee Joe and his customers. They were not "niggers" to him and he was not "whitey" to them. A man could be judged as a man seventy years ago in Trinidad. Trinidad is not South Africa nor even New York.'

Apart from Minee, the females in the play are generally kept-women who hope some day to marry and settle down. Meantime, they enjoy the exciting, masculine world of the gallant stick-men. Often they will develop a domestic skill such as needlework or pastrymaking which they do at home and which leaves them sufficient time to spend with their menfolk. They dress gaily, parade the town at the slightest excuse, indulge a passion for saucy repartee, and can be very beguiling or very fierce, some of them becoming as adept at stick-fighting as the men.

Writing this play was an experiment in integrating music, song and dance into dramatic action, and using the calypso form with its rhymed couplets to carry the rhythm throughout as an undercurrent. It is important in speaking the dialogue that undue stress is not given to the end-rhymes but that verbal emphasis should be dictated by the sense of the lines. The music used in the play is partly based on traditional folksongs with some original pieces, such as 'I love Petite Belle', 'Coolie Gone' and 'War and Rebellion', which were composed by the author. For musical accompaniment, a small orchestra of no more than five instruments, such as a flute, trumpet or saxophone, guitar, bass and drums, should suffice. Of course, Hannibal the calypsonian will accompany himself on his own cuatro or guitar when he sings.

In addition to its dramatic qualities it is clear that *Man Better Man* was also written to celebrate certain aspects of the folk experience which, under colonial rule, were at one time denigrated and which nowadays provide the means for the emergence of a national culture. Thus, translating elements of native expression into theatrical form serves both to preserve them as art and to contribute towards establishing the identity of the people responsible for their creation.

How well Hill's experiment may have succeeded depends ultimately on its reception by audience and critics. In its final form, the play was first produced by the Yale School of Drama in 1960 and revived by the school two years later. It was chosen to represent Trinidad and Tobago at the 1965 Commonwealth Arts Festival in Britain when, with a company recruited in Trinidad, it played in London, Croydon and Glasgow. The Negro Ensemble Company produced it in New York in 1969, and it has also been performed by numerous college and community theatre groups in the Caribbean, the United States and Canada.

Caribbean productions are uniformly popular and successful. Abroad, critical reviews have been generally favourable. Reviewing the Commonwealth Arts Festival production in London, *The Times* found that in its best moments the play turned into 'a blazing, electrifying feast of rhythm and colour. In the second act the company performed a stick-dance which had the whole audience rocking in their seats with delight [but] the writing is uneven, ranging from the endearingly humorous to the almost vulgarly folksy.'[13]

The *New York Times* critic compared the performance he attended to 'the wild innocence of an open water hydrant splashing in a neighbourhood street and the comic folk brilliance of Jorge Amado's novels about Negro life in northern Brazil ... The book is pungent, rhyming and metered poetry tailored to the West Indian speech.'[14] Several reviewers called for more music and dancing while others thought that the uniformity of the calypso verse dialogue might have been varied by the introduction of prose passages. Most agreed that the play succeeded in transporting them to another world and giving them an authentic view of a different culture.

Errol Hill

Footnotes

1 'Derek's "most West Indian play"', *Trinidad Guardian*, 21 June 1970, subsequent quotations are taken from the same article

2 *New York*, 14 August 1972

3 *Trinidad Guardian*, 26 June 1970

4 *The Daily News* Jamaica, 7 October 1973

5 'A Season of Plays', Handbook of the Trinidad Theatre Workshop, production of *Ti-jean and Dream on Monkey Mountain* at the Creative Arts Centre, Mona, Jamaica, April 1971

6 Programme flyer of premier performance at Creative Arts Centre, Mona, Jamaica, 1 May 1974

7 George Eaton Simpson, Jamaican Revivalist Cults, *Social and Economic Studies*, vol. 5, no. 4, December 1956, 379

8 Victor D. Questel, 'Unlocking the Gates of History', TAPIA, Sunday, 19 December 1976

9 *ibid*

10 Errol Hill, *The Trinidad Carnival*, Austin, University of Texas Press, 1972, p. 25

11 James Vinson, ed., *Contemporary Dramatists*, 3rd ed., New York, St Martin's Press, 1982, p. 394

12 Letter dated 13 July 1969, in author's files

13 *The Times*, London, 1 October 1965

14 *The New York Times*, 3 July 1969

Ti-Jean and His Brothers
Derek Walcott

For Peter Walcott

Characters

CRICKET

FROG

FIREFLY

BIRD

GROS JEAN

MI-JEAN

TI-JEAN

MOTHER

BOLOM

OLD MAN, or PAPA BOIS

PLANTER

DEVIL

Ti-Jean and His Brothers was first performed at the Little Carib Theatre, Port of Spain, Trinidad, in 1958 with the following cast:

GROS JEAN	William Webb
MI-JEAN	Horace James
TI-JEAN	Freddie Kissoon
MOTHER	{ Jean Herbert / Veronica Jenkin
BOLOM	Russell Winston
DEVIL	Errol Jones
FROG	Bertrand Henry

The musicians were: John Henderson, Gene Lawrence, Colin Laird and Michael Warren.

The play was revived by the Trinidad Theatre Workshop in June 1970 at the Town Hall, Port of Spain, with original music by Andre Tanker and with the following cast:

CRICKET	Adele Bynoe
FROG	Hamilton Parris
BIRD	Roslyn Rappaport
GROS JEAN	Claude Reid
MI-JEAN	Stanley Marshall
BOLOM	Belinda Barnes
TI-JEAN	Ellsworth Primus
MOTHER	Ermine Wright
PAPA BOIS	
PLANTER	Albert Laveau
DEVIL	

Prologue

[Evening. Rain. The heights of a forest. A CRICKET, *a* FROG, *a* FIREFLY, *a*
BIRD. *Left, a hut with bare table, an empty bowl, stools. The* MOTHER *waiting]*

FROG: Greek-croak, Greek-croak.

CRICKET: Greek-croak, Greek-croak.

    [The others join]

FROG *[Sneezing]*: Aeschylus me!

               All that rain and no moon tonight.

CRICKET: The moon always there even fighting the rain

               Creek-crak, it is cold, but the moon always there

               And Ti-Jean in the moon just like the story.

    [The BIRD passes]

CRICKET: Before you fly home, listen,

               The cricket cracking a story

               A story about the moon.

FROG: If you look in the moon,

               Though no moon is here tonight,

               There is a man, no, a boy,

               Bent by a weight of faggots

               He carried on his shoulder,

               A small dog trotting with him.

               That is Ti-Jean the hunter,

               He got the heap of sticks

               From the old man of the forest

               They calling Papa Bois,

               Because he beat the devil,

               God put him in that height

               To be the sun's right hand

               And light the evil dark,

               But as the bird so ignorant

               I will start the tale truly.

    [Music]

               Well, one time it had a mother,

               That mother had three sons.

The first son was Gros Jean.

That son he was the biggest,

His arm was hard as iron,

But he was very stupid.

[*Enter* GROS JEAN, *a bundle of faggots in one hand, an axe over his shoulder, moving in an exaggerated march to music. The* CREATURES *laugh*]

FROG: The name of the second son.

They was calling him Mi-Jean,

In size, the second biggest,

So only half as stupid; now,

He was a fisherman, but

Always studying book, and

What a fisherman; for

When he going and fish,

Always forgetting the bait,

So between de bait and debate ...

CRICKET: *Mi boug qui tait cooyon!*

(Look man who was a fool!)

[*Roll of drums. Comic quatro, martial*]

[*Enter* MI-JEAN *from the opposite side, carrying a book in one hand and a fishing net over his shoulder. Halfway across the stage he flings the net casually, still reading*]

BIRD: How poor their mother was?

[*Sad music on flute*]

FROG: Oh that was poverty, bird!

Old hands dried up like claws

Heaping old sticks on sticks,

too weak to protect her nest.

Look, the four of that family

[*Light shows the hut*]

Lived in a little house,

Made up of wood and thatch,

On the forehead of the mountain,

Where night and day was rain,

Mist, cloud white as cotton

> Caught in the dripping branches;
> Where sometimes it was so cold
> The frog would stop its singing

[*The* FROG *stops. Five beats. Resumes*]

> The cricket would stop rattling
> And the wandering firefly
> That lights the tired woodsman
> Home through the raining trees
> Could not strike a damp light
> To star the wanderer home!

[*The music stops. The brothers* GROS JEAN *and* MI-JEAN *put their arms around each other, and to heavy drums tramp home*]

CRICKET: I damned sorry for that mother.

FROG: Aie, cricket, you croak the truth!

> The life of an old woman
> With her husband cold in earth
> Where the bamboo leaves lie lightly,
> And smell of mouldering flesh,
> How well I know that story!
> Near where the mother was,
> Across the wet and melancholy
> Mountain where her hut was, O God,
> The Devil used to live!

[*Crash of cymbals. Shrieks, thunder. The* CREATURES *cower as the* DEVIL *with his troop of fiends, the Werewolf, the Diablesse, the* BOLOM, *somersault and dance across the stage. The sky is red*]

DEVIL: *Bai, Diable-là manger un 'ti mamaille!*

(Give the Devil a child for dinner!)

DEVILS: *Un, deux, trois 'ti mamaille!*

(One, two, three little children!)

[*They whirl around the stage leaping, chanting, then as suddenly go off*]

BIRD: Wow!

> Were they frightened of him?

FROG: If they were frightened?

> They were frightened of his skin,

                    Powdery as leprosy,

                    Like the pock-marked moon,

                    Afraid of his dead eye,

                    That had no fire in it ...

CRICKET: Of the terrible thunder

                    In his wood-shaking throat!

    [*Roar of devils off-stage*]

FROG: Just hear them in the hut ...

    [*Sad flute, as the light comes up on the three sons around the knees of the old woman*]

GROS JEAN: One time again it have nothing to eat,

                    But one dry bread to break;

                    I went out to chop some wood

                    To make a nice fire,

                    But the wood was too damp,

                    So I didn't use the axe

                    As I didn't want it to get wet;

                    If it get wet it get rusty.

MI-JEAN: Sense!

                    I went out to do fishing

                    For crayfish by the cold stones,

                    In the cold spring in the ferns,

                    But when I get there so,

                    I find I lack bait.

    [*Rising solemnly*]

                    Now for man to catch fish,

                    That man must have bait,

                    But the best bait is fish,

                    Yet I cannot catch no fish,

                    Without I first have bait,

                    As the best bait for fish

                    Is to catch fish with fish.

                    So I ...

GROS JEAN: Mi-Jean is a fool,
Reading too much damn book.

MOTHER: My sons, do not quarrel,
Here all of us are starving,
While the planter is eating
From plates painted golden,
Forks with silver tongues,
The brown flesh of birds,
And the white flesh of fish.
What did you do today,
My last son Ti-Jean?

TI-JEAN: *Maman, m'a fait un rien.*
(Mama, I didn't do a thing.)

GROS JEAN: We do all the damned work.

MI-JEAN: We do all the damn thinking.

GROS JEAN: And he sits there like a prince.

MI-JEAN: As useless as a bone.

GROS JEAN *and* MI-JEAN [*Jeering*]: *Maman, m'a fait un rien!*
Maman, m'a fait un rien!

MOTHER: Wait, and God will send us something.

GROS JEAN: God forget where he put us.

MI-JEAN: God too irresponsible.

MOTHER: Children!

[*Weird music. The* BOLOM *or Foetus rolls in unheard, somersaults around the hut, then waits. Sound of wind, rain, shriek of insects*]
Children, listen,
There is something listening
Outside of the door!

GROS JEAN: I don't hear nothing.

MI-JEAN: I hear only the rain,
Falling hard on the leaves,
And the wind down the throat
Of the gorge with the spring,
The crickets and the bull-frog,
And maybe one frightened bird.

MOTHER [*Standing*]: I tell you there is something

> Outside of the door,
>
> I tell you from experience
>
> I know when evil comes.
>
> It is not the wind, listen!

[*The* BOLOM *imitates a child crying*]

MI-JEAN: A young child out in the forest.

GROS JEAN: Looking for its mother.

MOTHER: The Devil has sent us

> Another of his angels!
>
> I prayed to God all day,
>
> While I scrubbed the hut bare,
>
> On the knuckles of my knees
>
> All day in the hungry house;
>
> Now God has sent me evil,
>
> Who can understand it?
>
> Death, death is coming nearer.

GROS JEAN: Line the step with fine sand

> To keep the evil out!

MI-JEAN: Turn over, Mother, the hem of your skirt!

GROS JEAN *and* MI-JEAN: Let two of our fingers form in
> one crucifix!

[TI-JEAN *steps outside*]

MOTHER: Spirit that is outside,

> With the voice of a child
>
> Crying out in the rain,
>
> What do you want from the poor?

[TI-JEAN *searches carefully*]

BOLOM: I have a message for a woman with three sons.

MOTHER: Child of the Devil, what is your message?

BOLOM: Send the first of your sons outside for it,

> They must die in that order. And let the youngest
>
> Return into the hut.

[TI-JEAN *steps back into the hut*]

MOTHER: We can hear you in the wind,

What do you want of me?

[*A weird light shows the* BOLOM. *Shrieks*]

ALL: Where are you? Where is it?

Hit it! There! Where is it?

BOLOM [*Leaping, hiding*]: Here, in the bowl!

Here, sitting on a stool!

Here, turning in a cup!

Here, crawling up your skirt!

MOTHER: I have done you no harm, child.

BOLOM: A woman did me harm,

Called herself mother,

The fear of her hatred

A cord round my throat!

MOTHER [*Turning, searching*]: Look, perhaps it is luckiest

Never to be born,

To the horror of this life

Crowded with shadows,

Never to have known

That the sun will go out,

The green leaf rust,

The strong tree be stricken

And the roaring spring quail;

Peace to you, unborn,

You can find comfort here.

Let a mother touch you,

For the sake of her kind.

BOLOM [*Shrieks, dancing back*]: Whatever flesh touches me,

Withers me into mortality;

Not till your sons die, Mother,

Shall this shape feel this life.

GROS JEAN [*Seizes axe*]: Kill it, then, kill it.

MI-JEAN: Curse it back to the womb.

DEVIL'S VOICE: *Faire ça mwen di ous!*

            (Do what I commanded!)

BOLOM: I hear the voice of my master.

DEVIL'S VOICE: *Bolom, faire tout ça mwen dire ous!*

            (Child, do all that I ordered you!)

BOLOM: Listen, creature of gentleness,

            Old tree face marked with scars,

            And the wounds of bearing children,

            Whom the earth womb will swallow,

            This is the shriek

            Of a child which was strangled,

            Who never saw the earth light

            Through the hinge of the womb,

            Strangled by a woman,

            Who hated my birth,

            Twisted out of shape,

            Deformed past recognition.

            Tell me then, Mother,

            Would you care to see it?

[*The* BOLOM *moves out of the light, shrieking*]

GROS JEAN: Let us see you!

MOTHER: The sight of such horror, though you are brave,

            Would turn you to stone, my strong son, Gros Jean.

MI-JEAN: Let us reason with you.

MOTHER: My son, the thing may be a ball of moving fire,

            A white horse in the leaves, or a clothful of skin,

            Found under a tree, you cannot explain that!

BOLOM: Save your understanding for the living,

            Save your pity for the dead,

            I am neither living nor dead,

            A puny body, a misshapen head.

MOTHER: What does your white master

            The Devil want from us?

BOLOM: The house looks warm, old woman,

            Love keeps the house warm,

From the cold wind and cold rain;

Though you bar up the door,

I can enter the house.

[*Thunder*]

MOTHER: Enter! You are welcome.

[*She flings open the door*]

GROS JEAN *and* MI-JEAN: Shut the door, shut the door!

[*Crash of cymbals. The* BOLOM *rolls in a blue light towards the hut, then enters; all freeze in fear*]

BOLOM: The Devil my master

Who owns half the world,

In the kingdom of night,

Has done all that is evil

Butchered thousands in war,

Whispered his diseases

In the ears of great statesmen,

Invented human justice,

Made anger, pride, jealousy,

And weakened prayer;

Still cannot enjoy

Those vices he created.

He is dying to be human.

So he sends you this challenge!

To all three of your sons,

He says through my voice,

That if anyone on earth

[DEVILS' VOICES *chanting*]

Anyone human

Can make him feel anger,

Rage, and human weakness,

He will reward them,

He will fill that bowl,

With a shower of sovereigns,

You shall never more know hunger,

But fulfillment, wealth, peace.

[*Increased drum roll to climax*]

But if any of your sons

Fails to give him these feelings,

For he never was human,

Then his flesh shall be eaten,

For he is weary of the flesh

Of the fowls of the air,

And the fishes in the sea,

But whichever of your sons

Is brave enough to do this,

Then that one shall inherit

The wealth of my prince.

And once they are dead, woman,

I too shall feel life!

[*Exit*]

DEVILS' VOICES OFF: *Bai Diable-là manger un 'ti mamaille,*

Un, deux, trois 'ti mamaille!

Bai Diable-là manger un 'ti mamaille,

Un,

   deux,

      trois ...

(Give the Devil a child for dinner,

One, two, three little children!

Give the devil a child for dinner,

One,

   two,

      three ...)

[*Fadeout*]

Act One

[*Daybreak. The hut. The* MOTHER *and her sons asleep.* GROS JEAN *rises, packs a bundle. His* MOTHER *stirs and watches. He opens the door*]

MOTHER: You will leave me just so,

            My eldest son?

GROS JEAN: Is best you didn't know.

MOTHER: Woman life is so. Watching and losing.

GROS JEAN: *Maman,* the time obliged to come I was to leave the house, go down the tall forest, come out on the high road, and find what is man work. Is big man I reach now, not no little boy again. Look this arm, but to split trees is nothing. I have an arm of iron, and have nothing I 'fraid.

MOTHER: The arm which digs a grave

            Is the strongest arm of all.

            Your grandfather, your father,

            Their muscles like brown rivers

            Rolling over rocks.

            Now, they bury in small grass,

            Just the jaws of the ant

            Stronger than them now.

GROS JEAN: I not even 'fraid that. You see,

            Is best you still was sleeping?

            I don't want you to wake my brothers.

            Ti-Jean love me and will frighten.

            Mi-Jean will argue and make me remain.

            The sun tapping me on my shoulder.

MOTHER: When you go down the tall forest, Gros Jean,

            Praise God who make all things; ask direction

            Of the bird, and the insects, imitate them;

            But be careful of the hidden nets of the devil,

            Beware of a wise man called Father of the Forest,

            The Devil can hide in several features.

            A woman, a white gentleman, even a bishop.

            Strength, *ça pas tout,* there is patience besides;

	There always is something stronger than you.
	If is not man, animal, is God or demon.
GROS JEAN:	*Maman,* I know all that already.
MOTHER:	Then God bless you, Gros Jean.
GROS JEAN:	The world not the same it was in your time,
	Tell my brothers I gone. A man have to go.

[*Marches from hut*]

[*Martial flute, quatro, drum*]

GROS JEAN [*Sings*]: There's a time for every man

> To leave his mother and father
>
> To leave everybody he know
>
> And march to the grave he one!

[*Enter the* CREATURES *hopping around him*]

> So the time has come for me
>
> To leave me mother and father
>
> To add my force to the world
>
> And go to the grave me one!

[*The* FROG *is in his path. He aims a kick*]

> Get out of my way, you slimy bastard! How God could
> make such things? Jump out under my foot, cricket, you
> know you have no bones! *Gibier! Gibier! montrez-moi
> sortir!* Bird-o, bird-o, show me a good short-cut, be quick!

[*Suddenly the* BIRD, *the* CRICKET *and the* FROG *all scurry shrieking,
croaking. The* OLD MAN *enters limping and rests a bundle of faggots
down.* GROS JEAN *watches. The* OLD MAN *lifts a comer of his robe to
scratch a cloven, hairy hoof.* GROS JEAN *emerges*]

GROS JEAN:	*Bonjour, vieux papa.*
OLD MAN:	*Bon matin,* Gros Jean.
GROS JEAN:	What you have with your foot?
OLD MAN:	Fleas, fleas, boy.

[*Covers it quickly*]

GROS JEAN:	Is man I am now. Chiggers in your flesh?
	Is man I am, papa, and looking for success.
OLD MAN:	The flesh of the earth is rotting. Worms.

GROS JEAN: Which way, papa?

OLD MAN: I cannot tell you the way to success;

               I can only show you, Gros Jean,

               One path through the forest.

GROS JEAN: I have no time to waste. I have an arm of iron,

               I have nothing, I 'fraid, man, beast, or beast-man,

               And more quick I get what I want, more better.

OLD MAN: I think strength should have patience. Look at me
               today.

               I was a strong woodman, now I burn coals,

               I'm as weak as ashes. And nearly deaf. Come nearer.

GROS JEAN [*Advances calmly*]: What you would say is the quickest way?

OLD MAN: The quickest way to what?

GROS JEAN: To what counts in this world.

OLD MAN: What counts in this world is money and power.

GROS JEAN: I have an arm of iron, only money I missing.

OLD MAN: Then I can't advise you.

GROS JEAN: You old and you have experience.

               So don't be selfish with it.

               Or you know what I'll do.

     [*Grabs him, hurls him down, axe uplifted*]

               Chop you and bury you in the bamboo leaves!

OLD MAN: With your arm of iron, the first thing to kill is
               wisdom?

GROS JEAN: That's right, papa.

OLD MAN: Well, the Devil always wants help.

GROS JEAN: The Devil boasts that he never get vex.

OLD MAN [*Rising*]: Easy, easy son, I'll help you if you wait,

               Just let me adjust the edge of my skirt.

               Well, I was coming through the forest now

               And I passed by the white spring, and I saw

               Some poor souls going to work for the white planter.

               He'll work you like the devil, but that's what you want,

               You and your impatience and arm cast in iron,

So turn to the right, go through the bamboo forest,

Over the black rocks, then the forest will open,

And you will see the sky, below that a valley,

And smoke, and a white house that is empty,

The old fellow is hiring harvesters today.

Remember an iron army may rust, flesh is deciduous.

There's your short-cut, Gros Jean, make the most of it.

GROS JEAN: Next time don't be so selfish.

   [*Exit* GROS JEAN, *marching*]

OLD MAN [*Sings, gathering bundle*]: Who is the man who can speak to
the strong?

Where is the fool who can talk to the wise?

Men who are dead now have learnt this long,

Bitter is wisdom that fails when it tries.

   [*To the audience*]

Ah well, there's wood to cut, fires to light, smoke to
wrinkle an old man's eyes, and a shrivelling skin to keep
warm. There went the spirit of war: an iron arm and a
clear explanation, and might is still right, thank God, for
God is the stronger. But get old father forest from the path
of the fable, for there's wood to cut, a nest of twittering
beaks to feed with world-eating worms. Oh, oh, oh.

   [*The* CREATURES *creep after him timidly*]

For they all eat each other, and that's natural law,

So remember the old man in the middle of the forest.

   [*He turns suddenly. Then hobbles after them*]

Eat and eat one another! It's another day. Ha, ha! Wah!
Wah!

   [*They flee. He goes out*]

GROS JEAN [*In another part of the wood*]: I have an arm of iron, and that's
true, but I here since the last two days working for this
damn white man, and I don't give a damn if he watching
me. You know what I doing here with this bag and this
piece of stick? Well, I go tell you. While I smoke a pipe.
Let me just sit down, and I won't lose my patience. [*He
sits on a log*] Well, you remember how I leave home, and
then bounce up this old man who put me on to a work?

Remember what the old son of a leaf-gathering beggar said? He said that working for the Devil was the shortest way to success. Well, I walked up through the bush then I come onto a large field. Estate-like, you know. Sugar, tobacco, and a hell of a big white house where they say the Devil lives. Ay-ay.

So two next black fellers bring me up to him. Big white man, his hand cold as an axe blade and his mind twice as sharp. So he say, 'Gros Jean, we has a deal to make, right?' So I say, 'Sure, boss!' He say the one that get the other one vex, the one who show the first sign of anger will be eaten rrruuunnnhhh, just like that, right? You think I stupid? I strong, I have some sense and my name not Gros Jean for nothing. That was two days ago. Well, Jesus, a man ain't rest since then! The first job I had, I had was to stand up in a sugar-cane field and count all the leaves of the cane. That take me up till four o'clock. I count all the leaves and then divide by the number of stalks. I must tell you there had times when I was getting vex but the old iron arm fix me, because there is patience in strength. The Devil ain't say anything. About seven o'clock, he tell me to go and catch about seventy fireflies. Well, you must try and catch fireflies! Is not easy. Had a time when I do so once, one whap with the hand! Thinking was a bunch but was nothing, only stars! So in the middle of all that, this man come up to me and say, 'What's the matter, Joe?' He always like he don't know my name, but I is me, Gros Jean, the strongest! And if you ain't know my name, you best don't call me nothing. Say, 'What's matter, Mac? You vex or sumpin?' O I say, 'No, I ain't vex!' Well, is two days now, and I ain't get a cent. I so tired I giddy. But I giving the old iron arm a rest from cramp, and breaking a little smoke. After all! If was only sensible work, if a man could get the work that suit him, cotton or sugar or something important! Plus he getting eighty-five per cent of the profit? Shucks, man, that ain't fair. Besides, I could just bust his face, you know. But me mother ain't bring me up so. After all, man, after all, a man have to rest man. Shime!

[*Enter* DEVIL *masked as a* PLANTER]

PLANTER: Well, how's it progressing, Joe, tired?

GROS JEAN: From where you was and now you come you hear me say I fagged? [*Slowly*] And Gros Jean is the name, boss.

PLANTER: Tobacco break? Whistle's blown past lunch, boy.

GROS JEAN: I taking a five here, chief. Black people have to rest too, and
                once I rest, chief, I do more work than most, right?

PLANTER: That's right, Mac.

GROS JEAN [*Gritting his teeth*]: Gros Jean ... Gros ... Jean ... chief ...!

PLANTER: You sound a bit annoyed to me.

GROS JEAN [*With a painful, fixed grin from now on*]: Have your fun.
                I know I ain't nobody yet, chief, but an old man tell me to
                have patience. And I ain't let you down yet, chief, hasn't I?

PLANTER: That's right, Gros Chien, Gros Jean, Gros Jean, sorry. Can't
                tell one face from the next out here. How's the work then?

[*Pacing up and down*]

GROS JEAN: Chief, why you don't take a rest too somewhat? You have all
                this land, all this big house and so forth, people working for
                you as if is ants self, but is only work, work, work in your
                mind, ent you has enough?

PLANTER [*Looking at his watch*]: Other people want what I have, Charley,
                and other people have more. Can't help myself, Joe, it's some
                sort of disease, and it spreads right down to the common man.

GROS JEAN: I not no common man, boss. People going hear about Gros
                Jean. Because I come from that mountain forest, don't mean
                I can't come like you, or because I black. One day all this
                could be mine!

PLANTER: Yes, yes. Well anyway, Horace, time is flying, and I want
                these leaves checked, counted, filed and classified by weight
                and texture and then stacked ... What's the matter, Francis?

GROS JEAN [*To the audience*]: You see how he provoking me, you don't
                think I should curse his ... [*Turns, bites hard on pipe,
                grinning*] Look, I haven't let you down yet, boss, have I? I
                mean to say I take two three hours to catch your goat you
                send me to catch. I mean not so? Wait, chief, wait, listen ... I
                ain't vex, boss. Ha-ha!

PLANTER: Sit down, Joe, relax, you can't take it with you, they say, only
                time is money, and the heights that great men reached, etc., and
                genius is ninety per cent perspiration and so forth ... So, sit
                down, waste time, but I thought you were in a hurry ... Henry.

GROS JEAN: Boss. [*Smiling*] You really impatianate, yes. Ha-ha! I mean
I don't follow you, chief. After I count and carry all the
cane leaves for you, ain't I, and look – when the wind blow
them wrong side I ain't say nothing, and I'm smiling ain't I?
[*Relaxes his expression, then resumes*] I'm smiling because I
got confidence in the old iron arm, ain't it? And if I do it and
have time to spare is the work and pay that matter, and is all
you worried about, *big shot!* Ain't it? Excuse me, I mean to
say, I'm smiling ain't I?

PLANTER: Sorry, Sorry, Gros Jean, sometimes we people in charge of
industry forget that you people aren't machines. I mean
people like you, Hubert ...

[GROS JEAN *is about to sit*]

GROS JEAN [*Rising*]: Gros Jean, chief, Gros Jean ... Ha-ha!

PLANTER: Gros Jean, very well ... [*Pause*] Have your smoke. [*Pause*]
Plenty of time. It might rain, people may be stealing from
me now. The market is unsteady this year. [*Pause*] But we're
human. [*Pause*] You don't know what it means to work
hard, to have to employ hundreds of people. [*Embracing
him*] You're worth more to me, Benton, than fifty men.
So you should smoke, after all. [*Pause*] And such a pleasant
disposition, always smiling. [*Pause, steps back*] Just like a
skull. [*Long pause*] But remember, Mervin, I'd like you to try
and finish this, you see I have a contract and the harder you
work the more I ...

GROS JEAN [*Exploding, smashing pipe in anger*]: Jesus Christ what
this damn country coming to a man cyant even get a
goddamned smoke? [*He tries to grin*] I ent vex, I ent vex,
chief. Joke, joke, boss ...

[*Explosion*]

[*When the smoke clears, the* DEVIL, *his* PLANTER's *mask removed, is
sitting on the log, calmly nibbling the flesh from a bone*]

DEVIL'S VOICE OFF: *Bai Diable-là manger un 'ti mamaille*

Un!

(Give the Devil a child for dinner)

(One!)

[*Blackout*]

40

Act Two

[*Music. Dawn. The forest. A cross marked 'Gros Jean'. The* CREATURES *foraging.* Enter MI-JEAN *walking fast and reading, a net slung over his shoulder*]

BIRD [*To flute*]: Mi-Jean, Mi-Jean, *bonjour*, M'sieu Mi-Jean.

    [*The* CREATURES *dance*]

MI-JEAN [*Closes the book*]: Bird you disturbing me!

    Too much whistling without sense,

    Is animal you are, so please know your place.

CRICKET: Where you going, Mi-Jean?

MI-JEAN [*To the audience*]: But see my cross, *oui*, ay-ay!

    Since from what time cricket

    Does ask big man their business?

FROG: You going to join your brother?

    You are a man's size now.

MI-JEAN [*Again to the audience*]: Well, confusion on earth, frog could talk!

    Gros Jean was one man, I is a next. Frog,

    You ever study your face in

    The mirror of a pool?

BIRD: Mi-Jean, Mi-Jean,

    Your brother is a little heap

    Of white under the bamboo leaves,

    Every morning the black beetles

    More serious than a hundred priests,

    Frowning like fifty undertakers

    Come and bear a piece away

    To build a chapel from his bones. Look, look!

    [*The* BIRD *shows the cross.* MI-JEAN *kneels and peers through his spectacles*]

CRICKET: Every morning I sit here,

    And see the relics of success,

    An arm of iron turned to rust,

    Not strong enough to stir the dirt.

FROG: Gros Jean was strong, but had no sense.

41

MI-JEAN [*Rising and dusting his clothes*]: He had the sin called over-confidence!
Listen, I …

BIRD: Run, run, Papa Bois, Papa Bois …

[*All run off*]

OLD MAN: *Bonjour, Mi-Jean, Mi-Jean, le philosophe.*

MI-JEAN [*To the audience*]: When my mother told me goodbye in tears,
She said, no one can know what the Devil wears.

[*To the* OLD MAN]

Bonjour, Papa Bois, how come you know my name?

OLD MAN: Who in the heights, in any small hut hidden in the ferns,
where the trees are always weeping, or any two men are
ploughing on a wet day, wrapped in old cloaks, or down in the
villages among the smoke and rum, has not heard of Mi-Jean
the jurist, and the gift of his tongue, his prowess in argument,
Mi-Jean, the *avocat,* the fisherman, the litigant? Come, come,
sir, don't be modest! I've been sitting there on the cold, crusty
log, rough as the armoured bark of a frog, waiting to exchange
knowledge with you. Ah, your brother's grave! How simple
he was! Well, I'm half-blind, but I see you have one virtue
more than your brother, fear. Nothing lives longer than brute
strength, sir, except it is human cowardice. Come nearer, come
nearer, and tell us why you left home? Sit down, you're among
equals.

MI-JEAN: I good just where I am.

I on my way to the sea

To become a rich captain,

The land work too hard.

Then to become a lawyer.

OLD MAN [*Softly singing*]: *On land on sea no man is free,*

All meet death, the enemy. I see,

Hence the net, the net and the book.

MI-JEAN: What?

OLD MAN: I say hence the book,

Hence the net, and the book.

MI-JEAN: *Ça c'est* hence? (What is 'hence'?)

OLD MAN: Same as whereas, and hereunto affixed.

These are terms used in tautology and law.

MI-JEAN [*Nodding blankly. Pause*]: I see you have a cow-foot.
Ain't that so?

OLD MAN: Yes, yes. A cow's foot. You have an eye for detail!
Born with it, actually. Source of embarrassment.
Would you like some tobacco? What are you reading?

MI-JEAN [*Opens the book*]: This book have every knowledge it have;
I checking up on man with cow-foot, boss,
In the section call religion, and tropical superstition.
Bos … Bovis … Cow … foot … foot, boss? Boss foot?
Bovis?

OLD MAN: Outside in the world they are wiser now, Mi-Jean:
They don't believe in evil or the prevalence of devils,
Believe me, philosopher, nobody listens to old men;
Sit down next to me and have a bit of tobacco.
And since you need knowledge, I'll give you advice …

MI-JEAN [*Still reading*]: I don't smoke and I don't drink,
I keep my head clear, and advice,
I don't need none, but will listen.

[*Shuts the book*]
This book is Latin mainly.
It have *bos,* meaning cow,
and *pes,* meaning foot,
Boss' foot, *bospes,* cow-heel perhaps,
It have plenty recipe
But it don't give the source! [*Sighs loudly*] So!
Yes, apart from wisdom, I have no vices.

OLD MAN: Life without sin. How about women?

MI-JEAN: The downfall of man! I don't care for women,
Women don't have no brain. Their foot just like yours.

OLD MAN: You believe in the Devil?
Oh, why don't you sit nearer,
Haven't you ever seen a cow-heel before?

MI-JEAN: Not under a skirt, no. [*Sighs loudly*] Yes!

I believe in the Devil, yes,
Or so my mother make me,
And is either that, papa.
Or no believe in God.
And when I meet this devil,
Whatever shape he taking,
And I know he is not you,
Since he would never expose
His identity so early,
I will do all that he commands,
But you know how I will beat him.

[*Sits near the* OLD MAN]

With silence, and a smile.

[*He smiles*]

Too besides when I meet him,
I will know if God exist,
We calling that in philosophy …

[*Checks in the book*]

We calling that in big knowledge,
Ah, polarities of belief,
When the existence of one object
Compels that of the other,
Bon Dieu, what terms, what terms!

[*Sighs loudly, rests the book down*]

Yes, Silence shall be my defence.

[*He sings 'The Song of Silence'*]

I

Within this book of wisdom
Hear what the wise man say:
The man who is wise is dumb
And lives another day,
You cannot beat the system
Debate is just a hook,
Open your mouth, de bait in!
And is you they going to juck

CHORUS: So when things dark, go blind
            When nothing left, go deaf
            When the blows come, be dumb
            And hum, hum.

                    II

            In Chapter Five from para-
            Graph three, page 79,
            This book opines how Socra-
            Tes would have been better off blind.
            God gave him eyes like all of we,
            But he, he had to look.
            The next thing, friends, was jail, *oui!*
            Hemlock and him lock up!
CHORUS: So when things dark, go blind, etc.

                  III

            The third set of instruction
            This self-said book declares
            Is that the wise man's function
            Is how to shut his ears
            Against riot and ruction
            That try to climb upstairs.
            If you can hear, don't listen!
            If you can see, don't look!
            If you must talk, be quiet!
            Or your mouth will dig your grave.

[*While he sings his song, the* OLD MAN *goes behind a grove of bamboo, leisurely removes his robe and his mask, under which is the mask of the* DEVIL; *then he changes into the mask and clothes of the* PLANTER]

PLANTER [*He sits on the log, legs crossed, smiling throughout the scene*]:
            Ah, finished all the work, I gave you, Mi-Jean?

[MI-JEAN *nods*]

            And menial work didn't bore you, a thinker?

[MI-JEAN *nods*]

            You're not one for small-talk, are you?

[MI-JEAN *nods*]

Did you catch the wild goat?

[MI-JEAN *nods yes*]

Frisky little bugger, wasn't he? Yes, sir, that's one hell of a goat. Some kid, what? Clever, however. How many canes were there on the estate?

[MI-JEAN *uses ten fingers repeatedly*]

Don't waste words, eh? All right, all right. Look, you don't mind a little chat while we work, do you? A bit of a gaff lightens labour. Good Lord, man, you've been here for over two days and haven't had the common decency to even pass the time of day. Where did you get your reputation as a bush lawyer, I mean it's only manners, blast it.

[MI-JEAN *cocks his head at the* PLANTER]

Oh, don't flatter yourself, young man, I'm not annoyed. It takes two to make a quarrel. Shut up, by all means. [*Rises*] Now, before it gets dark, I want you to come up to the house, check and polish the silver, rearrange my library and …

[*The goat bleats.* MI-JEAN *frowns*]

Aha, looks like the old goat's broken loose again, son. Better drop what you're not doing and catch it before it's dark.

[MI-JEAN *rises rapidly, runs off, returns*]

Ah, now you're smiling again, fixed him this time, haven't you?

[*The goat bleats*]

Not quite, cunning animal, that goat, couldn't have tied him.

[MI-JEAN *dashes out, annoyed, returns*]

Fast worker!

[*The goat bleats*]

Look, before you dash off, I'd like to say here and now …

[*The goat bleating as* MI-JEAN, *mumbling, smiling, points off*]

that I do admire your cheery persistence, your resigned nonchalance, so let me demonstrate something. There's a special kind of knot, and there's an end to that. Hence you take the rope thus, and whereas the goat being hereto affixed to the …

[*Goat bleating,* MI-JEAN *raging inside*]

but if that doesn't fix him, then my recommendation is …

MI-JEAN: Look!

PLANTER: Yes?

MI-JEAN: I think I know what I'm doing ... sir ...

PLANTER [*Above the sound of bleating*]: Oh, sure, sure. But I was simply
trying to explain just to help you out, that ... [*Goat bleats*]
You see? He's gone off again! Just a little more patience ...
[MI-JEAN *is about to run off*] It's simply a question of how
you tie this knot, don't you see? [MI-JEAN, *collecting himself,
nods, then tiredly smiles*] I mean, I've seen dumber men, not
you, fail at this knot you know, it's just a matter of know-how,
not really knowledge just plain skill ... [MI-JEAN *nodding,
nodding*] You look the kind of fellow who doesn't mind a
bit of expert advice. [*Goat bleats furiously*] And you'd better
hurry up before it gets dark. Wait, remember how to tie the
knot.

MI-JEAN [*Under control, nods*]: Yes, I remember.

[*Runs off, crosses the stage several times in a chase*]

PLANTER [*Walks up and down in a rage*]: Well, what the hell, I
thought I had him there, he's no fool, that's certain, for
the Devil comes in through apertures. He doesn't know
right from wrong, and he's not interested. The only
entrance I could have got through his mouth, I tried to
leave ajar, but the fool bolted it completely. There he goes
chasing the bloody goat like a simpleton, and not even
shouting at it. Good old Master Speak No Evil. I hope
he breaks his God-supported neck, the dummy! [*He sits*]
Here comes the comedy again, an eloquent goat and a
tongueless biped!

[*The goat cavorts across and around the stage to merry music, with
MI-JEAN behind him waving a rope and the net. MI-JEAN collapses*]

PLANTER: Tough life, eh?

[MI-JEAN *groans, nodding*]

Don't let it get you down.

[*Goat bleats*]

MI-JEAN: That goat certainly making a plethora of cacophony.

PLANTER: It's only a poor animal, in its own rut.

MI-JEAN [*Smiling*]:   Men are lustiferous animals also, but at least they
have souls.

PLANTER: Ah, the philosopher! The contemplative! An opinion at last! A man is no better than an animal. The one with two legs makes more noise and that makes him believe he can think. It is talk that makes men think they have souls. There's no difference, only in degree. No animal, but man, dear boy, savours such a variety of vices. He knows no season for lust, he is a kneeling hypocrite who on four legs, like a penitent capriped, prays to his maker, but is calculating the next vice. That's my case!

MI-JEAN: Nonsensical verbiage! *Bettise!*

PLANTER: It's not, you know, and you're getting annoyed.

MI-JEAN [*Shakes his head*]: You can't get me into no argument! I have brains, but won't talk. [*Long pause*] All I say is that man is divine!

PLANTER: You're more intelligent than the goat, you think?

MI-JEAN: I not arguing! Anything you want.

PLANTER [*Rises*]: Honestly, I'd like to hear what you think. You're the kind of chap I like to talk to. Your brother was a sort of politician, but you're a thinker.

[MI-JEAN, *rising, is about to lecture. The goat bleats*]

Steady-on. For all we know, that may be poetry. Which Greek scholar contends in his theory of metempsychosis that the souls of men may return into animals?

MI-JEAN: I never study Greek, but I ... [*Goat bleats. MI-JEAN pauses*] I was saying that I never study no Greek but I'd ... [*Goat bleats*] It getting on like to have sense, eh?

PLANTER: Why not?

MI-JEAN: Listen, I ent mind doing what you proposed, anything physical, because that's ostentatious, but when you start theorizing that there's an equality of importance in the creatures of this earth, when you animadvertently imbue mere animals with an animus or soul, I have to call you a crooked-minded pantheist ... [*Goat bleats, sounding like 'Hear, hear!'*] Oh, shut up, you can't hear two people talking? No, I'm not vexed, you know, but ... [*Goat bleats*]

PLANTER [*Advancing towards him*]: Your argument interests me. It's nice to see ideas getting you excited. But logically now. The goat, I contend, may be a genius in its own right. For all we know, this may be the supreme goat, the apogee of capripeds, the voice of human tragedy, the Greek ...

MI-JEAN: Exaggerated hypothesis! Unsubstantiated!

PLANTER: Since the goat is mine, and if you allow me, for arguments
             sake, to pursue my premise, then if you get vexed at the goat,
             who represents my view, then you are vexed with me, and the
             contract must be fulfilled.

MI-JEAN: I don't mind talking to you, but don't insult me, telling me a
             goat have more sense than I, than me. Than both of we!

PLANTER [*Embracing him*]: Descendant of the ape, how eloquent you
             have become! How assured in logic! How marvellous in
             invention! And yet, poor shaving monkey, the animal in you
             is still in evidence, that goat … [*Goat sustains its bleating*]

MI-JEAN: Oh, shut you damn mouth, both o'all you! I ain't care who
             right who wrong! I talking now! What you ever study?
             I ain't even finish making my points and all two of you
             interrupting, breach of legal practice! O God, I not vex,
             I not vex …

[*The* PLANTER *removes his mask, and the* DEVIL *advances on*
MI-JEAN]

[*Explosion*]

[*Blackout*]

[*The goat bleats once*]

DEVILS' VOICES OFF: *Bai Diable-là manger un 'ti mamaille*

                     (Give the Devil a child for dinner)

             Un!

             (One!)

             Deux!

             (Two!)

Act Three

[*Dawn. The forest. Two crosses marked 'Gros Jean' 'Mi-Jean'. The* OLD MAN *sits on the log, the* CREATURES *huddle near him.* TI-JEAN, MOTHER, *in the hut*]

DEVILS' VOICES OFF: *Bai Diable-là manger. un 'ti mamaille,*

> *Un, deux, trois 'ti mamaille!*
>
> *Bai Diable-là manger un 'ti mamaille,*
>
> *Un, deux, trois 'ti mamaille.*

OLD MAN: Aie! Feed the Devil the third, feed the Devil the third.

> Power is knowledge, knowledge is power, and the Devil devours them on the hour!

DEVILS: *Bai Diable-là manger un 'ti mamaille,*

> *Un, deux, trois 'ti mamaille!*

OLD MAN [*To the audience*]: Well, that's two good meals finished with a calm temper, and if all goes mortally, one more is to come.

[*Shrieks, points to where* TI-JEAN *is consoling his* MOTHER]

> Aie, ya, yie, a chicken is to come, a calf, a veal-witted young man, tender in flesh, soft in the head and bones, tenderer than old muscle power, and simpler than that net-empty atheist. For the next dish is man-wit, common sense. But I can wait, I can wait, gathering damp rotting faggots, aie!

MOTHER [*To flute*]: If you leave me, my son,

> I have empty hands left,
>
> Nothing to grieve for.
>
> You are hardly a man,
>
> A stalk, bending in wind
>
> With no will of its own,
>
> Never proven your self
>
> In battle or in wisdom,
>
> I have kept you to my breast,
>
> As the last of my chickens,
>
> Not to feed the blind jaws
>
> Of the carnivorous grave.

TI-JEAN: You have told me yourself

> Our lives are not ours,

That no one's life is theirs

Husband or wife,

Father or son,

That our life is God's own.

MOTHER: You are hard, hard, Ti-Jean,

O what can I tell you?

I have never learnt enough.

TI-JEAN: You have taught me this strength,

To do whatever we will

And love God is enough.

MOTHER: I feel I shall never see you again.

TI-JEAN: To return what we love is our glory, our pain.

OLD MAN: Oh, enough of these sentiments, I'm hungry, and

I'm cold!

TI-JEAN: Now pray for me, *maman*,

The sun is in the leaves.

MOTHER: The first of my children

Never asked for my strength,

The second of my children

Thought little of my knowledge,

The last of my sons, now,

Kneels down at my feet,

Instinct be your shield,

It is wiser than reason,

Conscience be your cause

And plain sense your sword.

[*The* BOLOM *rolls towards the hut. Drums*]

BOLOM: Old tree shaken of fruit,

This green one must die.

MOTHER: Aie, I hear it, I hear it,

The cry of the unborn!

But then have I not given

Birth and death to the dead?

[*The* BOLOM *dances off, shrieking.* TI-JEAN *rises*]

Oh, Ti-Jean, you are so small,
So small.

[*Exit*]

TI-JEAN: Yes, I small, *maman*, I small,
And I never learn from book,
But, like the small boy, David.

[*Sings*]

I go bring down, bring down Goliath,
Bring down below.
Bring down, bring down Goliath,
Bring down below.

[*He enters the forest*]

TI-JEAN: Ah, *bon matin, compère Crapaud*,
Still in your dressing-gown?

FROG: Ti-Jean, like your brothers you're making fun of me.

TI-JEAN: Why should I laugh at the frog and his fine bass voice?

FROG: You wouldn't call me handsome, would you?

TI-JEAN [*Kneels among the* CREATURES]: Oh, I don't know, you have
your own beauty.
Like the castanet music of the cricket over there.

CRICKET: Crak, crak. Now say something nice to the firefly.

FIREFLY: How can he? I don't look so hot in the daytime.

TI-JEAN: But I have often mistaken you at night for a star.

[*Rises*]

Now friends, which way is shortest to the Devil's estate?

FROG: Beware of an old man whose name is worldly wisdom.

FIREFLY: With a pile of sticks on his back.

CRICKET: … and a foot cloven like a beast.

TI-JEAN: If he is an old man, and mortal,
He will judge everything on earth
By his own sad experience.
God bless you, small things.
It's a hard life you have,
Living in the forest.

FIREFLY: God preserve you for that.

Bird, take the tree and cry

If the old man comes through

That grove of dry bamboo.

[*The* BIRD *flies off*]

CRICKET: Crashing through the thicket

With the cleft hoof of a beast.

FIREFLY: For though we eat each other,

I can't tempt that frog too close,

And we never see each other for dinner,

We do not do it from evil.

FROG: True. Is a long time I never eat a firefly.

FIREFLY: Watch it, watch it, brother,

You don't want heartburn, do you?

TI-JEAN: No, it is not from evil.

What are these crosses?

CRICKET: Nothing. Do not look, Ti-Jean.

Why must you fight the Devil?

TI-JEAN: To know evil early, life will be simpler.

FROG: Not so, Ti-Jean, not so. Go back.

[TI-JEAN *goes to the crosses, weeps*]

BIRD: Weep-weep-weep-weep-quick,

The old man is coming, quick.

FROG: If you need us, call us, brother, but

You understand we must move.

[TI-JEAN *stands over the crosses*]

OLD MAN: Ah, good morning, youngster! It's a damp, mournful walk through the forest, isn't it, and only the cheep of a bird to warm one. Makes old bones creak. Now it's drizzling, Damn it.

TI-JEAN: *Bonjour, vieux cor'*, I find the world pleasant in the early light.

OLD MAN: They say, the people of the forest, when the sun and rain contend for mastery, they say that the Devil is beating his wife. Know what I say? I say it brings rheumatism, I don't believe in the Devil. Eighty-eight years, and never seen his face.

TI-JEAN: Could you, being behind it?

OLD MAN: Eh? Eh? I'm deaf, come nearer. Come here and shelter. Good. Some people find me ugly, monstrous ugly. Even the small insects sometimes. The snake moves from me, and this makes me sad. I was a woodsman once, but look now. I burn wood into ashes. Let me sit on this log awhile. Tobacco?

TI-JEAN: No, thanks, sir.

OLD MAN: Tell me, boy, is your father living? Or your mother perhaps? You look frail as an orphan.

TI-JEAN: I think nothing dies. My brothers are dead but they live in the memory of my mother.

OLD MAN: You're very young, boy, to be talking so subtly. So you lost two brothers?

TI-JEAN: I said I had brothers, I never said how many. May I see that foot, father?

OLD MAN: In a while, in a while. No, I saw you looking at the two graves, so I presumed there were two. There were two, weren't there? Ah well, none can escape that evil that men call death.

TI-JEAN: Whatever God made, we must consider blessed. I'm going to look at your foot.

OLD MAN: Hold on, son. Whatever God made, we must consider blessed? Like the death of your mother?

TI-JEAN: Like the death of my mother.

OLD MAN: Like the vileness of the frog?

TI-JEAN [*Advancing*]: Like the vileness of the frog.

OLD MAN: Like the froth of the constrictor?

TI-JEAN: Like the froth of the constrictor.

[*He is above the* OLD MAN]

OLD MAN: Like the cloven cow's foot under an old man's skirt?

[TI-JEAN *sweeps up the skirt, then drops it*]

What did you hope to find, but an old man's weary feet? You're a forward little fool! Now, do you want some advice? Tell me how you'll face the Devil, and I'll give you advice.

TI-JEAN: O help me, my brothers, help me to win.

[*He retreats to the crosses*]

OLD MAN: Getting frightened, aren't you? Don't be a coward, son.

I gather twigs all day, in the darkness of the forest.

And never feared man nor beast these eighty-eight years.

I think you owe me some sort of apology.

[*The* BIRD *runs out and begins to peck at the rope, untying the faggots with his beak. The* OLD MAN *jumps up, enraged*]

      Leave that alone, you damned …

TI-JEAN: I'll help you, father.

[*Instead, he loosens the bundle*]

OLD MAN: I'll kill that bird. Why did you loosen my sticks?

      Haven't you any respect for the weariness of the old?

      You've had your little prank, now help me collect them.

      If you had a father you'd know what hard work was,

      In the dark of the forest, lighting damp faggots …

[TI-JEAN *pretends to be assisting the* OLD MAN, *but carefully he lifts his skirt and sees that below the sackcloth robe he has a forked tail*]

TI-JEAN: My mother always told me, my spirits were too merry,

      Now, here we are, old father, all in one rotten bundle.

OLD MAN: What's come over you, you were frightened a while back?

TI-JEAN: Which way to the Devil? Oh, you've never seen him.

      Tell me, does the Devil wear a hard, stiff tail?

OLD MAN: How would I know. [*Feels his rear, realizes*] Mm. Well, you go through that track, and you'll find a shortcut through the bamboo. It's a wet, leaf-rotting path, then you come to the springs of sulphur, where the damned souls are cooking …

TI-JEAN: You sure you not lying?

OLD MAN: It's too early in the morning to answer shallow questions,

      That's a fine hat you're wearing, so I'll bid you goodbye.

[TI-JEAN *lifts up a stick*]

TI-JEAN: Not until I know who you are, papa!

      Look, I'm in a great hurry, or I'll brain you with this;

      If evil exists, let it come forward.

      Human, or beast, let me see it plain.

[*The stage darkens. Drums. The* OLD MAN *rises*]

OLD MAN: Very well then, look!

[*He unmasks: the* DEVIL's *face. Howls, cymbals clash*]

DEVIL: Had you not gotten me, fool,

      Just a trifle angry,

      I might have played the Old Man

      In fairness to our bargain,

But this is no play, son.

For here is the Devil,

You asked for him early,

Impatient as the young.

Now remember our bargain,

The one who wastes his temper,

Will be eaten! Remember that!

Now, you will work!

TI-JEAN: Cover your face, the wrinkled face of wisdom,

Twisted with memory of human pain,

Is easier to bear; this is like looking

At the blinding gaze of God.

DEVIL [*Replacing the* OLD MAN'*s mask, and changing*]:

It is hard to distinguish us,

Combat to fair combat, then I cover my face.

And the sun comes out of the rain, and the clouds.

Now these are the conditions, and the work you must do.

TI-JEAN: Wait, old man, if is anything stupid,

I don't have your patience, so you wasting time.

OLD MAN: Then you must pay the penalty.

These are your orders:

I have an ass of a goat

That will not stay tied.

I want you to catch it

Tonight before sundown.

Over hill and valley

Wherever it gallops.

Then tie it good and hard.

And if it escapes

You must catch it again

As often as it gets loose

You try as many times.

If you should lose your temper …

TI-JEAN: Where the hell is this goat?

OLD MAN: Over there by the ... wait.

             The fool has run off.

             He won't last very long.

[*Exit* TI-JEAN. *The* OLD MAN *sits down, rocking back and forth with laughter.* TI-JEAN *runs back*]

OLD MAN: Finished already?

TI-JEAN: That's right. Anything else?

OLD MAN: Ahm. Yes, yes, yes. Best I've seen, though.

             Now I want you to go down to the edge of the cane field ...

[*The goat bleats*]

             Looks like you didn't tie him?

TI-JEAN: I tied the damned thing up.

             Something is wrong here.

             I tied the thing up properly.

[*The* OLD MAN *laughs.* TI-JEAN *runs off. The* OLD MAN *dances with joy. Goat bleats, then stops suddenly.* TI-JEAN *returns with something wrapped in a banana leaf and sits down quietly. The* OLD MAN *watches him. Pause. No bleat*]

OLD MAN: What's that in your hands?

TI-JEAN [*Proffers the leaf*]: Goat seed.

[*The goat bleats girlishly*]

OLD MAN: His voice is changing.

             I don't get you. Goat-seed?

TI-JEAN: I tied the damn thing.

             Then made it a eunuch.

[*The goat bleats weakly*]

             Sounds much nicer.

OLD MAN: You ... er fixed my one goat?

             Then you must have been angry.

TI-JEAN: No, I just couldn't see myself

             Chasing the damned thing all night.

             And anyhow, where I tied it,

             She'll never move again.

OLD MAN [*Walking around stage*]: You sit there calm as hell

And tell me you er … altered Emilia?

TI-JEAN: Funny goat, with a girl's name,

It's there by the plantain tree,

Just by the stones.

OLD MAN: Boy, you have a hell of a nerve.

TI-JEAN: It looks like you vex.

OLD MAN: Angry? I'm not angry. I'm not vexed at all.

You see? Look! I'm smiling.

What's an old goat anyhow?

Just the only goat I had.

Gave sour milk anyway.

TI-JEAN [*Rising. Rubbing his hands*]: Fine. Now, what's next on the agenda?

OLD MAN: What? Yes, yes … Fixed the goat …

TI-JEAN: Now look here, life is …

OLD MAN: Enough of your catechism!

TI-JEAN: Temper, temper. Or you might lose something. Now what next?

OLD MAN: Now, listen to this, boy.

Go down to the cane fields

And before the next cloud

Start checking every blade,

Count each leaf on the stalk,

File them away properly

As fast as you can

Before the night comes,

Then report back to me.

Well, what are you waiting for?

TI-JEAN: I got a bit tired chasing the goat,

I'm human you know.

OLD MAN: I'm going back to the house,

I'll be back at dawn to check on your progress.

[*Exit*]

TI-JEAN [*Goes to the edge of the cane field*]: Count all the canes, what a
            waste of time!

   [*Cups his hands*]

        Hey, all you niggers sweating there in the canes!

        Hey, all you people working hard in the fields!

VOICES [*Far off*]: 'Ayti? What happen? What you calling us for?

TI-JEAN: You are poor damned souls working for the Devil?

VOICES: Yes! Yes! What you want?

TI-JEAN: Listen, I'm the new foreman! Listen to this:

        The Devil say you must burn everything, now.

        Burn the cane, burn the cotton! Burn everything now!

VOICES: Burn everything now? Okay, boss!

   [*Drums. Cries. Caneburners' chorus*]

TI-JEAN: The man say Burn, burn, burn de cane!

CHORUS: Burn, burn, burn de cane!

TI-JEAN: You tired work for de man in vain!

CHORUS: Burn, burn, burn de cane!

   [*Exit*]

   [*The* FROG *enters*]

FROG [*Sings*]: And all night the night burned

        Turning on its spit,

        Until in the valley, the grid

        Of the cane field glowed like coals,

        When the devil, as lit as the dawn returned,

        Dead drunk, and singing his song of lost souls.

   [*Enter the* DEVIL, *drunk, with a bottle, singing*]

DEVIL: Down deep in hell, where it black like ink,

        Where de oil does boil and the sulphur stink,

        It ain't have no ice, no refrigerator

        If you want water, and you ask the waiter,

        He go bring brimstone with a saltpetre chaser,

        While de devils bawling.

   [*He is carrying the* OLD MAN's *mask. Now he puts it on*]

        Oh, if only the little creatures of this world could understand,
        but they have no evil in them … so how the hell can they?
        [*The* CRICKET *passes*] Cricket, cricket, it's the old man.

CRICKET: Crek, crek, boo!

CHORUS: Fire one! Fire one
Till the place burn down,
Fire one! Fire one.

DEVIL [*Flings the mask away*]: I'll be what I am, so to hell with you. I'll be what I am. I drink, and I drink, and I feel nothing. Oh, I lack heart to enjoy the brevity of the world! [*The* FIREFLY *passes, dancing*] Get out of my way, you burning backside. I'm the prince of obscurity and I won't brook interruption! Trying to mislead me, because I been drinking. Behave, behave. That youngster is having terrible effect on me. Since he came to the estate, I've felt like fool. First time in me life too. Look, just a while ago I nearly got angry at an insect that's just a half-arsed imitation of a star. It's wonderful! An insect brushes my dragonish hand, and my scales tighten with fear. Delightful! So this is what it means! I'm drunk, and hungry. [*The* FROG, *his eyes gleaming, hops across his path*] O God, O God, a monster! Jesus, help! Now that for one second was the knowledge of death. O Christ, how weary it is to be immortal. [*Sits down on log*] Another drink for confidence.

[*Sings*]

When I was the Son of the Morning,
When I was the Prince of Light.

[*He picks up the mask*]

Oh, to hell with that! You lose a job, you lose a job. Ambition. Yet we were one light once up there, the old man and I, till even today some can't tell us apart.

[*He holds the mask up. Sings*]

And so I fell for forty days,
Passing the stars in the endless pit.

Come here, frog, I'll give you a blessing. [*The* FROG *hops back, hissing*] Why do you spit at me? Oh, nobody loves me, nobody loves me. No children of my own, no worries of my own. To hell with … [*Stands*] To hell with every stinking one of you, fish, flesh, fowl … I had the only love of God once [*Sits*] but I lost that, I lost even that.

[*Sings*]

Leaning, leaning,
Leaning on the everlasting arms …

To hell with dependence and the second-lieutenancy! I had a host of burnished helmets once, and a forest of soldiery waited on my cough, on my very belch. Firefly, firefly, you have a bit of hell behind you, so light me home. [*Roars at the* CREATURES] Get out, get out, all of you … Oh, and yet this is fine, this is what they must call despondency, weakness. It's strange, but suddenly the world has got bright, I can see ahead of me and yet I hope to die. I can make out the leaves, and … wait, the boy's coming. Back into the Planter. [*Wears the* PLANTER's *mask*]

TI-JEAN [*Enters, also with a bottle*]: Oh, it's you, you're back late. Had a good dinner?

DEVIL: You nearly scared me. How long you been hiding there?

TI-JEAN: Oh, I just come through. Drunk as a fish.

DEVIL: Finished the work?

TI-JEAN: Yes, sir. All you told me. Cleaned the silver, made up the fifty rooms, skinned and ate curried goat for supper, and I had quite a bit of the wine.

DEVIL: Somehow I like you, little man. You have courage. Your brothers had it too, but you are somehow different. Curried goat? …

TI-JEAN: They began by doing what you suggested. Dangerous. So naturally when the whole thing tired them, they got angry with themselves. The one way to annoy you is rank disobedience. Curried goat, yes.

DEVIL: We'll discuss all that in the morning. I'm a little drunk, and I am particularly tired. A nice bathtub of coals, and a pair of cool sheets, and sleep. You win for tonight. Tomorrow I'll think of something. Show me the way to go home.

TI-JEAN [*His arms around the* DEVIL]: Oh, show me the way to go home,
I'm tired and I want to go to bed,
I had a little drink half an hour ago …

DEVIL [*Removing his arm*]: Wait a minute, wait a minute … I don't smell liquor on you. What were you drinking?

TI-JEAN: Wine, wine. You know, suspicion will be the end of you. That's why you don't have friends.

DEVIL: You have a fine brain to be drunk. Listen, I'll help you. You must have a vice, just whisper it in my ear and I won't tell the old fellow with the big notebook.

61

TI-JEAN [*Holds up bottle*]: This is my weakness. Got another drink in there?

DEVIL [*Passing the bottle*]: This is powerful stuff, friend, liquid brimstone. May I call you friend?

TI-JEAN: You may, you may. I have pity for all power. That's why I love the old man with the windy beard. He never wastes it. He could finish you off, like that ...

DEVIL: Let's not argue religion, son. Politics and religion ... You know, I'll confess to you. You nearly had me vexed several times today.

TI-JEAN: How did my two brothers taste?

DEVIL: Oh, let's forget it! Tonight we're all friends. It gets dull in that big house. Sometimes I wish I couldn't have everything I wanted. He spoiled me, you know, when I was his bright, starry lieutenant. Gave me everything I desired. I was God's spoiled son. Result: ingratitude. But he had it coming to him. Drink deep, boy, and let's take a rest from argument. Sleep, that's what I want, a nice clean bed. Tired as hell. Tired as hell. And I'm getting what I suspect is a hell of a headache. [*A blaze lightens the wood*] I think I'll be going up to the house. Why don't you come in, it's damp and cold out here. It's got suddenly bright. Is that fire?

TI-JEAN: Looks like fire, yes.

DEVIL: What do you think it is, friend?

TI-JEAN: I think it's your house.

DEVIL: I don't quite understand ...

TI-JEAN: Sit down. Have a drink. In fact, I'm pretty certain it's your home. I left a few things on fire in it.

DEVIL: It's the only house I had, boy.

TI-JEAN: My mother had three sons, she didn't get vexed. Why not smile and take a drink like a man?

DEVIL [*Removing the PLANTER's mask*]: What the hell do you think I care about your mother? The poor withered fool who thinks it's holy to be poor, who scraped her knees to the knuckle praying to an old beard that's been deaf since noise began? Or your two damned fools of brothers, the man of strength and the rhetorician? Come! Filambo! Azaz! Cacarat! You've burnt property that belongs to me.

[ASSISTANT DEVILS *appear and surround* Tl-JEAN]

TI-JEAN: You're not smiling, friend.

DEVIL: Smiling? You expect me to smile? Listen to him! [*The* DEVILS *laugh*] You share my liquor, eat out my 'fridge, treat you like a guest, tell you my troubles. I invite you to my house and you burn it!

TI-JEAN [*Sings*]: Who with the Devil tries to play fair,

Weaves the net of his own despair.

Oh, smile; what's a house between drunkards?

DEVIL: I've been watching you, you little nowhere nigger! You little squirt, you hackneyed cough between two immortalities, who do you think you are? You're dirt, and that's where you'll be when I'm finished with you. Burn my house, my receipts, all my papers, all my bloody triumphs.

TI-JEAN [*To the* DEVILS]: Does your master sound vexed to you?

DEVIL: Seize him!

[*The* BOLOM *enters and stands between* TI-JEAN *and the* DEVIL]

BOLOM: Master, be fair!

DEVIL: He who would with the devil play fair,

Weaves the net of his own despair.

This shall be a magnificent ending:

A supper cooked by lightning and thunder.

[*Raises fork*]

MOTHER [*In a white light in the hut*]: Have mercy on my son,

Protect him from fear,

Protect him from despair,

And if he must die,

Let him die as a man,

Even as your Own Son

Fought the Devil and died.

DEVIL: I never keep bargains. Now, tell me, you little fool, if you aren't afraid.

TI-JEAN: I'm as scared as Christ.

DEVIL: Burnt my house, poisoned the devotion of my servants, small things all of them, dependent on me.

TI-JEAN: You must now keep
             Your part of the bargain.
             You must restore
             My brothers to life.

DEVIL: What a waste, you know yourself
             I can never be destroyed.
             They are dead. Dead, look!

[*The* BROTHERS *pass*]

             There are your two brothers,
             In the agony where I put them,
             One moaning from weakness,
             Turning a mill-wheel
             For the rest of his life,
             The other blind as a bat,
             Shrieking in doubt.

[*The two* BROTHERS *pass behind a red curtain of flame*]

TI-JEAN: O God.

DEVIL [*Laughing*]: Seize him! Throw him into the fire.

TI-JEAN [*With a child's cry*]: Mama!

DEVIL: She can't hear you, boy.

TI-JEAN: Well, then, you pay her what you owe me!
             I make you laugh, and I make you vex,
             That was the bet. You have to play fair.

DEVIL: Who with the devil tries to play fair ...

TI-JEAN [*Angrily*]: I say you vex and you lose, man! Gimme me money!

DEVIL: Go back, Bolom!

BOLOM: Yes, he seems vexed,
             But he shrieked with delight
             When a mother strangled me
             Before the world light.

DEVIL: Be grateful, you would have amounted to nothing, child, a
             man. You would have suffered and returned to dirt.

BOLOM: No, I would have known life, rain on my skin, sunlight on my
             forehead. Master, you have lost. Pay him! Reward him!

DEVIL: For cruelty's sake I could wish you were born. Very well then, Ti-Jean. Look there, towards the hut, what do you see?

TI-JEAN: I see my mother sleeping.

DEVIL: And look down at your feet,
Falling here, like leaves,
What do you see? Filling this vessel?

TI-JEAN: The shower of sovereigns,
Just as you promised me.
But something is wrong.
Since when you play fair?

BOLOM: Look, look, there in the hut,
Look there, Ti-Jean, the walls,
The walls are glowing with gold.
Ti-Jean, you can't see it?
You have won, you have won!

TI-JEAN: It is only the golden
Light of the sun, on
My mother asleep.

[*Light comes up on the hut*]

DEVIL: Not asleep, but dying, Ti-Jean.
But don't blame me for that.

TI-JEAN: Mama!

DEVIL: She cannot hear you, child.
Now, can you still sing?

FROG: Sing, Ti-Jean, sing!
Show him you could win!
Show him what a man is!
Sing Ti-Jean ... Listen,
All around you, nature
Still singing. The frog's
Croak doesn't stop for the dead;
The cricket is still merry,
The bird still plays its flute,
Every dawn, little Ti-Jean ...

TI-JEAN [*Sings, at first falteringly*]: To the door of breath you gave the key,

Thank you, Lord,

The door is open, and I step free,

Amen, Lord ...

Cloud after cloud like a silver stair

My lost ones waiting to greet me there

With their silent faces, and starlit hair

Amen, Lord.

[*Weeps*]

DEVIL: What is this cooling my face, washing it like a

Wind of morning. Tears! Tears! Then is this the

Magnificence I have heard of, of

Man, the chink in his armour, the destruction of the

Self? Is this the strange, strange wonder that is

Sorrow? You have earned your gift, Ti-Jean, ask!

BOLOM: Ask him for my life!

O God, I want all this

To happen to me!

TI-JEAN: Is life you want, child?

You don't see what it bring?

BOLOM: Yes, yes, Ti-Jean, life!

TI-JEAN: Don't blame me when you suffering,

When you lose everything,

And when the time come

To put two gold coins

On your eyes. Sir, can you give him life?

DEVIL: Just look!

BOLOM [*Being born*]: I am born, I shall die! I am born, I shall die!

O the wonder, and pride of it? I shall be man!

Ti-Jean, my brother!

DEVIL: Farewell, little fool! Come, then,

Stretch your wings and soar, pass over the fields

Like the last shadow of night, imps, devils, bats,

Azaz, Beelzebub, Cacarat, soar! Quick, quick the sun!

We shall meet again, Ti-Jean. You, and your new brother!
The features will change, but the fight is still on.

[*Exit*]

TI-JEAN: Come then, little brother. And you, little creatures.
Ti-Jean must go on. Here's a bundle of sticks that
Old wisdom has forgotten. Together they are strong,
Apart, they are all rotten.
God look after the wise, and look after the strong,
But the fool in his folly will always live long.

[*Sings*]

Sunday morning I went to the chapel
Ring down below!
I met the devil with the book and the Bible.
Ring down below!
Ask him what he will have for dinner.

CHORUS: Ring down below!

TI-JEAN: Cricket leg and a frog with water.

CHORUS: Ring down below!

TI-JEAN: I leaving home and I have one mission!

CHORUS: Ring down below!

TI-JEAN: You come to me by your own decision.

CHORUS: Ring down below!

TI-JEAN: Down in hell you await your vision.

CHORUS: Ring down below!

TI-JEAN: I go bring down, bring down Goliath.

CHORUS: Bring down below!

[*Exit. The* CREATURES *gather as before*]

FROG: And so it was that Ti-Jean, a fool like all heroes, passed
through the tangled opinions of this life, loosening the rotting
faggots of knowledge from old men to bear them safely on his
shoulder, brother met brother on his way, that God made him
the clarity of the moon to lighten the doubt of all travellers
through the shadowy wood of life. And bird, the rain is over,
the moon is rising through the leaves. Messieurs, creek. Crack.

[*Curtain*]

An Echo in the Bone
Dennis Scott

Characters

RACHEL   Wife of the dead murderer, Crew. A pretty woman, in her late 40s.

BRIGIT   Her daughter-in-law, two months pregnant, lightfooted, in her 20s.

SONSON   Rachel's son, a boxer's build, 25.

JACKO   Rachel's younger son, 21, lithe and quiet.

RATTLER   The village drummer. A mute. Late 20s.

MADAM   Shopkeeper, friend of Rachel. Wiry. Late 60s.

LALLY   Madam's grand-daughter. Saucy. In her 20s.

DREAMBOAT A hard-drinking, womanizing peasant, 26.

P   The district's largest producer of 'grass'. Sturdy, gnarled, 64.

STONE   Ironmonger. A heavyweight. Reserved. 45.

The play was first presented by the University Drama Society at the Creative Arts Centre, Mona, Jamaica, on 1 May 1974, as part of the University's twenty-fifth anniversary celebrations. It was directed by Carroll Dawes. The cast was as follows:

RACHEL   Isoline Blackwood

SONSON   Dennis Morrison

BRIGIT   Diane Evering

RATTLER   Vernard Johnson

MADAM   Bernadette Allum

P   Justin Vincent

LALLY   Carolyn McPherson

DREAMBOAT Teddy Price

STONE   Keith Noel

JACKO   Jimmy Hall

The action of the play originates in the old sugar barn behind Crew's cottage, nine nights after the killing of the estate owner, Mr Charles, and the disappearance of Crew. The action moves through the present, a ship moored off Africa in 1792, MADAM's shop two days ago, an auctioneer's office in 1820, woods near an estate in 1833, Crew's house four years ago, a Great House in 1834, a field in 1937, and outside the Great House last week.

All characters are black. Objects present in the beginning of the play (i.e. the present) may be used as substitutes for props used in scenes from the past. Similarly, the set should provide playing areas needing a minimum of resetting to suggest the various places of the action.

The barn is large, with thick but deteriorating walls, and anonymous articles of rusting metals creating a feeling of age and disuse. Perhaps the ceiling slopes. Four huge girders rusting, support the roof and its gaping holes. The stage is dominated by a huge chain that is looped to the roof in two places, falling to the ground in coils past a broken shelf of wood a few feet across on one side, and ending in mid-air on the other. A table has been roughly hammered – wood on empty barrels but with a clean table-cloth. On it are bread, cheese, a basin and pitcher of water, a paper bag with 'grass', a couple of bottles of rum and a few mugs and cups. Near, are a broom, a pile of hessian bags, a box or two, and a chair. A large rough window opens on to a view of the hills, The Blue Mountains of Jamaica. A door on another wall leads to a forked path, one road to Crew's house a quarter mile from the village, one to the village.

Unseen to the side of the house and village, are miles of sugar cane, a few small peasant holdings, and the old Great House of the estate owner. Night has recently fallen. The moon will rise later.

Act One

[*Blackness*]

RACHEL [*Off; sings*]: Me alone, me alone, in de wilderness, [*Repeat*]
          Forty days and forty nights in de wilderness, [*Repeat*]

[*Lights up. RACHEL enters. A pretty woman. Strong. Tired. Proud.
She carries a hurricane lantern. Places it on the table in silence.
She stands beside the table gripping the old clothes tightly. Rocks a little.*]

    Aiee, Crew.

[*Replaces the clothes softly, turns the lamp down, moves to the window.
The moonlight silhouettes her.*]

BRIGIT [*Off*]: Ma!

RACHEL [*To herself*]: Don't call me tonight, child. I have business. If you
    want me, find me. Tonight I belong to the dead.

BRIGIT [*Off*]: Ma Rachel!

[SONSON, *a violent man of 25. Brooding. Seeing* RACHEL *stops.*]

RACHEL: You late.

SONSON: I had was to go all the way to the corner for the cheese and
    de money you give me wasn't enough. Why you didn't sent
    to Madam?

RACHEL: I shame to ask her. She is a guest in the house tonight. You find
    food on the table.

SONSON: I not hungry.

RACHEL: I tell the girl to leave for you. Wash yourself and go eat.
    The moon rise already. Night getting old.

SONSON: Wash? Is a dance I going to?

RACHEL: Is respect you must show. You not no dutty old nigger that
    don't know better. Where's you pride.

SONSON: There. [*Puts cheese on the table*] The chinawoman say I could
    credit it till month-end. Them say tell you don't forget this time.

RACHEL: Feisty, them couldn't say it to me face though.

SONSON: If you poor, dog eat you name.

RACHEL: I should send Jacko for things like that. You so bitter.

SONSON: Is me madda I learn it from. And – and him [*Nods towards
    the table*]

RACHEL: Run to clean yourself up. Change your shirt and call the others.

[*He turns to go.* BRIGIT *is at the door.*]

BRIGIT: Oh! You come back? You food on the coal stove. Ma, ah cyan find the bag with the candle.

RACHEL: Ah have to do everything meself?

SONSON: You better find dem or you gwine have to go shop dis time.

RACHEL: Sonson hush you mouth! Don't interfere wid what is not your business.

SONSON: Is my business, Ma. I is de man of the house now, you better know that Miss Brigit.

BRIGIT: I do you anything? Ma, I don't say a word to the man, him come here wid him striking self and bad talk me. Whey you want eeh?

SONSON: Whay you do all day? Who clear up this old shack and get the place ready, scrub de table when I should be cooling me head, before I go back to clearing the field. Who build the benches and patch the roof so good? Don't blow out all the candles while I praying. All a dat who responsible? Me and she!

BRIGIT: But wait!

SONSON: All you want to do is fix you face and laugh wid the man down de village.

BRIGIT: Damn liar!

SONSON: I don't know how Jacko stand you.

BRIGIT: Is him a married to, not you.

SONSON: You cyan find nothing in de house, you don't know where nothing is, all you do is chat, chat, and leave de work to you mother-in-law.

BRIGIT: You don't own me mouth.

SONSON: You damn right, thank God I don't own no part of you.

BRIGIT: Das the trouble –

RACHEL: Sonson, Brigit!

BRIGIT: Das what bun you!

RACHEL: Hush! You hear me? One likkle question cause that? You run you mouth too much, de two of you. I see the candlestick on top of the dresser in the kitchen. Go bring dem come. No you Brigit.

[SONSON *stands angrily for a moment, then goes. Pause.*]

When I am a old woman, what you going to do eeh? The three of you.

[BRIGIT *starts to cry*, RACHEL *goes to comfort her*.]

This is a hard time for him. Him did look to his father. Hush, hush now, don't make Jacko see you crying. It's bad for him child, besides we have worse things to cry about. If you eye going shed water, make it rain down for the dead man.

BRIGIT: I do like you say, Ma. I stay far from him. I keep myself quiet when he around. And still I can't do nothing to please him. Is like somebody curse him.

RACHEL: A family must be able to live in de same house and don't fight people so all the time. I will talk to Jacko in the morning.

BRIGIT: Don't do that, Ma Rachel. Him will say I only make trouble in de house and blame me.

RACHEL: Well then, don't fret. Bide your time. Is the child getting heavy in you belly that make things hard to bear. Don't fret. Go call Jacko before people start to come.

BRIGIT: Ma, what you doing this for? Why you don't make the dead stay dead? Is best the village forget him now, and forget how he spill the blood of another man.

RACHEL: And I am to forget him too! Is my man, I going satisfy his ghost with whatever respect I have to give him. You think you can wipe out thirty years of him together just so?

[*At the window a face*]

Hurry now, chile. The drum is here already. Call you husband.

[BRIGIT *exits*]

[RATTLER *enters, the drum is hung at his back. He swings it around and beats a note. Grins at her.*]

RACHEL: My old friend. You the first one. Welcome. I know what you looking for. Here. You have your own bottle.

[*She gives him a bottle of white rum. He eyes it again and again, uncorks it and drinks.*]

RATTLER: Ahhhh!

RACHEL: Take a seat Rattler. Just by the door. An warm yourself on the 'whites' till is time to speak.

[*He sits by the door at his drum and relaxes, watching her*]

You have plenty 'waters' tonight, ease yourself before the others come. Rattler, you keep the house. I soon come, and the children too. I going to put on my company clothes.

[*Exit*]

[RATTLER *beats a tentative rhythm, swings the bottle. Voices outside. Listens. Quickly makes a large cross on the door with a finger wet in the rum. The voices are outside the door. He hugs the drum. Two women and two men come in.* MADAM LOVE, LALLY, DREAMBOAT *and* P. RATTLER *signs to them to keep out.*]

MADAM: Miss Rachel!

DREAM: What wrong, Rattler boy?

MADAM: You see Miss Rachel, Rattler?

LALLY: Don't bother ask him nothing, Ma. I can't stand when him make that noise inna him throat.

[P *starts to sit down, wheezing*]

DREAM: Hey gimme some of that, friend. Is a hot walk up the hill.

MADAM: Wait. [*Sniffs the air*] Mass P don't sit down yet. The place not bless yet.

LALLY: I did tell you we was early.

P: Not bless yet? Lawd help me, mek me go sit down outside till she come.

DREAM: Chu, Rattler, is only a small drink a begging.

MADAM: You hear me, Dreamboat? Leave the man bottle alone.

LALLY: Is how you drink so Dreamboat?

P: Such a long walk for a old man.

DREAM: Gimme the bottle. [*Wrestles playfully with* RATTLER]

LALLY: Lick him wid the drum, Rattler. Don't mek him tek it from you.

MADAM [*At the door*]: Miss Rachel!

P: Dreamboat behave yourself!

DREAM: Shut you tail, grampa. All I asking is a little drink.

LALLY: I will hold the drum for you, Rattler. You can settle up with Dreamboat.

P: You damn fool, you want to bring curse on all of us. [*Pushes feebly at* DREAMBOAT]

DREAM: I say don't interfere with me [*Struggles more seriously with the other two men. The bottle falls, breaks, pouring rum out on the floor.*]

[RACHEL *off screams. Pause.*]

[DREAMBOAT *in the silence, pants loud and fast. The others watch him motionless. His head begins to swivel on his neck, slowly till the whole body is weaving on the spot. His feet shuffle a little, then …*]

[RATTLER *crouches over the drum, picks up the beat softly, moaning a little with concentration*]

MADAM: Lally.

LALLY: Yes, Granny.

MADAM: Go down to the house. See if Miss Rachel is alright.

LALLY: Yes, Ma.

[*Exits quickly*]

MADAM: Mass P. You see any oil on the table?

[P *hunts nervously*]

Is the rum cause it.

Hurry.

[*He brings a small bottle to her*]

Hold him now, Mass P. [*To* RATTLER] Don't stop.

[*The drum gets louder*]

[P *pours a little oil into her hand*]

P: Is a old man I can't hold him!

MADAM: You have to! The spirit on him back. It will tear him. You was smoking before you come here, nuh?

[DREAMBOAT *moves in circle around the drum.* RATTLER *turns on his heels so as to be always facing him.*]

RATTLER [*In a high voice*]: Ah ah ah ah ah …

STONE [*At the door, panting, a paper in his hand*]: Crew, show yourself!

P: Crew? Where?

MADAM: Hold him, Stone, him going kill himself!

STONE: Jesus! Dream, what happen?

P: The spirit take him, just so, and him start to dance.

STONE: Then is him I see!

P: Who?

STONE: Is the dead man walking in the air. Is Crew! From the bottom of the road I see this man walking and I say that is Crew, I would know that walk anywhere, and I run up here as fast as I can.

P: What we going to do, eh? What we going to do?

MADAM: Is the rum that pour out on the floor and the place sacred now the dead man come home.

STONE: He walk right into here. I see him with my own eyes.

MADAM: Hold him Stone! He inside the boy trying to get out, and the heart will break open if the oil is not put on his head and his mouth soon.

STONE: Help me, then.

MADAM: Hold the candle in front of his face.

[*P does so. STONE grapples with DREAMBOAT. They lurch together then fall. STONE pins him down, the candle is held close triumphantly, MADAM makes the sign of the cross on the boy's head, then wets his lips with the oil. DREAMBOAT arches onto his shoulders, shuddering, lies quiet. RACHEL is at the door, gripping the arm of SONSON, the two girls behind them close. RACHEL enters dressed in white, with her head tied. The drum is still. Pause.*]

RACHEL: This is the house of the dead. This is the house of the dead. I welcome you. [*Pause*] It is the will of the man that is dead.

MADAM: Oh me Gawd, Rachel – [*Goes to her swiftly, comfortingly*]

RACHEL: Madam Love, I know. Look after the boy. They were friends, him and Crew.

P: We was all his friend, woman.

RACHEL: P, you most of all.

BRIGIT: Ma.

RACHEL: Yes, daughter.

BRIGIT: Jacko coming, Ma. I see him coming through the cane.

RACHEL: Ah.

P: That's good. A man's sons should mourn him.

RACHEL: How is he now?

STONE: How you feel, Dream?

[*P brings a cup of water. DREAMBOAT is dazed and weak.*]
           Here, drink it.

LALLY: Is all right Dream, is not rum this time. [*Laughing at him*]

MADAM [*To RACHEL*]: You saw something? [*Pause*]

BRIGIT: There was a shadow at the window. [*Pause*] The curtain …

SONSON: Breeze. The door was open.

RACHEL [*Pityingly*]: He is here.

DREAM: … dream … [*Shivers*]

P: Don't talk.

[JACKO *passes outside the window*]

DREAM: Dark. [*Cries softly*]

[LALLY *impulsively moves to him*, BRIGIT *snickers*]

LALLY: Ma, come we go home.

MADAM: Child.

LALLY: Suppose it was me …?

JACKO [*At the door*]: 'Evening. 'Evening. I came as fast as I could, Ma.
           A truck gave me a ride part of the way from town. Lally.

BRIGIT: The food is on the coal stove.

JACKO: We had a flat, and I had to help him fix it. Rattler. Mass P.
           Madam.

BRIGIT: What about me, Jacko?

JACKO: Evening.

BRIGIT: Go eat.

JACKO: I not hungry. I could hear the drum all the way across the cane
           field.

SONSON: What they ask you?

JACKO: Same thing as before. If I ever plant grass. Or my father. Or you.
           How I make the money for the shoes I wearing. Where my
           father is hiding. If I was there when he kill the white man.

P: What you tell them, boy?

JACKO: I tell them my father is dead, and I going home to mourn him.

           [*Silence*]

RACHEL: All o' you, sit yourself down.

           [*They sit quietly*]

           Those that want to refresh themselves, make yourself easy.

           Sonson.

           [SONSON *opens the paper bag, hands it around. They help themselves to*
           the 'spliffs'.]

P: Dream! Mind. Remember what happen to you the last time
           you smoke the weed?

DREAM: Chu, man!

           [DREAMBOAT *first. Lights it from the candle eagerly, inhales.*
           P *ceremoniously lights* JACKO's *before his own.*]

MADAM: I will share it with my grand-daughter, thank you.

           [RATTLER *playing, very softly, broken rhythms*]

JACKO: My face want washing.

           [BRIGIT *brings him a wet rag, after she has poured a little water from a*
           jug on it]

STONE: He grew the best in the district, except for you, Mass P.

[*Small approving laughter from the others*]

[RACHEL *stands at the window, half lit by the moon.* LALLY *sits close to* DREAMBOAT *staring at him. She drags at his smoke once or twice.* JACKO *goes to* RACHEL, *offers his 'spliff'. She motions him away. Takes one for herself.* STONE *lights it.*]

RACHEL: My friends. My children.

[*In turn she goes to each, stands before him a moment, bows dippingly, so that the motion carries through her whole body in a ripple. As she bows,* RATTLER *makes the drum cry in a ciyé. She seats herself.*]

P [*Waveringly, sings. The others join in, one by one. The drum joins them.*]:

He was tempted by the devil in de wilderness, [*Repeat*]

Forty days and forty nights inna de wilderness, [*Repeat*]

[*The verse becomes a humming, sustained under the litany*]

MADAM: Who is dead?

RACHEL: A man.

P: What is his name?

RACHEL: Crew.

DREAM: Where him come from?

RACHEL: Darkness.

SONSON: Where him gone to?

RACHEL: Darkness.

JACKO: What him life was like?

RACHEL: Sorrow.

STONE: What his life was?

RACHEL: Smoke.

BRIGIT: Who going remember him?

RACHEL: Friends.

STONE: Who going remember him?

RACHEL: Sons.

P: What him leave with us?

RACHEL: What is his memory?

RACHEL: Smoke. [*Silence. The tune lifts again.*] All right now, we going to talk about him a little. Who first will witness? Who going to speak and let him hear? [*Silence*] If you have forgiveness to ask, speak it now.

Those that have debts to pay, wipe them away this very time. [*Silence*]

P: He was the strongest man in the area. Stone. Stronger than even you.

STONE: I always wanted to fight him. But he wouldn't take me on.

LALLY: You think he was afraid of you eh?

JACKO [*Laughs*]: He wasn't afraid of nobody, my father.

BRIGIT: Such a good-looking man. Handsomer than you, Sonson.

LALLY: He used to come into the chinaman shop sometimes, before he fire me and said I was feisty to them customers. You should see the white woman them watching him from the corner of dem eyes. You know that old pair of tight trousers him wear? Woeeeee! [*Laughing*]

RACHEL: Crew …

MADAM: Rachel. You know what happened that day up at the Great House? [*Silence*] I wonder if anybody see him? I wonder what de white man, Missa Charles, do him? Mek him kill him.

JACKO: Don't talk of death, that's not what we come here to do, right, Ma?

DREAM: Lawd God, him spirit go peaceful-like to rest. Do Lawd.

ALL: Amen.

DREAM: Miss Rachel, he have a knife I used to ask him for all the time, the handgrip make of bone, you think I can take it now?

P: What a man did like knife! Anything sharp, like he couldn't resist it.

JACKO: Beat something a man can laugh with, Rattler.

BRIGIT: The police keeping the machete, nuh Jacko? I remember how him used to keep it sharp and thin.

JACKO: Ras, woman, you don't hear me say that it not the right talk? Ma, tell her. When I talk to her is like the water washing over stone in the river.

RACHEL: Hush, speak soft to your woman.

STONE: Watch out she don't leave you Jacko. [*It's a joke that falls flat*] Especially like some fellas making all kinds a money doing metal work on the estate.

P: All that going change now, though. The estate pass away from the family now that Mr Charles is dead and buried. New times coming. The next owner going to put in machines all over, and what will happen to you and me then?

STONE: Iron work is a good trade, I going to town next week, and set myself up.

LALLY: And you going to, Dreamboat? You can take me with you.

MADAM: How you tongue so loose, girl? You too forward.

LALLY: Even if you not so strong and good looking like Crew.

DREAM: He was a good friend, Miss Rachel.

RACHEL: He was a poor black man like all 'o we. And my house feel empty and cold without him.

[SONSON *moves away. Strips his shirt off. Puts the dead man's clothes on deliberately.*]

P: Is a terrible thing to go out like a fire that the rain put out. This is what a man must live for, eh? You cut down the canes for a lifetime, every year you drag the sweetness out of the ground with you bare hands and pray the next season will be easy. Three hundred years crying into the white man's ground, to make the cane green, and nothing to show.

MADAM: Hush P!

P: Nothing to show! That's what he always said. And then they plough you back into the canes, and nobody remember how strong you was. And when they squeeze the canes nobody knows how much blood it takes to make the rum hot and sweet.

RACHEL: I remember. I remember. Thirty years long like three hundred.

[*Hums and the others follow*]

[SONSON *walks softly into the light. He is Crew.*]

SONSON: Rachel. [*Silence*]

P: Sonson.

[*The others back away. SONSON moves forward. Someone overturns the mug of water. It splashes at his feet. He stops, it is like a wall in front of him. The sea roars suddenly in the air.*]

SONSON: I could hear the drum all the way across. [*Pause*]

STONE: Smoke.

[RACHEL *kneels*]

JACKO: Sonson …

SONSON: Crew!

RACHEL: My husband. What you want?

SONSON: I lose my cutlass. Rachel you see it anywhere?

MADAM: Crew. In the name of Christ, if you come with hatred in you, may you never rest in peace. What you want?

SONSON: I have to wipe it off. But when I wake up I couldn't find it anywhere. You remember it, Jacko? It have blood all over it.

JACKO: Pa, they have it in town at the station. They take it away, Pa.

STONE: You kill the white man with it, and them find it, Crew.

SONSON: Don't cry, Rachel, I had to do it. He was a bad man, and the earth was calling out for his blood for what he do to us. [*Pause*] All of us …

[BRIGIT *comforts* RACHEL]

LALLY: Is what do him, Rattler?

SONSON: Don't cry, woman. I not the first one the white man kill with his lies. Nor the last one … I would like to touch you, again. [*Reaches out to her. It is an impossibly long distance. Sways, distressed, rambling.*] Such a long way I had to go to find you. Miles and miles of green. All the way home. Going home so fast so far, the heart inside me was like a drum smelling the ground in the moonlight. Home.

[*Drums. He begins to dance.*]

P: Rattler, don't!

MADAM: Make him rest, the spirit will go away when him ready.

BRIGIT: Stop it, Rattler!

[RATTLER *shows his empty, idle hands. He isn't beating. But the drums build. Darkness. Then quiet a little.*]

[*The sound of the sea against the ships timbers. 1792. The slave coast on board a ship. P is up in the crow's nest, swaying, squinting against the sun's glare.*]

P: Mother of God! What a way for a Christian subject of His Majesty to die. Those damn drums night and day, the beach out of bounds and the black bastards stinking in the hold already. It's not too good up here either. [*Smells his armpit*] If the sun would only let up for a minute! It's on their side that's what. God help me, if I ever get home to London it's Thameside for me this time. All that green. The place is too rich, it's too hot, and those heathen brutes. Aye, old fellow, you're getting too crabby to be perched up here four bells at a stretch, baking your blood away. Too old … One day you will fall and nobody will miss you. Aye, well … What's this now? [*Trains his glass down on the deck*] A new batch of females. Naked as the day. That's what I should do. Three voyages now, all that money saved, careful I am not like Daniel down there, spending it all on grog. If I add my share for this venture, I could buy me a young black and settle in the islands. Hire her out maybe. Then retire for a quiet old age, and nothing to do. [*Crackles*] Look at them pissing themselves in sheer fright. And not a stitch on them. Daniel! Save me some ...! Ah the wind's against me. An hour to go. But the sun! [*Looks slowly out to sea*] Yes, that's what I'll do ...

[*Drums down and out*]

[*In the hold the others are crouched, sitting, tight-packed. Humming 'Sumulay ...' pause. Silence. Except for the sea.*]

JACKO: Wife. Wife.

[*Voices whisper it, echoing*]

LALLY: Whydah? Is it you?

JACKO: Where is my woman? Does she sleep? Nana! [*Silence*]

LALLY: Whydah, my brother, I was awake when they came for her. I called out to you, but the fat one the one like pork, he hit me. I did not say anymore.

JACKO: Didn't anyone of you see, or hear? Ah ah, they have taken my woman.

LALLY: Be still, if they hear, they will whip us again. My back is cracking like wood still from the last time. And yours, my sister, how do you feel?

[DREAMBOAT *moans in fever*]

RACHEL: He worse than me.

SONSON: What does he say?

LALLY: Listen yourself, how much breath do you think I have to gossip?

RACHEL: It will soon be over. It must end.

SONSON: One way or the other, Mother.

JACKO: Then my son is dead too.

SONSON: What does he say? His son is dead too. The woman was pregnant. Be glad. He's out of it.

LALLY: If we stay here longer, we'll learn to speak the same tongue. All the tribe. Of Dahomey.

SONSON: We will die first.

RACHEL: You talk too much.

LALLY: Yes, be like my brother here, who says nothing from one eating time to the next.

JACKO: But I will speak. Hear me, oh Gods of my fathers. If you have travelled by the water with us, hear how I curse you.

RACHEL: Fool!

LALLY: He may be right. The Gods are dead or gone away. Or too far to hear what we speak.

RACHEL: Only a mad man rails at the Gods. They have their reasons.

JACKO: May your altars be ever empty, and the holy places pull down. May the beasts spoil your offerings and the fires be cold under pots. May your priests wither and die, and their stool be empty and the drums tear and become silent. For you have forsaken your people and the houses of those that trusted you. And we are strangers in a dark place.

RATTLER: Peace, my brother!

SONSON: Ah! So he has a tongue after all!

RATTLER: I saw when they took her. It was no worse than I seen your people do to mine in the year of the war between us. When there was a raid on my village. I was only a boy then. And your warriors killed my mother. It was quick, I have no complaints. And then they dragged her outside, through the food she had been cooking, and put fire to the hut.

RACHEL: Someone is coming!

RATTLER: But a chief's son learns early how to make the best of things. I will tell you. Once the house is empty, what happens to it is of no importance. I saw your woman. When they loosed the chain, she fell on her face onto the ground, and they dragged her with her mouth opened through the shit we lie in, and took her away. Do not weep for her, my brother. She tasted nothing.

SONSON: That one is a cold one. He will live long.

RACHEL: Shhh!

[*During the following conversation they crawl up a length of chain on the stage, and out of the hold into the blazing sunlight. On deck, under a parasol, perhaps,* BRIGIT. *She is in the care of* STONE. P *stands by.*]

STONE: Ma'am, are you sure you want to watch this?

BRIGIT: Bosun, I have already obtained the captain's permission. I shall be absolutely still, I merely wish to observe them. After all, if I am to spend the rest of my life in the islands it is best for me to know precisely what kind of … er, people they are.

STONE: Aye aye, Ma'am. You haven't seen them before Ma'am?

BRIGIT: No, I have not. It is a lucky thing our ships crossed so near to the port, or I might have arrived from England quite green, as to the nature of the creatures! One had such conflicting reports from various writers!

STONE: Here they come now. Excuse me, Ma'am, please to stand over here.

BRIGIT: Will you please ignore me, I shall be quite safe here!

STONE [*Stolidly*]: The cap'n said –

BRIGIT: Bosun, I know what the captain said, and I assure you –

[*As the contents of the hold appear, hands still chained in front of each one, she chokes, gasps, retches and runs to the rails*]

STONE [*His amusement hardly shows*]: It's best to stand leeward, up wind of them, Ma'am. Are you all right, Ma'am?

BRIGIT: Quite alright, thank you. I never expected … that's all.

STONE: Very good, Ma'am.

BRIGIT: But – oh! They're quite … naked, most of them.

STONE: Yes, Ma'am.

BRIGIT: How dare you – the Captain – oh!

STONE [*Puzzled*]: Well, Ma'am, it's like the bulls you see – I mean cow, animals. You don't expect them to be wearing clothes like people. That's different.

BRIGIT [*Pauses*]: Oh. Oh. Yes, I see.

JACKO: Where is he? Where is the one who saw her taken away?

BRIGIT: Bosun. That one is saying something! What is he saying?

STONE: Some kind of local talk, Miss. Alright put the hoses on them.

BRIGIT: But they're filthy. What dreadful animals!

JACKO: Where is he?

RACHEL: Quiet fool! They're watching.

BRIGIT: It's disgusting, I hope my father's are better looking. The men …

JACKO: Is it you, eh? Is it …? As soon as I can see.

STONE: Keep them together, there. And keep you fingers on the triggers!

[*The bodies are buffeted this way and that by the streams of water*]

BRIGIT [*Pleased*]: Well, this is most interesting.

[DREAMBOAT *falls.* STONE *nods to* P. P *prods* DREAMBOAT *who scarcely reacts.* P *looks questioningly at* STONE. STONE *frowns.*]

STONE [*Turning* BRIGIT *away, pointing*]: There's a lad that's going to be a strong specimen, Ma'am.

BRIGIT: Oh I'd like to have him, perhaps when we arrive Papa will get him for me!

[P *quickly kicks* DREAMBOAT *in the head, then rolls him over the side of the ship. Nobody notices, really.*]

BRIGIT: I have a volume by Mr Bryan Edwards, just published, about the islands. Do let me read you what he says about them.

STONE [*Sighs*]: Very good, Ma'am.

[*While* BRIGIT *reads,* JACKO *stumbles against* RATTLER, *peers into his face*]

BRIGIT: 'The Papaws, or people of Whydah, are unquestionably the most docile and best-disposed slaves that are imported from any part of Africa. Without the fierce and savage manners of the Caromantyn Negroes, they are also happily exempt from the timid and disponding nature of the Eboes ...'

JACKO: You ...

[*Lifts his hand to hit* RATTLER. RATTLER *swings clubbed fists.* JACKO *doubles up.* RATTLER *knees him. They fall.* P *is over them pointing his gun.* STONE *is at his side.*]

STONE: That's private property! Don't lay a hand on each other or I'll have both your hides!

P: They don't know what you are saying, Bosun!

STONE: They'd better learn to hear the voice.

[RATTLER *deliberately turns and spits on* STONE. *Pause.*]

STONE: Look at me. Look at me.

[*It is a quietly contained fury. They look to the group of four.*]

Knife, Danny –

[STONE*'s hand is out to* P, *though* STONE *watches* RATTLER. *The knife is placed in his hand. He shoves* RATTLER *on to his back,* P *presses the gun into* RATTLER*'s belly,* STONE *kicks* RATTLER *in the head.* RATTLER *relaxes into unconsciousness.* STONE *reaches into his open mouth pulls at his tongue, straddling* RATTLER*'s body. Slices it with one movement.* BRIGIT *gasps. He turns to face her, blankface. They stare at each other, pause.*]

BRIGIT: Filthy beast. How dare he! [*Pause*] I think I'll go below now. I shall tell the Captain how well you escorted me, Bosun.

[BRIGIT *smiles at* STONE. *Goes. Sits in her cabin at the table, thoughtfully nibbling at a bit of meat.*]

STONE: Very good, Ma'am. [*To all the sailors*] Not a word of this on shore. The owners don't like it when we spoil the goods.

P [*Chuckles*]:   He'll find it hard to spit now, without a tongue.

STONE: Now, below.

[*The group shuffles, clambers, drifts, marches, stumbles back to the hold.* RACHEL *stops, looks back at the body of* RATTLER. *Pause. Looks at* SONSON. SONSON *goes back to him cautiously, watched by* STONE *and* P. *Lifts, drags him over to the hold. The group pass him silently between themselves, very gently, down into the hold, along the chain. Follow him down. Crouch in place. Darkness. Sea sound. Silence.*]

[MADAM's *shop in the village two days ago*]

P [*Outside*]: Madam? You open yet?

MADAM: P, is you? What you want? I just getting ready to sweep out the place.

P: Well, you leave the broom outside. See it here.

MADAM: Ohuh. So that is where it is. I couldn't find it anywhere. [*Goes to the door*] Come in then, nuh. Take what you want off the shelf and leave the money on the counter. You have the right amount?

P: Yes. You get up late this morning, though? Monday morning. Sun upstairs two hours ago.

MADAM [*Sweeping*]:   I … take the trip to town Saturday, and I get back late last night.

P: Then you don't hear what happen yesterday?

MADAM: Lawd Jesus! Them find the killer?

P: I don't know 'bout that, but them find something down by the deep part of the river.

MADAM: What you saying?

P: And them say is Crew kill the white man.

MADAM: Crew kill him! Poor Miss Rachel. How them know?

DREAM [*Bursts into the shop*]:   Madam! Lally sleep by you last night?

MADAM: Dreamboat, you forgetting you manners. Say mawning!

DREAM: Mawning, Ma'am, P. You don't see Lally anywhere?

MADAM: Look nuh, I not interfering in the girl business.

DREAM: Don't she is your grand-child?

MADAM: Well, so, but she have her own room down the street, and her own life to lead. [*To* P] What they find?

P: They find a cutlass, and it have Crew's name on the handle. You member how him carve it on the handle in here one night, when we was drinking a rum together?

MADAM: Dreamboat. I don't want you fas'ing around the back of the yard, when I see Lally I will tell her you looking for her.

P: The blood dry on the blade.

MADAM: Then a where is Crew?

P: Can't find him anywhere, Ma'am.

DREAM: I come out of my yard without my morning tea, looking for the damn girl. Sell me a piece of cheese, Madam.

MADAM: You have money?

DREAM: Chuh, Madam, just trust me for the one little piece o'cheese, nuh?

MADAM: Trust, trust, all the time, how you think I can live when de whole village taking food out of my shop and not a penny coming back in? All right, see a cut piece there.

DREAM: T'anks. [*Helps himself*]

P: If you spend less on rum, you would have something in you pocket to pay for what you want.

DREAM: I ask you anything, old man? Take you mouth off me.

P: Some thing get Crew in trouble.

MADAM: You can't say that, Mass P.

P: Well them find a rum bottle beside the machete, and there was blood on it and on the clothes too, that's what Lally tell the police.

DREAM :   Lally? How come she mix up in this business?

MADAM: Where my grand-daughter come into that?

P: Then, don't is she that find the things down by the river?

MADAM: But when this happen, P?

P: I tell you Saturday in the afternoon!

DREAM: What the hell she was doing down by there?

P: How I must know that?

DREAM: Who she was with?

P: By herself.

MADAM: What you trying to say, boy?

DREAM: Me? I not trying to say nothing. Only that she know I was going out hunting this weekend, and I warn her not to go out with anybody else.

P: She come back along the road, and first thing you know a police van pass her going up towards Port Valley, and stop. She wrap up the shirt and the machete and have it under her arm.

DREAM: But that's not the way to the village.

P: She was carrying them straight to Miss Rachel.

MADAM: Aye, that girl have a good heart.

DREAM: Well, what happen?

P: Same time the police see the bundle, they want to know what happen.

MADAM: And she tell them?

P: She couldn't do nothing else, Madam. It wasn't dark yet so they make her lead them back to the place where she find them, and next thing them say is proof that Crew kill the white man, and run 'way.

MADAM: Lawd Jesus!

DREAM: Poor Lally, then she still with the police?

P: I hear say they bringing her back. I suppose if she don't sleep at her house last night, they have her up in town.

DREAM: Well, as long as she wasn't down by the river with somebody …

MADAM: Boy, anybody ever tell you, you have a nasty mind?

DREAM [*Sadly*]: I know her, Madam.

MADAM: And a hard heart, you can't think of anybody else but yourself!

DREAM: A man have to look out for himself, woman.

P: My son, all of we poor, and all of we black, but sometimes life put the stone down harder on some than the rest. Then you have to stop and think yourself lucky that you is alone in the world, and young and strong. Then if the stone crush you, is only you suffer.

   [RACHEL *is at the door*]

MADAM: Sshhh! … Morning, Miss Rachel.

RACHEL: Morning to all.

P [*Sadly goes to her*]: Aye, me child …

RACHEL: Madam, I bring a roast breadfruit and a fowl.

MADAM: You shouldn't bother, Miss Rachel.

RACHEL: I have an account in the shop, and I don't like to be in debt. Here, take this towards what I owe you already. I will bring you some ground provisions at the end of the week, when my son finish reaping the yams.

MADAM: Thank you. [*Pause*] You need any tinned milk? I bring some back from town.

RACHEL: I think I will take two tins …

P: Over here, Rachel. Dreamboat help the lady!

DREAM: Miss Rachel, I sorry to hear about Crew.

MADAM: Dreamboat!

[RACHEL *sits suddenly, crumpled*]

P: Respect the woman's privacy, boy.

DREAM: What I do now? Is only sorry I saying!

RACHEL: They going to search the river for him. That's what the policeman say. And bring him to trial.

MADAM: Please god he is alright.

RACHEL: Don't pray for nothing like that! You hear me? You think I don't know him is dead? From last Monday evening when I wait for him to come home from the field and eat, I know what happened. They going to search for him all over the district, but they not going to find him, I know that. Crew dead P, Crew dead and gone, and the only place to look is the bottom of the river.

P: Then you know all along that he kill Mass Charlie?

RACHEL: You want them to find him and bring him to trial? You think that is how to end his life, hanging from a rope because of a dirty white man?

P: Hush. Hush.

RACHEL: I beg him not to go, you see, but he was a good man, and the only way he could find to save the little piece of land and feed us was to shame himself in front of that man. So he take a piece of cane to eat on the way, and stick the machete through his belt, and I knew I wouldn't see him again.

DREAM: Madam, she must cry, that's what my mother always say, cry and ease your heart.

RACHEL: I don't have no tears left inside me, boy. For thirty years this land take all the moisture that is in me, and now it take my man too. I don't have nothing left to give. [*Silence*] Tomorrow will make nine nights since he gone. I holding a wake for him, to watch over his spirit for the last time. You will come?

MADAM: You can't stand the expense, Rachel.

RACHEL: Is not plenty people, just you, and Lally, and the ironmonger that was a good friend of his. I will have some bread, kill a fowl, and a bottle of something strong [*Smiles at* DREAMBOAT] and we can smoke a little and talk. I going to clean out the old barn behind the house, that they used to store the cane in, and we can talk about him for a little. That is all. I will take three tins of milk, instead, if is alright by you.

[*Leaves shop quietly*]

MADAM: P, if you see Rattler today, tell him to bring the drum tomorrow night. It will be a good thing to have some music.

P: All right, Madam. Behave yourself, Boat!

[*Exits*]

DREAM: I will be going too. I can take another piece, Madam? [*Silence. She looks at him.*] All the same I not too hungry. Thank you, Madam.

MADAM: You catch any wild hog in your hunting?

DREAM: Well, them kind of scarce this time of year.

MADAM: Answer me, Dreamboat!

DREAM: One ...

MADAM: Well, when you finish roast it, just remember the old woman that feed you all the time for free, you hear me. You must give back someting once in a while.

DREAM [*Sheepishly*]: All right, Madam. You will get a joint. [*Grabs another piece of cheese*] Thank you!

[*Quickly exits*]

MADAM: Going come to an early end, you wait. [*Sits. Silence. Darkness.*]
[*In the dark, street cries:*]

Orange. Sweet and mellow, orange green and yellow! Buy you ripe banana; fresh fish, fresh orange, orange, butter fish, fresh fish!

[*Fading away*]

[*Lights warm on an auctioneer's office in town, 1820*]
[DREAMBOAT *ushers in* STONE]

DREAM: A chair, sir.

[STONE *removes his gloves fastidiously, doesn't sit, raises a brow impatiently*]

DREAM: Tea, sir? The master yesterday received a pound of very fine mixture, a very delicate flavour. Perhaps you would care to try it.

[STONE *snaps his fingers*]

DREAM: Ah, of course, the day's business waits. We must not waste time. [*Snaps his fingers*] These three are excellent, the master knows how careful you are – only the best for the owner he told me, of course, and indeed you've never had a complaint have you, sir? No, no, these are the healthiest of the last lot, I assure you. The master guarantees them.

[LALLY, BRIGIT *and* RATTLER *are at the door. They enter.*]

           Yes, over there.

[STONE *sits attentively. Languid.*]

DREAM: Now sir, to business. The females, you will wonder what the other does here. Now the master, Lord bless him, he's prepared a fine surprise for you sir – this one fell into his hands from Barbados, a gentleman going home and had to sell out everything and here we come upon – but I shan't tell you, you shall judge for yourself. But these – ah. [*Sighs with pleasure. Hands* RATTLER *a blank sheet, ink and pen.*] Sisters. Hardly more than nineteen, no bad habits yet. Now let me see. [*Consults a paper*] You want one for breeding, one for er, a houseworker. Of course. Nervous you see, but that's always a good sign, like a good hunter, the master says, don't you agree sir? Now my pretties, stand steady, this is your lucky day. Show your best side. A fine problem, sir indeed I hardly know how to advise you. Now this – [*To* BRIGIT] please make note, the wide hips, the breasts just fulling out. Teeth of course … docile. No offspring yet. Do you wish to see proof of virginity – or perhaps you'll wish to see for yourself – indeed, that's hardly necessary, we have a long association of trust, don't we, sir. Calves, well muscled, exceedingly well turned, you will notice. Now, now! Stand quiet, no harm will come to you! Ah. I remember the day of my selling, just a small boy, and so frightened. There was such a lot to learn. But my master, oh, a wiser gentleman you couldn't find … such a lot he thought of me! Ah yes. Notice how he holds the pen, sir. Ah, a fine surprise when he finishes.

[STONE *gestures – turn them around*]

DREAM: Of course, slowly, my beauties.

[*The girls are sobbing a little*]

Come, come! The other … Here is the doctor's certificate, equally untouched. Notice the nipples. Fire in this one sir, you'll forgive my saying so. But the clear eyes show how easily she can be taught. All kinds of things.

[STONE *goes to* LALLY. *Puts on a glove. Feels her shape, presses on her jaws to make them open. Runs his hands up between her legs. She gasps and tenses. Considers her head on one side.*]

DREAM: That's enough. [*Takes paper from* RATTLER *who stands stiffly with the ink and pen in two hands*] Now sir, we in the business know how difficult it is to find a good reckoner. This one falls into your lap. He can read, write and reckon like a schoolmaster. The master thinks to give you proof and turn your head with good luck, no hesitation. This is what he has been writing while we spoke here, sir. If I may read?

[STONE *nonchalantly assents*]

DREAM: 'My dear sisters, give thanks now to the Lord for your good fortune, in falling to the hands of this most kind gentleman. One of you shall be assured shelter, kindness and the blessing of a full womb – what more can you ask of Providence? The other, in circumstances even happier, may in time rise to the respect and affection accorded to the housekeeper in a great-house such that slaves run to do your bidding, and she is answerable only to the master, whose needs she shall see to with loyalty and good grace. These are opportunities seldom given to poor creatures such as we are. And under the same master! Show thanks and willingness therefore, and learn quickly the ways of christian children!' There and he dumb from birth! Is that not the finest address you have heard in months?

[STONE *takes the paper with a gloved hand*]

DREAM: And on the other side, the account sir. For that one, £65 3s., for the other, £54 9s. 7d. and for himself, £78 6s. 2d. Figures laid down by the master, sir, when he left his morning. Total as you will see it, £197 18s. 9d. A bargain, sir, a bargain!

[STONE *taps the paper thoughtfully*]

DREAM: Of course, the additional expense is unfortunate, but the master felt sure that you'd not want to pass up such a windfall! It would be a great pity to have to auction him for field work – he's in his prime, but what a waste! Ah sir, if I must advise you –

[STONE *gestures, 'Be still'. In great indecision inspects the girls again. Lounging staring at all three. Sighs, points to* LALLY, *hesitates … the girls hold tightly to each other.*]

DREAM: Ah, they cannot understand yet, of course, but you see how they look forward to being taken together! And on the other hand, of course, what learning is so cheap …!

[STONE *points to* RATTLER. RATTLER *throws himself at* STONE's *feet, kisses his hand.* STONE *takes it away gently.*]

DREAM: Oh! [*Rushes to the table, brings a towel and a basin of water*] STONE *wets his hand, wipes it carefully on the towel, while* DREAMBOAT *continues*]

DREAM: An excellent decision, sir, if I may so. Outside now, all of you. [*Shoos them out*] We'll take your note for the amount sir, of course, your bond is always good, not like some of the gentlemen from some of the other estates. The master always says it's a pleasure to do business with an owner that knows his own mind. You won't regret it, sir. Well, if you'll just follow me to the office across the street. Excellent excellent …

[STONE *leisurely puts on both gloves*]

DREAM: Going to be a fine day, sir, hot but fine!

[*They leave*]

[*Outside fading away down the street, the vendors cry again. Darkness.*]

[*1833. Woods near an estate. Hounds are baying in the distance.* P *staggers to his knees between the trees; he's been running; clutches a bottle. Uncorks it, upturns it. It's empty. Hurls it away, weakly. Listens. Silence. There is a wound on his leg. Inspects it, takes off his shirt. His back is covered with white scars. Ties the shirt in a tourniquet around the leg. Stretches out, exhausted, face down. The dogs again, farther away this time. Sits up slowly. Grins. Chooses his direction. Sets off.*]

STONE [*Off*]:   Hooooo! Call off! Call away! [*Limping on*] The deaf fools. [*Stares around him*] You won't find him now, not with night coming on! Hallooo! Took to the trees for a while, that's for certain, else the dogs, would have kept the trail 'til doomsday, no matter how fast he went. [*His ankle buckles under him*] Damn! Which way's home? [*Eyes the tree he's leaning against*] No choice. Well …

[*Begins to climb, carefully not using his twisted foot. Slips, falls, hurting himself. Tries again.* JACKO *appears and watches him.*]

JACKO: What you doing?

[STONE *loses his balance, falls, holds himself tight against the pain*]

JACKO [*Laughing*.]: Easy now, Busha. Softly, softly, catch monkey, eh?

STONE: You, boy. What's you name?

JACKO: My name? You don't know me, Busha?

STONE: Where you come from? Who you belong to?

JACKO: I don't belong to anybody, Busha.

STONE: Another damned runaway.

JACKO: Me? No sah. I born a free man. From up in the hills behind here.

STONE: A Maroon!

JACKO: Thas right, Busha. [*Pause*] You come far from home, though. What you doing out here, Busha?

STONE: Hunting. Hunting wild pig.

JACKO: Alone! On foot?

STONE: The horse fell, I had to leave him, and the others were too far ahead. You ask a lot of questions, boy.

JACKO: Is so I stay, Busha. What you going to do now?

STONE: Depends on you, boy.

JACKO: Oh. How that?

STONE: You look like a smart fellow. How you like to earn a free pardon?

JACKO: Pardon, Busha? For what?

STONE: You'd know that there's a reward out for any Maroon who comes down from the hills?

JACKO: Reward! Yes … I hear something about that. But they never catch any of us, Busha. Chu, all that money and nobody can get it! You looking to catch some of it, Busha?

STONE: I need to find the trail home, that's all.

JACKO: True you don't need money. You rich, eh? Not like me. If you ever know how hard I have to work find food. Aeieeee …

STONE: How much?

JACKO: How much what, Busha?

STONE: Don't play the fool with me, boy. How much to show me the way?

JACKO: Well I don't really have no use for the money, you know, Busha.

STONE: What the hell do you mean, money is money!

JACKO: Well the only place to spend it is in town, an' plenty people woulda like that reward, you see. Not everybody rich like you, Busha. So the money not going to do me any good. What else you have?

STONE [*Reluctantly*]: A knife. It's a good one.

JACKO: A knife! But what about your gun? I don't see it.

STONE: With the horse back there, the stock broke when I fell.

JACKO: Well I will just have to go back and see if I find it.

STONE: No! It went down in a gulley, you'll not find it before it's dark! Here take the knife. [*Unsheathes it, tosses it a step away, recoils in pain at the effect of his movement on the ankle*]

[JACKO *goes to take it up*, STONE *trips him*, SONSON *steps from cover, straddles* STONE, *holds his knife at* STONE's *neck. Pause.* STONE *looks around slowly, is stopped by the point of* SONSON's *weapon. Drops his slowly.* JACKO *rolls out from under* STONE, *laughing. Pause.* JACKO *sticks his knife in his belt.*]

SONSON: You take too many chances.

JACKO [*Shrugs*]: You was there.

SONSON: One day I not going to be there. You going get you throat cut.

STONE: Goddam niggers.

SONSON: Shhh. White man. [*The point of the knife is into* STONE's *neck*] I find the pig he was hunting.

JACKO: Big one?

SONSON: Two legs. Tracks down to the river.

JACKO: Uh. Smart, Busha. Him get away?

SONSON: Maybe. Didn't stop to see.

JACKO: What we going to do with him?

SONSON [*Shrugs*]: What else.

JACKO: Wait. [*Pause*]

SONSON: On you belly, white man.

[STONE *obeys cautiously*]

SONSON: Put your hands together. [*Knots twine around his thumbs. Turns him over.*] Now.

JACKO: Suppose we take him to the compound?

SONSON: Kill him here, just as easy. Besides him very heavy to carry.

STONE: If you kill me every man in the district will hunt you down till they find you. No blasted nigger is going to get away with killing a white man.

SONSON: I told you!

JACKO: Is true, man. They not going to stand for it. As long as we
            hunt and keep up in the hills they will leave us to hide.
            But the whole island will blow up if it look like we can molest
            the landowners and get away with it.

SONSON: You belly weak, my brother.

JACKO: You calling me a coward?

SONSON: You hear me say the word?

JACKO: What you think we going to gain by killing him?

SONSON: One less.

JACKO: That's not enough.

SONSON: You feel he would think twice 'bout it if he was holding
            the knife?

JACKO: You going to kill and kill till the whole island run red, and
            then what?

SONSON: Then we can start again.

JACKO: So that is the only way. Brother I can't see it so.

            [*Far off the sound of the dogs*]

STONE: Here! To me!

            [*Immediately they are both at his side*]

JACKO: White man, white man, make another sound, and all argument
            cease. They far off.

SONSON: But not too far. The gun. I want something for all this trouble.

JACKO: Open your mouth, just once, white man. You think is blood I
            'fraid of?

SONSON: Don't say anything. Just point. Where is the gun?

            [STONE *points*]

SONSON: This partnership finish if him get away from you, you hear me?

JACKO: Don't fool man, I waiting for you.

            [SONSON *slips away*]

            They hunting you now ey? Don't fret, Busha? Well, look, mark
            the face. In case we buck up again make sure is the right man,
            white man. That way you will be sure who is opening your
            belly like a spring to water the ground.

STONE: Don't cross my path again, boy. I have a lot of bitter things to
            pay back since I came back to this country.

            [*The dogs are nearer now*]

JACKO [*Anxiously*]: Is you, brother?

STONE: Hope that he hurries, Sambo.

JACKO: Sticks and stones will break my bones … [*Laughing*]

STONE: A white man saying, Sambo.

JACKO: A black day for you when you taught us your tongue. Busha.
          All the tribes coming together, under the one language.
          The word is freedom, and one day the whole country going
          stand up and shout it out.

[*The dogs again.* SONSON *off whistles twice.*]

JACKO: My father was a white man, Busha, but the woman run away
          before he could lay claim on me. I white too, Busha. And so
          when the day come to count up the rich and the poor, that is
          why I give you a chance. Maybe you will know more then and
          not talk about black and white so loud. And if you don't know
          better than that then, the gun and the knife will decide who
          is right.

[SONSON *runs in empty handed*]

JACKO: The gun.

SONSON: No time the dogs are too close. Hold him.

[JACKO *guards* STONE. SONSON *takes off* STONE's *belt. Ties his
hands to his feet. Stuffs his handkerchief in his mouth, throws him face
down on the ground.*]

JACKO: Good hunting, Busha.

[*Exits fast*]

[SONSON *lingers, thumbing the blade of his knife.* JACKO *off whistles
twice.* SONSON *after a moment spits, turns and exits fast. The dogs are
very near. Darkness.*]

Act Two

[*Later this night*]

[RATTLER *taps out a light rhythm. They are lying about loosely.* P *keeps time with one hand, while* MADAM *croaks/hums the tune.* RACHEL *dozes with a hand on either son.* DREAMBOAT *whispers to* LALLY. STONE *is not there.*]

P: The boy sleeping now.

[JACKO *stirs, tries to rise, fails*]

MADAM: Woaie! Me voice feeble these days. I can't carry a tune anymore …

P: Hold strain, boy. Where Stone? He will help you sing.

LALLY: He stops outside a while ago for air.

JACKO: You all here still?

LALLY: Then wait, you was really sleeping the whole time!

JACKO: You all talk and talk till a man wasn't certain what the darkness was saying to him.

P: Sometimes you have to stop and remember what is dead and gone. Then there is today …

DREAM: Is Rattler do it. The drum was telling a story all by itself.

MADAM: Boy, you father would glad to see we making the night pass in memory of him. Is a long time I don't take a smoke with a few friends.

P: True, true. Play louder, Rattler. You fingers nimble!

JACKO: You going to wake them.

MADAM: Chu, she just dozing off, she not sleeping seriously.

LALLY: What that you singing, Granny?

MADAM: Lawd almighty, you young people don't know a thing about the past. You 'member it, P?

DREAM: The place too dead! Let we liven it up, ee Lally?

[*Claps to the tune*]

MADAM *and* P: Moonshine tonight, come le' we dance and sing, [*Repeat*]
               Me de rock so, you de rock so, under Banyan tree. [*Repeat*]

DREAM [*On his feet pulling* LALLY *to join him, sings and dances*]:
               Ladies may curtsey, gentlemen may bow, [*Repeat*]
               Me de rock so, you de rock so, under Banyan tree. [*Repeat*]

*[All except RACHEL and SONSON are on their feet by this time,
subdued with laughter]*

[JACKO finds a flask of rum on the table, tosses it over]

JACKO: Here Rattler, you deserve one for that beat.

DREAM: You mean to say you have it there all the while an' never say a
          word? What a hard man, sah!

P: You drink too damn much, Dreamboat.

DREAM: Aye, man, what a man to do? You work sun up to dark, and
          the money come in trickling and go out like the river washing
          down in spate. You grow a little corn and potatoes, and take it
          to the market, how much you can sell it for? The white ladies,
          all of them go into the town to buy their goods, nobody in the
          market to take the provisions off you hands except poor people
          like you, hungry same way, poor same way. You laugh a little,
          drink a little, trust a little, eh Madam? Who is to say a man
          should hold his life to the straight path all week, year in, year
          out? That is the way the world is friend.

[Enter STONE]

          Look me, I young, no? And strong. So sometimes on a
          weekend I go up into the mountains, and wait for the wild pig
          to pass by. When luck and the Lord on my side, I take home a
          side of meat, and roast it to feed me for a week or so, and my
          friends. What else to do?

STONE: You should get yourself a little piece of land, that's what Crew
          tell me, last time we was together. Settle down, Stone, he say,
          and raise a crop. For what? I ask him that, you see. I watch how
          the big land-owners they corner up with their own and sell the
          sugar back to us for four times what it cost us to raise. I know.
          I see the inside of the offices sometimes, and the big house that
          they build from two hundred years ago, when all of us worked
          the land for nothing, like animals. You think things change any?

P: We free now, Stone. That is a big change.

BRIGIT: You feel so? You skin white, then Mass P? To them you is still
          dirt, nothing you can say will change the way they look at you.
          No respect, you know that. How can a man live easy without
          respect? *[Silence]*

LALLY: The talk getting too serious again. Come, Granny, another
          song!

MADAM: Hush you mouth, child.

DREAM: One day they going catch up with you, Mass P. How long you think you going sell ganja before they find out?

P: Is a steady market, me son. Every week the man come from town and take all I have off my hands, selling it to the sailor boy down in the harbour. It don't have no trouble in it, just grow the plants and tie the leaves up, ready to take away.

STONE: He pay you good, Mass P? Answer me that.

P: It small but is steady, me son.

BRIGIT: Is a white man, P?

P: Fairskin.

STONE: Worse yet. That kind stand between the rich and the poor, and they would sell out their own grandmother to get closer to the rich. You watch, one day he going to ask you to lower the price, and say no if you bad. First thing you know, the police have information where to find you, and the game is over.

MADAM: Stone, don't set goat mouth on Mass P!

STONE: I not saying nothing Madam, I not the one using him to make a living.

P: Then what I am to do, Stone, answer me that?

STONE: I don't know, Mass P. But someday there is going to be blood. This land is used to it, and it is crying out for rain, for two thousand years that is what the cane grow with, and I 'fraid to see into the future. It looking too much like what gone before … There is any more, Miss Rachel?

BRIGIT: Don't wake her, Stone, she is sleeping.

STONE: Aye. [*Helps himself to it*] A last stick and I going to me yard. [*They pass out the joints*] Play, Rattler. The drum sweet tonight.

LALLY: Is a new skin you stretch on it, not so Rattler?

[RATTLER *plays Nago.* RACHEL *stirs, wakes, goes to the drum, stands before it.* RATTLER *smiles up at her. She shakes her head nervously.*]

BRIGIT: Madam!

[MADAM *goes to her quickly, touches her forehead with oil, steps back.* RACHEL *hugs* BRIGIT *to her.* DREAMBOAT *clicks his tongue to the drum's beat.*]

[*As lights warm,* RACHEL *is humming the tune, preparing a meal, late morning four years ago. Pause.*]

SONSON [*Storming in*]: Ma, is lunch ready?

100

RACHEL: Then what wrong with you? That's how you come into the house nowadays?

SONSON: Sun hot outside, Ma, I just come in from the field.

RACHEL: Where you father and you brother?

SONSON: Pa say him have to come up later. Jacko leave the work early this morning. I don't see him for the last two hours. Look like serious business take him away.

RACHEL: Take a plate from over there. Walk soft nuh, me son! You're like a bull in the place today. What business?

SONSON: I don't know, Ma! I expect him will tell you when him ready!

RACHEL: Give thanks [*He bows his head for a second*] Uhuh, you hands dirty.

SONSON: I wash them just a while ago, Ma.

RACHEL: Here, I took some wet sugar and made a cool drink.

SONSON: Pa say to send 5/ – when I coming back. Damn feisty white man.

RACHEL [*Sits*]: Oh. Who trouble you?

SONSON: Nothing, Ma, is alright.

RACHEL: Oh. [*Pause*] When you finish eat, lie down in the cool for a while. Sun hot.

SONSON: You know bottom field, where we just start to plant? [*She nods*] Pa wasn't there, he had to go sharpen the hoe, and I was down there chopping out some grass. All of a sudden I look up and saw this blasted man on a horse watching me. I don't pay him no mind, I have my work to do. Then I look up again and he was just getting down.

RACHEL: I hope you remember you manners.

SONSON: Manners! I say morning! He sort of nod his head at me and start to feel the soil.

RACHEL: He is a government man?

SONSON: Not no government man, Ma. Wait till I tell you. Next thing I know he walking across to me, stepping straight across the land that belong to us.

RACHEL: Then what he wanted?

SONSON: That's what I ask him. He say what's my name? I say that is for me to know, you have business with me? He say watch me tongue. I tell him he don't have any damn right standing on my property and telling me how to speak to trespassers.

He sort a look at me and smiled. 'You're a little young to be so loudmouthed,' he sing out.

RACHEL: True, is you father land, you should express yourself properly.

SONSON: Ma! I have my hand round the machete, and little more I would a chop him with it, when he say 'Keep you temper, fellow, I am Mr Charles.'

RACHEL: From the Great House?

SONSON: Him same one!

RACHEL: You certain, Sonny?

SONSON: Ma, same time he say that, I recognize him from the stories they tell about him. Big and heavy, red in the face, and looking all the time like butter wouldn't melt in his mouth.

RACHEL: Eat you dinner. You are a growing boy!

SONSON: Ma! You not hearing what I saying to you!

RACHEL: Sonson I hearing you, but good food not suppose to waste.

SONSON [*Flings himself away from the table*]: That is how they go on, eh? Like the Lord put them on the earth to walk all over the rest of us. Ma, from slavery days them don't change, they still think they better than the rest. Why the hell he don't stay in town and leave us alone?

RACHEL: He was in England.

SONSON: Eh?

RACHEL: He wasn't here, son.

SONSON: Then what he come back for? The estate don't need him, the place stand up without him all this time, just the old lady and the overseer! I feel in my bones he carry trouble with him.

RACHEL: It's his right to be here, you know.

SONSON: I know, Ma, but the minute his eye and mine make four my spirit turn against him. If he never say a word to me, I would know. Why is that, Ma?

RACHEL [*After a while she tries to smile and pats his cheeks*]: Go lie down, if you sleep I will wake you.

SONSON: I can't sleep, Ma. But I will ease me back a while.

[*Goes*]

[RACHEL *crosses to the window and stares out. Slowly clears the table, replaces the ware and clean plate, spoon, cuts another piece of bread. Stops in mid-action once or twice. She is humming 'Moonshine tonight'. JACKO and BRIGIT enter.*]

BRIGIT: Good day, Miss Rachel.

RACHEL: Brigit me chile, how you do? You late today, Jacko?

BRIGIT: Well, thank you Ma'am.

JACKO: I eat already, Ma.

RACHEL: Is so? Siddown me dear, take something cool.

BRIGIT: Thanks.

JACKO: Ma –

RACHEL: Soon come Jacko, I don't see you such a long time, Brigit.

JACKO: Chu Ma, scarcely three days now, and you call that long!

RACHEL: Take this chair, it is more comfortable. I used to see you everyday almost, just a short while eh! Look long! I giving you a long glass.

JACKO: I can't stay long, Ma, Pa working alone.

RACHEL: Where you eat anyhow? You have money to buy outside? You get enough?

JACKO: Belly full, Ma.

RACHEL: You mother cooking not good anymore, eh?

BRIGIT: I had a little piece of fish cook up and give him, Miss Rachel. I hope you don't mind.

RACHEL [*Laughing*]: Mind, chile! Lawd no! Feed him all you want, the boy eat me out of house and home.

JACKO: Sit down, nuh Ma!

BRIGIT: Is true, you know. He polish off the fish clean and ask for more.

JACKO: Alright, I going leave you then.

RACHEL: Wait nuh! You so in a hurry. Is something you can talk in front of a visitor?

BRIGIT [*Laughs*]: Jacko, you go on, I will talk to you mother.

JACKO: You are the hardest person to talk to I ever meet.

BRIGIT: No, go on. You done say you piece already.

JACKO: Where I will find you?

BRIGIT: Down at Madam's shop. Walk good, you hear?

JACKO: You too. [*Pause*] All right, Ma.

    [*Pauses. Goes.*]

BRIGIT: Miss Rachel.

RACHEL: Yes me, chile.

BRIGIT: You know what Jacko was trying to tell you. [*Pause*]

RACHEL: The drink sweet enough, Brigit?

BRIGIT: Yes, Miss Rachel. He ask me to marry him.

RACHEL: You tell him yes?

BRIGIT: I see it coming, and I make things take their course. I tell him yes.

RACHEL: Girl, I don't understand you.

BRIGIT: He come by me yard today, late in the morning, like he couldn't hold out any longer, and he beg me. [RACHEL *goes to the window*] You going stop him?

RACHEL: Me? After I not mad, chile. The two of them have the same father. Stubborn like him through good and through bad. Is the two of you decide. Nobody going say nothing.

BRIGIT: I think you would be glad. You knowing me a long time, Miss Rachel.

RACHEL: When you going to tell Sonson?

BRIGIT: Jacko will make him know.

RACHEL: You have a right to make him know yourself!

BRIGIT: Why is that? It don't have nothing between us, Miss Rachel.

RACHEL: Nothing? Three months back he was carrying straw for you, the whole village see that. And now this.

BRIGIT: Sonny is you son too. You mean you don't know him?

RACHEL: Enough to see how hard this going to hit him.

BRIGIT: I don't break my promises, I can swear to that.

RACHEL: If is what you want, well. But it don't smell good to me, and I don't have to pretend to that.

BRIGIT: Why you set against Jacko?

RACHEL: Set against him? He is my son!

BRIGIT: But is not him you want me to marry eh?

RACHEL: Answer me this, Brigit. You love him?

BRIGIT: Yes!

RACHEL: I not talking about Sonny.

BRIGIT: I know who you talking 'bout! How you mean, love? He offer to put a ring on my finger, the other one not even mention that. No, he quiet and kind to me, you ever see Sonny when he get vexed? Which one of them have more liking for the land? Jacko will settle down and raise him family, and you grandchildren

104

will know where the father is all the time. What more you want?
I not looking to raise no man's wild oats, Miss Rachel!

RACHEL: You take Jacko to you bed yet?

BRIGIT: You is him mother, but is none of you damn business! Why you
don't ask me the same thing about the other one?

RACHEL [*Sits*]: Excuse me, chile. [*Silence*]

BRIGIT: I not a young girl anymore, Rachel. Is time for me to close
the door on me own house, even if it's only a room in your
husband yard, till my man make his own place to keep me in.
I see the other women, how the world take them and use them,
and throw them back in the canepiece. Look Lally.

RACHEL: Don't talk about Lally. She is me friend Madam grand-
daughter, and she don't do anything worse than the rest of you.

BRIGIT: That is what I must content myself with? She is my friend
too, but that is not the way I choose. Lally will say yes to any
man that young and strong and ask her. Black or white, the
field worker or the man passing through the village and stop
to show himself on the bankside. But I born poor, you hear
me, and black and the only thing I have is my pride. That is
what Jacko see, even if him is quiet and soft talking. And if the
owner of this estate should call me and say lie down girl, you
don't have nothing to lose, is the same thing I will tell him like
I tell all the others – I don't have anything but I have a right
to answer no. Black people used to work this land for nothing
and they used to treat them like beast, they coulda mount them
anytime. I not breeding for any man just because of pleasure.
I is not an animal. I is a human being.

[SONSON *is at the door yawning.* BRIGIT *turns to* RACHEL *and buries
her head in her bosom,* RACHEL *comforts her.*]

SONSON: Brigit. What she crying for, Ma?

RACHEL: Don't mind, my son. Is happiness. She coming into the family.
Shoo, shoo don't cry … I old enough to know when something
wrong. I was wrong. Now don't fuss. I couldn't want for a better
daughter. Sonson! What you standing there for? You don't have
you work to go and do?

SONSON: The money, Ma.

RACHEL: What you talking about?

SONSON: The 5/ – my father say to send for him.

RACHEL: Oh. [*Pulls hanky out of her bosom*] Is only a 10/ – I have. Come go next door with, Mass P will change it.

SONSON: I coming, Ma. I just getting a drink.

RACHEL [*At the window*]: He leaving the yard, going to catch him first. [*Exits with a moment's hesitation*] Mass P! Mass P!

SONSON [*Making no move to her*]: You satisfy now, Brigit? A whole church wedding, eh?

BRIGIT: Sonny he ask me today.

SONSON: Uhuh, I not bitter. That's how people stay sometimes. [*RACHEL enters, pauses*] I hope you will be very happy.

[*BRIGIT bows her head*]

RACHEL [*Watching them*]: I just catch him in time. Go on now, Sonson.

SONSON [*Takes the 5/ –*]: The drink too sour, Ma.

[*Exits*]

RACHEL: You have courage, girl. Good. Looking for rain. Take off you shoes and lie down inside. I have some mending to do.

[*STONE's face appears at window*]

BRIGIT: Is pay day. I have to go by the parsonage and collect my few shillings, even though it's my day off. Thank you, Ma.

RACHEL [*Pats her face tenderly*]: Come back later, my husband going to want to see you. Him like you off, you know.

[*They smile together, BRIGIT goes*]

STONE [*Off, singing softly*]: 'Moonshine tonight,' [*He is at the door. RACHEL is frozen with her back to him.*] Good afternoon, Rachel. [*She turns slowly*] May I come in? [*Silence*] And sit down? It's a long walk over the back meadow, but I wasn't sure I wanted to see anybody on my way. [*Sits*] Still a fine woman …

RACHEL: Mass Charlie.

STONE: How many years now, Rachel? [*Pause*]

RACHEL: Three, Mass Charlie.

STONE: Respectful as ever. Is anybody here? [*Shakes her head*] That's a fine boy you have. Three years? How they grow.

RACHEL: Not a boy anymore, sir.

STONE: Jack, wasn't it?

RACHEL: Isaac, we call him Sonson.

STONE: Ah yes, could I bother you for a drink? [*She moves to get it*] Insolent though. You must be proud of him, has your spirit.

RACHEL [*Levelly*]: Is his father in him, Master Charles. [*Pours*]

STONE: Yes, I remember there are two. [*Takes the glass*] Thank you. Ah, country tastes. The best, always. I have missed this place.

RACHEL: My husband is not here now, sir. I can direct you to the acreage if you want.

STONE: Sit down, Rachel.

RACHEL: You want him to come up to the Great House tomorrow and see you?

STONE: Sit down. [*She sits*] How have you been, Rachel?

RACHEL: Things are the same as ever.

[*He takes it at face value*]

STONE: From I was a boy, I found it strange that things changed so slowly here, or not at all. Tell me how things are, Rachel.

RACHEL: Mr Charles –

STONE: I want to know. [*Silence*]

RACHEL: The farm is doing well.

STONE: Have you roofed the house yet?

RACHEL: Last April.

STONE: In time for the rains.

RACHEL: But it was a dry season.

STONE: I heard. [*Silence*]

RACHEL: What you want, Mr Charles?

STONE: I have come home, Rachel.

RACHEL: You staying long, Mr Charles?

STONE: For good. I've come back to my people. [RACHEL *laughs. After a moment he laughs too.*] Nice and sour.

[*She takes the glass*]

RACHEL: What you want, Mr Charles?

STONE: I'd like to talk business for a while. [*Goes to the window*]

[STONE *moves back, she smiles*]

STONE: The old house is falling to ruin. It's a disgrace. Built well, mind you. Your ancestors worked hard at it. I'm sorry. I say the wrong things to you without meaning to. It's a fact, you know.

RACHEL: It don't have nothing to do with me, Mr Charles.

STONE: Now that I'll be here all year round, I'm going to find a staff for the place. Reliable people I can depend on. I need a good housekeeper to start with. The job is yours.

RACHEL: I have a family, Mr Charles.

STONE: You'll have a staff of about four, I think, it's a big old house, though I'll probably close down half of it. Maybe make it into a museum. There's some fine stuff there from the past. My wife never appreciated it. Solid stuff. Enduring.

RACHEL: Thank you for the offer, sir. I will ask around in the village if you want.

STONE: Ask around, hell! I know what I want. Of course it will take a while to change the place into the kind of house it should be. But there's no reason to wait, I need some good home cooking right now to fatten me up. I'd forgotten how much I missed it.

RACHEL: I have a husband and two sons, Mr Charles. And one of them marrying soon. The house to keep and clothes to mend and food to prepare. That is a big enough job for one woman. You will have to find somebody responsible from town, a single woman.

STONE: The pay is good. And you wouldn't have to sleep in except once or twice a week, perhaps, when I happen to have guests. You can do a lot to help your family, it's a responsible job, Rachel. The whole district will look up to you.

RACHEL: Is so?

STONE: You understand the job I'm offering you, Rachel?

RACHEL: Yes.

STONE: It's cold in England, Rachel. And with my wife dead, I was lonely. Did you like her?

RACHEL: It wasn't my place to like or not to like.

STONE: But you saw her with me sometimes. You could tell from the mouth alone, couldn't you. She was an ugly woman. But you get used to people.

RACHEL: How you speak ill of the dead like that?

STONE: I'm trying to tell you, I would have stayed away out of sheer habit if they could have stopped the cancer. But I kept seeing your face on every frosted window in London after she died. Calling me home. Different from winter. Different from white. Warmer than snow.

RACHEL: How you can talk this way!

STONE: Rachel, it's not as if we were strangers! We grew up here in the village, remember, long before you came to the back of the Great House selling corn. We're part of this place, I can talk to you. You know that! If it's not true, what was it that make you so weak three years ago? So eager?

RACHEL: You is a dirty, dirty man.

STONE: Eh? Don't be so goddamn innocent! Are you ashamed, now? Where the hell do you get this sudden virtue from?

RACHEL: I didn't know what I was doing, so help me God.

STONE: You didn't know what you was doing! [*Laughs raucously*]

RACHEL: I was feeling so sorry for you, with that white bitch of a wife, that the whole district did know 'bout.

STONE: Try again. Married how many, twenty years? And a great sorrow and sympathy takes hold of you, right in the middle of the stable, with the horses watching us steeplechase for a whole hour. Confess the truth, wasn't it the thought of the white man that made your skirt so easy to lift up? Eh, Rachel? Didn't you feel proud that you'd caught the richest man around here in between your legs?

RACHEL [*She moves to the window*]: You finish?

STONE: You country slut. Oh, you had a good time that afternoon. And the next week too. One might have been an accident, but two! You remember what you said, eh? Lawd, it big! I did think is only black man make so!

MADAM [*Is at the door*]: Rachel my dear, I hear the news! – Beg pardon! Mass Charlie! I will come back later, Miss Rachel! Sorry sah, I didn't know anybody was here.

STONE: That's alright. I'm going, don't go.

RACHEL: Mass Charlie!

STONE: Yes, Rachel?

RACHEL: Maybe Madam know the person you looking for.

MADAM: What dat sah?

RACHEL: He looking for a housekeeper to take over the Great House.

MADAM: But that's a big job!

STONE: Yes. I stopped by to ask whether she knew of anyone who might be interested.

RACHEL: No, no … I can't think of a soul just now, Mass Charlie.

MADAM: Me neither. I too old, eee?

RACHEL: Chuh Madam, you joking! Mass Charlie looking somebody respectable, not like we! Don't is so, sah?

STONE: It's getting late, I've got some business to attend to.

RACHEL: But if I hear of a person, I will send to you, sir.

STONE: Thank you, Rachel.

MADAM: I glad you coming back here to stay, Mass Charlie. We did miss you. You marrying again, sah?

RACHEL: Madam! How you mean to ask him that kind of a question?

MADAM: Tchh! After I know him from him was a young boy! Ah glad you come home, sah.

STONE: Thank you, Ma'am. Tell your husband I'm glad to see you looking so well, Rachel.

RACHEL: Thank you, sah! The corn ripe now, I going tell him to bring some up to the house for you next evening. [*Pause*]

STONE: That won't be necessary. But I won't forget you offered.

[*Exits*]

MADAM: Rachel! Him is a fine man, ee? Rachel, I hear 'bout the wedding! What a celebration, chile!

[*1834. Black. In the dark, half a mile away, drums. They are heard throughout the scene. A great house.*]

P: Girl! Girl [*Silence*] The light is out. Girl!

[LALLY *enters with lit candles and a glass*]

P: Dammit, stay close! Nothing has changed. Freedom, my backside.

LALLY: I bring your medicine, sir.

P: Must have fallen asleep. Woke up and not a damn light to be seen. There, that's a good girl. Now tuck me in. Night's getting chilly.

LALLY [*Adjusting blanket around him in the chair*]: Gentleman to see you, sir.

P: At this hour?

LALLY: Come from town, sir.

P: Not a decent hour. Tell him I was sick?

LALLY: Yes. Sey he come from town.

P: Know him?

LALLY: New.

P: Hell of a long way for a social call. Well, a strange face. Show him in, eh? And finish packing.

LALLY: The boxes are ready.

P: Lazy bitch.

LALLY: Sick-Sick!

P: Show him in.

LALLY: They steal some of the silver.

P: No more stealing! They can have the house when I'm gone, everything! But pack it all away, hear?

[LALLY *exits*]

P: Nearly said come with me. Old fool. [*Calls after her*] And come back, here? That's what you're here for, to look after me. Cold. Cold. [*Nods off*]

LALLY [*At door with* JACKO]: He's sleeping, sir. He sleep a lot.

JACKO: I'll not wake him.

LALLY: Talk to him, sir. He's dying.

P: Who's there? Come man, come. Hear them? Been making that racket all evening. Like a drug. But it keeps them quiet. You get to like it after a while. Company, like.

JACKO: Colonel Charles, I take it.

P: There y're. Come in, come in. Can't rise. I'm afraid.

JACKO: My card. [*Offers it*]

P [*Squinting at card*]: Well, Doctor. A sawbones, eh? Queer time to call, but you're welcome. Sit down.

JACKO: This is not a social call, I'm afraid, sir.

P: Want to look me over? Never sent for anybody. Girl's good enough. Just a touch of weakness from the fever.

JACKO: I'd be happy to examine you, sir.

P: Dammit man, take off your beside manner and get off your feet. Girl, get the gentleman a glass and some biscuits.

JACKO: Thank you, no. I stopped with a message from the Reverend Draper.

[LALLY *exits*]

P: Pretty face, eh.

JACKO: Sir.

P: New out here, Doctor?

JACKO: Two months, sir.

P: Aye, you can always tell them. Haven't got used to our ways yet, eh. Morals a little looser than in London, lad.

JACKO:	I have observed it, sir.
P:	You'll be glad enough for a little bit of fire to warm you at my age, if you stay here long enough. And it's free. [*Laughs*]
JACKO:	Colonel –
P:	Ah, message. Yes. Draper's that fellow in the Governor's Council. What's he want?

[LALLY *enters with sherry*]

JACKO:	A warning, sir. The new Act is to be strictly imposed. The slaves are free as from tomorrow. All landowners will be held accountable for the peaceful carrying out of the Crown's order.
P:	Girl?

[LALLY *exits*]

JACKO:	Mr Draper asked that I impress on you – there is a need to disappoint those who have it that you intend to disobey the edict. The consequences may be severe.
P:	Doesn't matter, Doctor. I'm leaving. I've packed, and it's London for me in a day or so. Show the Doctor to a room.
JACKO:	That won't be necessary, sir. I'm staying at Tivoli, just behind the hill – there's a sick man there who needs my attention urgently, I've come with drugs to save him, in fact.
P:	Good god, don't tell me the old gentleman is sick too!
JACKO:	One of the workers, actually.
P:	And you're breaking your neck for that? I have me doubts about your sense of values, man. Show him out.
JACKO:	I'll bid you goodnight, sir.
P:	Girl, the salts.
JACKO [*Helps him*]:	Breathe deeply.
P:	Where's the girl?
JACKO:	What's her name?
P:	Name, what name. Girl, that's her name.
JACKO [*Examining him*]:	Hold still. Don't talk.
P:	Damn feet are cold. Girl!
JACKO:	I think she's gone, Colonel.
P:	How can she be gone when I need her? What's wrong with me, eh?
JACKO:	They're all gone, I'm thinking.
P:	Send for two of the big fellows, they'll get me to bed.

JACKO:	The place was all dark when I came. Lie still.
P:	Took her out of the fields, made her a favourite! Pretty little thing.
JACKO:	Are you in pain?
P:	Gone! I'll have her whipped to an inch of her life!
JACKO:	She's free tomorrow, Colonel.
P:	Free! What's that mean? What'll they do without me, eh? Who'll feed them, and look after them when they get sick?
JACKO:	You're going, anyway!
P:	What should I stay for?
JACKO:	Quiet. Don't talk. I have to go.
P:	Get out, get out, then!
JACKO:	I'll be back early morning.
P:	I'm a white man.
JACKO:	My job is to save lives, mister.
P:	Boy! [*Silence. JACKO hesitates.*] Hold my hand. [*JACKO comes to him*] Don't stay long.
JACKO:	Come morning, I'll be back.
P:	No, no. I mean here. It catches you, you see? Quietly. You won't understand at first.

[JACKO *tucks him in, blows out one candle, eases off his shoes. Goes quietly, unnoticed by P.*]

P:	Queer place, this Island. You come to it like a woman, full of all the possible things you dream of. Young and green and fertile. It's so rich, so rich. It works its way into your blood like the drums, and you think it's yours. It belongs to you, you sweat for it and love it and form it to what you want. And the years pass, and you won't admit it but you belong to it. It claims you, bends under you, and smiles, but you stay a stranger. You never really understand it, you see. And you dare not admit that you know how much she hates you. Smiling and fighting you every inch of the way. And then one day you're old, you look around and it's still so young, so green. You want to give in, to say how much she means to you, but she just smiles through you, and there's no way to touch her. That's the lonely part. Then you know how strong she is. And it was all such a waste … Girl! [*Sleeps*]

[LALLY *stares from the door, as P.'s head falls, she smiles. JACKO turns, sees her. Turns away. She is gone. Lights down slowly as he dozes. The candles. Black. Drums up.*]

[*In the dark, voices humming cane-cutters' song. Even the drums. Lights warm to noon, last Monday, 1937 on Crew's farm. A bare space in the field. Cane stretching away into the distance around him, from the boundaries of the place.*]

[SONSON *sounding down and out, as he drinks deeply from a bottle, stands, turns, looking around him intently, corks the bottle. Sits slowly.*]

SONSON: Thirty years. Thirty years of a man's life. [*Picks up his cutlass, sharpens it shrilly against a hand file. The glare is in his eyes.*] Father sun is your time now. Jesus, I dry! [*Drinks again. Looking off, sees* RACHEL.] Rachel! Over here! Wait, she dress up! Is a good looking woman you have, Crew.

[RACHEL *enters*]

RACHEL: What you doing, Crew?

SONSON: Sharpening my blade.

RACHEL: You drinking again?

SONSON: A few. Here, take one. [*Offers her the bottle*]

RACHEL: You want you wife walk round the place stinking of rum?

SONSON: Heh! Don't want my wife walking round the place at all.

RACHEL: Come, don't lie down in the direct sun!

SONSON: Chuh, no harm in that. Him and me is old friends.

RACHEL: It will give you fever, my husband. Come now, lean up against this. [*Nudges him into the shade*] I look for you all over, you not working?

SONSON: I come out to see the farm. You see it?

RACHEL: I see it. [*Pause*]

SONSON: I don't think I can make it up the hill. Send Jacko to see me. I will just rest here till him come.

RACHEL: Jacko leave the house early this morning, Crew, gone up in the bush to hunt wild pig. We don't have no meat in the house, Crew.

SONSON: Send the other one then.

RACHEL: Sonny? He just leave for town.

SONSON: Town? Whar him have there? [*Pause*]

RACHEL: Looking for work, Crew. Nothing round here to do anymore.

SONSON: Well, him and me going have words when him come back. Him belong to the country. Town is not a good place, you know that.

RACHEL [*Sighing.*]: Yes, Crew.

SONSON: They violent! All they can do is talk about killing. I tell you. When I go last November a big black man chop down a white woman just so, thief everything in the house, and dash down the little baby that was in the bed with the woman. Town is not a nice place anymore.

RACHEL: Yes, Crew, you did tell us. [*Pause*]

SONSON: They don't have no work there either. [*Loudly*] Those that raise on the land must stay on the land! That is where we belong!

RACHEL: All that finish now …

SONSON: Hanging, das what going happen.

[RACHEL *turns a handful of soil in her fingers, sadly*]

SONSON: Kill, kill, look like everybody following the white people ways. Is only white people love butchery so! I going tell him so when he come back.

RACHEL: He should stay in town.

SONSON: He is you son, Rachel!

RACHEL: You so blind, Crew. When you don't want to see. The house too small for all of we.

SONSON: Don't it have three rooms? Is really the biggest cottage in the village, even if the roof over Jacko's room still leaking.

RACHEL: Ah Crew, you don't know. The three of them eating their heart out through living so close. Is only God know why nothing bad happen yet.

SONSON: Sonson giving trouble?

RACHEL: No, Crew.

SONSON: I warn him already you know. He is to have good manners towards him brother's wife. I don't care how long he know her.

RACHEL: I wish … I wish we had some money to send Jacko and Brigit to live in their own home.

SONSON: But I think is Sonson you want to send away?

RACHEL: Ah Crew, go sleep, you hear.

SONSON: I doze off, but the heat meking the blood go up in my head like a drum. So dry … [*Silence*] Rachel. You see the watercourse? [*She nods sadly*] First time I ever see it dry, in thirty years. [*Looks around hopelessly. She rises.*] Where you going?

RACHEL [*Not looking at him*]: Up the hill.

SONSON: Which hill?

RACHEL: To the Great House.

SONSON: Yes, that is a good idea. Take two hands of bananas as well as the corn, see if you sell them. People always say is the sweetest fruit the district produce.

RACHEL: I going to ask for a job. [*Pause*]

SONSON: You what?

RACHEL: They want a housekeeper up there, Crew.

SONSON: You? Housekeeper?

RACHEL: How long I looking after you house? Eh?

SONSON: Das different. Das not your house. They looking for somebody with experience to run the place. They don't want no poor nigger.

RACHEL: I never tell you, they ask me about it over a year ago, Crew.

SONSON: Who ask you?

RACHEL: Madam was there at the time, ask her if is not true.

SONSON: Then tell me something. What is to happen to the rest of us when you up there in white Massa house?

RACHEL: Brigit in the house, Crew, she will do whatever you say! I only going to be away in the days. And one night a week, or two …

SONSON: You sounding as if everything settle already!

RACHEL: I don't know, Crew! I going up there to find out!

SONSON: When you asked me 'bout this?

RACHEL: I never ask you …

SONSON: Well, you can haul yourself back to the house and put it out of your mind.

RACHEL: You making joke!

SONSON [*Threatening*]: Try me out!

RACHEL: You never raise you hand to me once yet. This is not the time to start.

SONSON: You think a man have no pride? I must let my woman support me, eh?

RACHEL: Show me another way then! What happen to the cultivation?

SONSON: Them turn the river to flow back round the hill, nothing can grow in the farm without water. You don't see the earth dry up since August?

RACHEL: And what you doing about it? Every day you come out here and lie down, drink the stinking rum, and when day get too

hot you go to sleep, like you have all the time in the world
to spare.

SONSON: I have a little save up, that will carry us until I get a loan from
the government.

RACHEL: The money finish! When last you look?

SONSON: Then what you want from me?

RACHEL: Find a job, go to town, and I will work here to do what I can.

SONSON: Leave here? I can't do that! How I will live? My navel string bury
here, woman. Give up the land? You don't want me to do that?

RACHEL: The two of we don't have to give up, after all these years.

SONSON: I know every step of it. Every bush; like the back of me hand.
Is a history behind every foot of it. Look at me, woman! I don't
have nothing except what I get from the ground. I born by it
and marry by it and one day it going to kill me. Maybe even
now, but is what I know, it is what nothing can change. I trying
to tell you, and I don't have the word to tell you, I am like a
dumb man trying to tell you what happen to him. I only can
trace the line here in the hard dirt, see? And the line going
from here to there, and this end is where them bring my great
grandfather, here, and this is me. If you take away the line from
the ground I am nothing. I am nobody!

RACHEL: The land don't have to take the bread out of your mouth.
The land is not everything!

SONSON: It is everything! Everything! I will tell you! My father and
his father sweat for it, year after year. It is my birthright that
say I am not a slave anymore. I don't have to work for no
man, I don't have to beg no man for bread to pass down to
my children. And my woman don't have to go slave in any
whiteman house, I don't care how much they pay you! Rachel
me love, don't take that away from me. I will find a way out.
Trust me. [Pause] Mass Charles. I going to talk to him.

RACHEL: Him is a white man too, Crew.

SONSON: Don't him born here? Grow up here same as me and you.
Him is a white man yes, but he know how a man like me feel
about the land, and him will listen. The river rise on his land,
and when the landfall turn it from the property, it still flowing
through the estate. Mass Charlie have water, and to spare. I will
work out something with him. You will see. Wife, go take off
you good clothes and wait for me. I will be back before dark.

RACHEL: Crew, you can't go up to the Great House like that.

SONSON: I don't have nothing to be ashamed of. This how a man look
            when he work for his living. I is a cultivator, I look like one and
            I smell like one. Is a honest thing, and I don't have no need to
            hide it, even if is only begging I going to do. Lawd, sun beating
            like a drum on me head …

RACHEL: Crew, walk good.

SONSON: Go on now.

[RACHEL *moves away from him. He brushes off his trousers, stacks
the machete in his belt, empties the flask, wipes his mouth on his hand,
throws the bottle away. Waves her off grinning. She backs away, then
turns and goes quickly. He blinks up at the sky.*]

            Hold on, father. Is a long walk I making, so cool off little bit, eeh?

[*Exits*]

[*The drum is beating the Mahi slowly as lights cool to black. In the dark the
roaches burn in the hands of* DREAMBOAT, JACKO, LALLY. *When the lights
are up again, all are as they were when* RACHEL *was anointed.* BRIGIT *leads*
RACHEL *to a seat.*]

P: Somebody outside. [*Silence except for the drum*] I sure I hear
            somebody call.

[*Lights a candle, close by* SONSON. SONSON *wakes.*]

SONSON: Hot. Hot. [*Shades his eyes against the candle*] Oh Lawd.

[SONSON *swings his hand at it.* P *lifts it high, backs away from him.
He follows, keeping the same distance.* P *moves again, he follows, shielding
his eyes all the while. It brings them to* STONE *where he is slumped.*
P *trips against* STONE.]

STONE: What you want, man?

[*As* P*'s attention shifts to* STONE, SONSON *blows out the candle. Black.
Drum.*]

[*Hard spot on* SONSON. *He is trudging on the spot … Staggering a little,
but in time to the drum*]

SONSON: Take the short cut. I soon make it. Just keep in a straight line.
            Straight line in the dirt. One. Two. Three.

[*He counts aloud throughout. The others stand/crawl/crouch/roll … in
his way. He moves through them and around them, never touching them,
towards his destination. Simultaneously at intervals they whisper.*]

CHORUS: What's one more nigger more or less

Lazy bitch

[*Laughs*] Lost your tongue? You dumb?

Don't cross my path

Teach him

Nothing

The women are no better

You, boy, fetch the dogs

With a stranger passing, with a husband's brother

Here! To me!

Took in washing for a white man named

Warmer than snow

Rebellious

Overboard, and tell the Captain

Bitter things

Nothing between us, nothing

Black

And insolent

Don't cross my path!

SONSON [*His intensity drives them back slowly, spiralling out from him*]:
I not a criminal. I come to beg. I can cut a lickle canal from the estate, I can lead the water just a lickle at a time, not much for my land, it don't cost him nothing, him have water an to spare. I have a wife an two sons and a lickle piece of land, I not asking for nothing that don't belong to me, nothing that don't belong to me.

[*The* CHORUS *are still. He is in a clear space. Each in turn, facing away from him when they've spoken, except for* STONE.]

So. Ask.

[*Silence. Drums, softly. He is on Great House steps.*]

Mass Charlie! [*Silence*] Mass Charlie! Is me, Crew!

[*The* CHORUS *part in the middle leaving* SONSON *standing at the top of the steps*]

STONE: What you want, man?

SONSON: I sorry to talk like this, sah. I come to beg a small help out.
I don't have hardly anything to eat in the house, you see sah, and my son wife carrying a child now. Two months gone. I not

complaining but thas how things go now. And me own wife saying how she will go out to work, to bring in money – a man can't live like that, Mass Charlie! So I come to ask you a favour, sah – my land dry up since the river turn –

STONE: How you mean to come to the front door, man? Go round the back and wait.

[*The* CHORUS *laughs, building.* STONE *turns away.* SONSON *grabs the shirt, spins him around.* STONE *pushes him away furiously.* SONSON *falls,* STONE *moves to kick him.* SONSON *brings him down pulling his feet from under.* STONE *falls.* SONSON *grabs his machete, raises it high to swing down. Freeze action. Drum ceases. A long building scream from the* CHORUS. *Black.*]

P [*In the dark*]: Sonson! One o'you pick up the candle, nuh!

DREAM: What happening?

LALLY: Where is the matches?

BRIGIT: Ma!

RACHEL: What happening?

DREAM: Him gone mad now!

[MADAM *strikes a match, lights a candle.* P *pushes the door open, moonlight streams in.* SONSON *has a machete in his hand but we can't see it. He is crouched wearily. He doesn't see them unless they move. Then they register as danger.*]

SONSON: They going come and find me. I not going to jail for this, you hear me! I suffer too long – three hundred years! Three hundred!

P: Stone wake up!

RACHEL: Madam, what I must do?

SONSON: Poor Rachel. What I must do.

JACKO: Him gone crazy now!

SONSON: Somebody coming! Lawd he bleeding like a wild pig. They coming this way! [*Stares at the chain*] The tree. I can get up to the roof, and get round to the back!

MADAM: You can't hold a man when him under the weed like that!

[SONSON *climbs up the chain, travelling fast up to the top of the hanging down section. Onto the beam that juts out from the wall. Pauses.*]

LALLY: Is alright Miss Rachel, he soon get back him senses and come down.

RACHEL: None of you couldn't stop him!

BRIGIT: Is who cause it? Why you can't leave the dead in peace?

DREAM: Look, he going further!

[SONSON *climbs out on to the chain length that loops across the roof*]

RACHEL: Jesus, have mercy!

[SONSON *almost falls, swings from the chain for a moment, pulls himself back up, rests. Then, on to the end of it, where it hangs down, the last link several feet from the floor.*]

SONSON: Is a long way down, Mass Charlie. Oh Gawd! I not going back there!

BRIGIT: You have to get him down!

SONSON: Is too far. I going to catch me breath, and then I will try it. Mass Charlie, why you did say that?

RACHEL: Jacko! Is you brother!

JACKO: You think I can fly all of a sudden? How? The damn fool going to break him neck and I can't help him.

BRIGIT: Jacko!

[JACKO *turns sharply to her. Looks from* BRIGIT *to* SONSON, *slowly, and back.*]

          Now is the time to show yourself, Jacko, my husband. You was always the clever one, you remember? You brother fight and curse to get what him want, but you bide you time, and make people like you, and then you have you way. Not so?

JACKO: That is so. That is what you think about me. Why you never tell me from the first?

BRIGIT: You think I judging you, Jacko? Maybe that is the better way. I don't know. But that is your way, and maybe it will help you now to figure out how to save him.

[JACKO *looks at them again*]

          What you thinking, Jacko? What you been thinking all these months? Speak you mind. [*Silence*]

JACKO [*He can hardly say it*]:   If it was me, you would 'fraid for me same way?

BRIGIT: You know it. But I would know it wasn't any use to ask him for help. He have a good heart, Jacko, he don't have enough patience, he don't have enough love to take time, and find the right way.

SONSON: I can't wait any longer ... [*Dries his palm on his trousers, tries to balance his weight so he can stand, before crouching to jump*] The sun too damn hot! [*Takes his cutlass from his belt, holds it*]

BRIGIT: What I have to say to make you understand, Jacko? The white man is right after all. Is only brute force can make us change our ways! Is only blood that people like us understand, is only revenge that satisfy us. And we is no better than the beast in the field, that don't know nothing about love!

JACKO [*Turns from her, after a moment, moves to below* SONSON. *Quietly.*]: Sonny. Is me, Jacko. What you doing, man?

[SONSON *ignores him*]

[STONE *is awake now, starts to join* JACKO. MADAM *stops him, whispers.*]

Crew! Pa!

[*Startled*, SONSON *crouches hiding*]

SONSON: Jacko? You?

JACKO [*Easily*]: Pa? Where you?

SONSON: Shhh! Up here.

JACKO: What you doing up there? Everybody waiting for you.

SONSON: Waiting for me? Jacko, them going hang me!

JACKO: Who going hang you, Pa?

SONSON: Them going throw me in jail for murder, Jacko! I kill the white man out in front of the house!

JACKO: Is true, then?

SONSON: Them find him, no? I was trying to get away, but the roof so high!

JACKO: Stone say you wouldn't take him challenge!

SONSON: What?

JACKO: We was down at the shop taking a quick one, and I bet Dream say you couldn't wrestle Stone to a fall, two out of three.

SONSON: Jacko, them going hang me! Go home before somebody come and find you here with me!

JACKO [*Laughing*]: Chuh, Pa! Don't bother with that! Mass Charlie say him give you permission to pick breadfruit from the tree in the front, so I know you must be up here somewhere.

SONSON: Mass Charlie?

JACKO: Pa, I bet a whole five dollars on you! Come down quick, we set up the match for this evening!

SONSON: Mass Charlie dead! I chop him straight cross the chest! Jacko, the blood spurt out like a river …

JACKO: Chuh Pa, stop talk stupidness, and come down! I going lose my money if you turn down the challenge. Is only a friendly match, Pa!

SONSON: The sun turning me head I can hardly see …

JACKO: I sure you stronger than Stone, Pa. I feel you is the strongest man in the whole village!

SONSON: Jacko …

JACKO: Yes, Pa.

SONSON: I have blood all over my shirt and mi hands … I can smell it.

JACKO: I bring you a clean shirt, Pa. Ma say you not to walk around the district with hog blood all over your shirt, you will give her a bad name!

SONSON: Clean shirt … I can hide this one …

JACKO: Come back over by the tree, Pa! This sun so hot! I nearly fall down on the way over.

SONSON: Hog blood. Maybe I was killing hog.

JACKO: Pa, hold on, I hear somebody calling me.

SONSON: Jacko, you lying to me! I don't know. I don't know.

JACKO: Is Mass Charlie, wait for me, Pa. [*Moves off around the corner of the house*] Stone. Go wait for him when he come back across.

[STONE *moves to the chain, and up it to the platform*]

Pa, Mass Charlie say I must bet a five dollar for him! You see that!

SONSON: True, everybody know I can beat Stone any day. Jacko?

JACKO: I going round to the front, meet me by the tree, Pa.

SONSON: Wait! Jacko, is true?

JACKO: Five dollars! [*Laughing*] Don't bother make me lose it!

[SONSON *nods his head slowly, puts back the 'cutlass' in his belt, starts to crawl back along the chain.* BRIGIT *hugs* JACKO *and* RACHEL.]

RACHEL: Ah, mi son …

DREAM: I never see nothing like that!

P [*Watching* SONSON]: Careful … Careful …

LALLY: You think him will make it?

MADAM: Lally don't make any noise.

LALLY: No, Granny!

SONSON: I going home and lie down before the match. I don't feel so good …

JACKO: Pa! You alright?

SONSON: I don't feel so good son …

JACKO: Little more and you can come down! Stone waiting for you!

SONSON: You wait, I bet him three out a three …!

[SONSON *is at the ledge.* STONE *reaches to help him but he doesn't see.*]

JACKO: No, leave him, wait till he comes down …

SONSON [*Reaches the floor, staggers*]: Jacko … [*Fumbles to take off the cutlass*] Help me with this –

STONE: What you want, man?

SONSON [*Tenses. Pause.*]: I sorry to talk like this sah, I come to beg a small help out. I don't have hardly anything to eat in the house, you see sah, and my son wife carrying a child now. Two months gone … [*Stares at his hands*] I have to wash. Killing pig is a dirty business … The shirt cover with it. The river. I will run down and wash it off …

MADAM: Is so …

JACKO: See a clean shirt here. [*Gives* SONSON's *shirt to* SONSON]

RACHEL: An water.

[RACHEL *hands out the basin.* SONSON *puts in his hands. Wets his face. Washes hands. Stops. Stares at her. Slowly relaxes, smiles. Touches her face.*]

SONSON: Don't cry, Ma. Don't cry. [*Looks up at chain. Shivers.*]

RACHEL: Is so.

[SONSON *goes to* BRIGIT. *Stares at* JACKO. *Pushes her gently towards her husband.* JACKO *nods silently.* RACHEL *holds* SONSON *tenderly.*]

          Thas good. Thas good.

[RATTLER *quietly beats* 'Ratatata, Ta ta ta, Ratatata, Ta Ta, Tatatum, tatatum tum, tum']

[MADAM *stops him.* RACHEL *gestures 'no' to her.*]

RACHEL: Sometimes is not a good thing to cry too long. My man is dead yes. But not all the crying in the world going bring him back. And I 'fraid to lose what leave. We is here, don't is so? And tomorrow the sun going come up same as ever. No matter what is past, you can't stop the blood from drumming, and you can't stop the heart from hoping. We have to hold on to one another. That is all we can do. That is what leave behind, after all the rest. Play, Rattler. Play for what leave behind. Play for the rest of us.

[RATTLER *beats louder and louder. They pass* SONSON *from hand to hand increasingly joyful. When the stage is full of their celebration, somewhere in the ritual.*]

[*Curtain*]

Man Better Man
Errol Hill

Characters

(In order of appearance)

TIM BRISCOE

PORTAGEE JOE

SWIFTY

INEZ BRISCOE

HANNIBAL

TINY SATAN

CRACKERJACK

PETITE BELLE LILY

CUTAWAY RIMBEAU

DAGGER DA SILVA

ALICE SUGAR

COOLIE

PELOO

POGO

DIABLE PAPA

MINEE WOOPSA

VILLAGERS

The play was first presented by graduate students at the Yale School of Drama, New Haven, Connecticut, in an experimental theatre production on 21 April 1960. It was directed by Michael E. Rutenberg with music arranged and directed by Julian C. Barber.

The cast was as follows:

TIM BRISCOE	Vern Hinkle
PORTAGEE JOE	Leslie J. Stark
SWIFTY	Paul Weidner
INEZ BRISCOE	Wendy Howe Oehlert
HANNIBAL	Jerry Phillips
DAGGER DA SILVA	John Krich

TINY SATAN	George White
POGO	Ken Parker
CRACKERJACK	Arlen Digitale
PETITE BELLE LILY	Barbara Reid
CUTAWAY RIMBEAU	David Bray
ALICE SUGAR	Judith Ebert
COOLIE	Arthur Athanason
PELOO	Stephen Coy
DIABLE PAPA	David M. Keller
MINEE WOOPSA	Joyce Elliott

Musicians were: Ian Underwood (flute), Don Hitchman (guitar), Steve Swallow (drums), Charlie Keil (bongo drums), Melvin Esdaile (congo drum).

The first performance with a Trinidad cast took place at Queen's Hall, Port of Spain, Trinidad, on 30 August 1965. It was directed by Errol Hill with choreography by Beryl McBurnie and the music master was G.A. Prospect. The cast was as follows:

TIM BRISCOE	Leo Ruffino
PORTAGEE JOE	Peter Pitts
SWIFTY	Winston Gaye
INEZ BRISCOE	Marina Maxwell
HANNIBAL	Lennox Lake
DAGGER DA SILVA	Kenneth De La Rosa
TINY SATAN	Sydney Hill
POGO	Ken Parker
CRACKERJACK	Russell Winston
PETITE BELLE LILY	Vilma Ali
CUTAWAY RIMBEAU	Hugh Bonterre
ALICE SUGAR	Molly Ahye
COOLIE	Ronald Williams
PELOO	Andrew Dupigny

POGO	Freddie Kissoon
DIABLE PAPA	Errol Jones
MINEE WOOPSA	Jean Herbert

Musicians were: Fitzgerald Jemmott (flute), George Scott (clarinet), Eugene Phillips (guitar), John Henderson (cuatro), John 'Buddy' Williams (bass), Rennie Cooper and Carlton Francis (drums).

Synopsis of scenes

The action takes place in a small village on the island of Trinidad, West Indies, at the turn of the twentieth century. It covers a period of two days.

Prologue
Act One

Scene 1: 'El Toro', a general store and rumshop owned and operated by Portagee Joe.

Early afternoon.

Scene 2: A room in the dwelling-house of Diable Papa, obeahman.

The following day. Early morning.

Act Two

Scene 1: 'El Toro' store.

The same day. Late afternoon.

Scene 2: The stick-playing Arena.

The following day. Noon.

Act Three

Scene 1: 'El Toro' store and nearby woods.

The same day. Several hours later.

Scene 2: Diable Papa's house and nearby woods.

The same day. Late afternoon.

Scene 3: 'El Toro' store.

The same day. Evening.

The songs

Prologue

Canboulay Chant: 'Out In The Road'

Act One

Scene 1: Stick-fighting Chorus – *in background (optional)*

'Tiny, the Champion' (*Hannibal, Tiny and Chorus*)

'I Love Petite Belle' (*Briscoe*)

Scene 2: 'One Day, One Day, Congotay' (*D. Papa and Minee*)

Act Two

Scene 1: 'One, Two, Three' (*Hannibal and Male Chorus*)

'Man Better Man' (*Minee and Male Chorus*)

Scene 2: Stick-fighting Chorus – *in background (optional)*

'Petite Belle Lily' – *calypso (Hannibal, Lily and Chorus)*

'Girl in the Coffee' – *stick-fighting chorus (The Company)*

Act Three

Scene 1: 'Coolie Gone' (*Inez and Male Chorus*)

'War and Rebellion' (*The Company*)

Scene 2: 'Beautiful Heaven' – *revivalist hymn*

(*D. Papa, Minee, Coolie and Peloo*)

Scene 3: 'Briscoe the Hero' – *reprise of 'Tiny the Champion'*

(*Hannibal and Chorus*)

Prologue

The Prologue evokes the carnival 'canboulay' procession of olden times. A chorus of women led by HANNIBAL, *the calypsonian, dance onto the forestage singing a traditional stick-fighters' chant. The women are dressed in white with white headbands and carry lighted bottle-flambeaux.* HANNIBAL *sings the two-line verses, accompanying himself on a guitar or cuatro, and the women answer in chorus. During the singing, images of the stick-fighters appear behind a scrim. They mount a small platform, one at a time, and assume characteristic stick-fighting positions. At the end of the Prologue, the chorus of women dance off, the calypsonian makes his exit, and the scrim is raised to reveal the setting for Scene 1: 'El Toro' general store.*

Canboulay Chant: 'Out In The Road'

CHORUS: Out in the road,

Come out in the road, warrior.

VERSE 1   Out in the road, warrior,

Rouse yourself for the great encounter.

2   Foreday morning is no time to slumber,

Grab your poui and join in the slaughter.

3   Blow the conch-shell and beat the calinda,

Face the foe without fear or favor.

4   Call on the brave Captain Baker

To salvage your soul for your Maker.

5   Out in the road, warrior,

Band your belly but never surrender.

6   Say goodbye to your mooma and poopa,

Beg a prayer and plenty novena.

7   Carray, sauter, is licks like fire,

Blade for blade but no time to retire.

8   Down on your knees to your master,

No retreat from certain disaster.

9   Freddy, Fitzi, Tiepin and the Tiger,

Lie, Moscobee, Mybone and Myler.

10   Out in the road, warrior,

Rouse yourself for the great encounter.

Act One

Scene 1

'El Toro', a general store and rumshop owned and operated by PORTAGEE JOE, *in a small village in Trinidad, West Indies, at the turn of the century.*

The store supplies most of the physical needs of the community and is situated in the centre of the village at a wide cross-roads known as the 'square'. It is a favourite haunt of the inhabitants, especially at night when brightly-lit hurricane lanterns hanging from the rafters attract a crowd of carousing patrons.

Within the shop, a broad counter runs the length of the building. Behind this are rows of shelves containing foodstuffs, dry goods and drinks in separate stalls. There are tables and chairs, some spilling over onto the boardwalk in front of the shop which is protected from the weather by wide over-hanging eaves of galvanized iron supported on wooden posts. JOE's *private quarters adjoin the store and there is a door in the wall next to the bar which leads to them.*

JOE *employs two helpers.* SWIFTY, *a coloured youth of 17, serves as bartender and general handyman.* INEZ BRISCOE, *19, works as store clerk and waitress.*

PORTAGEE JOE *is popular with the villagers. About 50 years old, he hails from Madeira and, from the first, has lived and worked among the people until he is considered one of them.* JOE *has never married but, following local practice, has kept several mistresses in rotation. At present,* INEZ BRISCOE *appears to be next in line.*

AT CURTAIN

Three o'clock of an afternoon. The saloon is deserted. The central floor area is cleared and a small rostrum, decorated with flags and coloured kerchiefs, stands at one end. In the rostrum is a richly-ornamented tinsel crown on a stand. The noise of drumming and chanting in the distance.

TIM BRISCOE *enters the saloon and sits. He is a clean-shaven, youthful-looking blade of about 20, dressed inconspicuously in open-necked shirt and khaki pants, tennis shoes and with a kerchief tied round his neck. He calls to the barman.*

BRISCOE: Swifty! A drink! Swifty!

[*No answer. He crosses to the bar and pours himself a drink. Then he turns to inspect the decorations, takes up the crown, tries it on, looks at himself in a piece of glass.*]

Jeezu-web! A natural fit!

[*He finds a poui-stick and begins to go through the motions of a stick-fighter in the ring. Not satisfied with his display, he takes a long drink,*

131

changes his own neckerchief for a gaudy one from the rostrum, assumes
a fierce expression, looks in the mirror again and, apparently satisfied, he
shadows with the stick once more, this time going through the pantomime
more ferociously. Carried away, he emits a shrill yell which brings
PORTAGEE JOE *hurrying out from the back of the store.*]

JOE: What the hell … hey, who you be!

[BRISCOE *stops, embarrassed. He puts down the crown and poui-stick,*
and returns the kerchief he had borrowed.]

     Ah, Senor Briscoe!

BRISCOE: The shop was empty.

JOE: Swifty not here?

BRISCOE: Nor Inez either.

JOE: She in the tent, but where he disappear?

BRISCOE: You expecting him to miss the fight?

JOE: Don't I employ him and have the right
     To say if he can go?

BRISCOE: In Trinidad
     A stick-fight send everybody mad.

JOE: Excepting you? I think the whole village
     Down in the tent to witness a barrage
     Of blows. Say, how come you exclude
     Yourself from all that?

BRISCOE: I ain't in the mood.

JOE: You grieving still over Petite Belle Lily.
     Forget her, my friend, that is a frisky
     Girl who looking fame, not romance,
     All you can offer is perseverance.
     Tell me, you know to fight stick at all?

BRISCOE: It run in my blood. You ever hear tell
     Of the great Moscobee? He was my poopa
     And teach me all the science of war
     From the time I could walk.

JOE: That is bygone days.
     I, too, was famous for all kind of crazy
     Things. But reason take over now.

BRISCOE: To win Petite Belle I could recall how

To braix and charge –

JOE: I wouldn't start

Up again, Briscoe boy. Console your heart

That it, have plenty fish in the sea.

So one get away, that is no tragedy.

BRISCOE: You taking a drink?

JOE: Pass me over this one.

BRISCOE: I notice you make big preparation

To crown the champion.

JOE: Is Inez idea,

She trying to liven up things 'bout here.

And I go along.

BRISCOE: Who you back to win?

JOE: No difference to me.

BRISCOE: You still avoid betting?

JOE: To throw away the little money

That I put by?

BRISCOE: Well, I back Tiny.

The talk went around he got a mount stick.

JOE: Meaning what?

BRISCOE: That it charm! You know – black magic!

JOE: Ho-ho-ho! You island-people too funny,

In every shadow you spy a jumbie,

If a cock crow one night, a dead baby born,

Say a donkey bray hard, somebody life gone,

You frighten for blight, juju and maljo,

And the obeahman thiefing your money for so.

BRISCOE: You don't believe in obeah, eh Joe?

JOE: Obeah? Ha-ha, since I was a po-po,

Knee-high to a grasshopper, I finish with that.

But here you can't turn before somebody scattering

Pepper on the doorstep, rice on the floor –

BRISCOE: You should worry, seeing they buy from your store.

JOE: If I had the power I would drive from the land
            Every kind of witch doctor and obeahman,
            And I tell you, first to go is Diable Papa.

BRISCOE [*fearfully*]: Easy, Portagee, beware of that mister,
            He is one man not to tangle with ever.

JOE: So you believe the superstition?

BRISCOE: Supposing I do? I ain't the only one!
            Diable Papa plant here like an old sugar-mill,
            You try to uproot him at your peril,
            And though I can't swear to his villainy
            I hear some terrible testimony.
            Take for instance, when Soucouyant Jane denounce him
            As a fake, brother, she went out on a limb.

JOE: Soucouyant Jane?

BRISCOE: A notorious witch
            Used to fly through the night without a stitch
            On her body, like a ball of fire.
            Anyway, she quarrel with Diable Papa,
            Three days later they find her – is hard
            To believe it – stone dead in her yard
            Under a silk-cotton tree that people believe
            Is the devil own umbrella. So, pardner, leave
            Well alone is my motto from then.

JOE: Strange to talk so and call yourself men.

BRISCOE: Portagee Joe, when you live in a place
            You learn how to run to keep up in the race.

JOE: Well, is only with you I make free
            And, truth to tell, obeah don't bother me
            Except when I find it growing in my yard.
            Every person I take in the store have it bad.
            Sometimes is the girl, sometimes is the man,
            Sometimes my woman and all put her hand
            In the cash-box to pay this vagabond.

BRISCOE: You don't have to worry, you could trust Inez,
            She's a good little girl.

JOE: I ain't displease

With your sister. In fact my intention

Could be honest with a little persuasion.

If she would friends-up a little more

And don't flirt with all who come in the store.

[*Prolonged shouting and cheering off. The chanting and music stop.*]

BRISCOE: Excitement in blood! The fight done over

And the village have a new conqueror

In the person, come bet, of Tiny the Terror.

JOE: Well, so be it. Help me prepare

For the crowd who will soon invade me here.

I tell Swifty fix-up before he go,

That boy! Fill the glasses, a dozen or so,

While I set the tables.

[BRISCOE *pours rum liberally into glasses while* JOE *arranges the tables and chairs in a semi-circle facing the rostrum on which he places a single chair.*]

BRISCOE: You know something, Joe,

That crown take my head in a natural fit

As if the stars pick me for a favourite

And sooner or late, I will rule the ring.

What you say to that?

JOE: I say you deceiving

Yourself, you just don't rank in the game.

Think how much warriors you have to tame

Before you could challenge the champion.

BRISCOE: Not so much. Maybe nine or ten.

JOE: Ten names too terrible to pull down,

Ten giants barring the way to the crown.

BRISCOE: You can't blame me for trying.

JOE: It could mean your death.

BRISCOE: What is for a man, that he must get.

[SWIFTY *and* INEZ BRISCOE *enter quickly. He is a precocious youth of 17, inclined to be excitable, but well-meaning.* INEZ, *19, already has the air of a mature coquette. She is attractively dressed in a gay coloured cotton dress with a low neck and frilled skirt over stiff petticoats.*

The background music is now a victory chorus as the stick-fighting crowd make their way to 'El Toro' to celebrate.]

SWIFTY: They coming! Singing the victory chorus!

          Everything ready?

JOE: You have plenty brass.

SWIFTY: It was battle royal!

JOE: Now look here, you –

INEZ: Joe, don't get upset.

SWIFTY: What the hell I do?

JOE: You walk off the job. Leave the shop wide

          Open.

SWIFTY: But I leave you relaxing inside!

JOE: Jesu-Marie!

INEZ: Remember your pressure!

JOE: The boy talk as if he owning the store!

BRISCOE: Who win the fight?

INEZ: Tiny Satan.

SWIFTY: With a blow

          So swift you only hear when it pass

          Like a breeze. He is stick-man of class!

[*He takes up a poui-stick to demonstrate.* JOE *snatches it away.*]

JOE: Go busy yourself out in the back,

          From tomorrow you could take all day to slack.

SWIFTY: Oh, Mr Joe! Miss Inez, please!

INEZ: Give him a chance, Joe. He didn't mean

          To aggravate you. Swifty, see and clean

          Up the place. Come on, make yourself handy.

SWIFTY: Yes, mum!

JOE [*to* BRISCOE]: She take over the business already.

          Just like I say. Is only the key

          To the strong-box I still call my own.

INEZ: Portagee Joe, when you use that tone

          I must be on guard. Like a borne creole

          You know all the tricks to fool-up a girl.

[*She gives him a gentle hug.*]

SWIFTY: The female fans mob Tiny with kisses,

          First to besiege him was Miss Inez!

INEZ: If you can't keep quiet, bite on your tongue.

          You have too much lip for one so young.

BRISCOE: The crowd in sight!

JOE: Get your carnival

          Over quick, Inez, and come back to normal.

[*The* CROWD *come into view shuffling down the road, singing, led by* HANNIBAL, *the calypsonian, on his cuatro. They carry aloft the new champion,* TINY SATAN. *He is about 25, short in stature with powerful shoulders and legs, and decked out in traditional costume. He holds a poui-stick. Beside* HANNIBAL *is* PETITE BELLE LILY, *in her early 20s and the belle of the village. Others of the crowd are* ALICE SUGAR, *elder sister to* LILY, CRACKERJACK, *28, a leading contender,* CUTAWAY RIMBEAU, *of French creole descent and* DAGGER DA SILVA *of Portuguese stock, both about 30. Also in the crowd are* COOLIE, *35, of East Indian extraction, and* PELOO *an ancient, arthritic Negro. These two latter men work as agents for* DIABLE PAPA *unknown to the other villagers. A few extras of both sexes complete the company.*]

HANNIBAL [*singing*]:   Tiny Satan born with a poui,

          Tiny blade the enemy,

          One and all cry 'surrender',

          Tiny is the conqueror.

CHORUS: Who win? Tiny!

          Who Tiny? Tiny Satan!

TINY [*singing*]:   I raise my rod and I rule the ring,

          Give the victory shout and crown me king.

HANNIBAL [*singing*]:   Tiny battle all in town,

          One by one they tumble down,

          Tiny prove the better man,

          Tiny is the champion.

          Tiny harder than old iron,

          Tiny strong as any lion,

          Tiny muscles form like spring,

          Tiny fast as lightning.

Tiny eyeing every chick,

Tiny out to take his pick,

Not a girl to tell him no,

Tiny is the world's hero.

[*The crowd enter the saloon and dance around the new champion. Then they perch informally on tables and chairs facing the rostrum.* TINY *and* CRACKERJACK *stand before them.* JOE, INEZ *and* SWIFTY *pass the drinks.* BRISCOE *remains in the background.*]

CRACKERJACK: I promise this will be short and sweet,

Everybody know why for we meet,

Tiny Satan win a glorious encounter

Today as befits a great warrior.

SEVERAL: Prove he is king

Of the stick-man ring ...

Tiny Satan is hero

Today and tomorrow ...

CRACKERJACK: He reach the top without losing a war,

A feat never equalled in annals before,

Therefore we gather to celebrate

His victory for he is truly great.

SEVERAL: Carve his name

In the book of fame ...

None to compare

With a fighter so rare ...

CRACKERJACK: We have a crown, and now it must sit

On the head that never taste defeat.

Which lovely girl will win the honour

To crown the champion? Tiny, show your favour!

TINY: I pick Petite Belle; she possess two eyes

Where sun and moon shine in constant surprise

Of each other, one minute glazing with scorn,

The next, tender as a baby new-born,

So with a stick-man, furious in fighting,

But calm as a church outside of the ring.

CRACKERJACK: Spoken like a hero. Lily, take your stand

> Beside the champion, crown in hand.
>
> Tiny Satan, conqueror of the field,
>
> Swift as lightning, sharper than steel,
>
> Wizard of wood, a terror in war,
>
> Brave as a lion whose mighty roar
>
> Spell death and destruction to the enemy,
>
> We crown you king!

[POGO, *the defeated champion, runs into the store. He wears a bandage round his head.*]

POGO: Is a lie! All lies!

CRACKERJACK: Who disturb the proceeding?

POGO: Me, Pogo, beaten but not disgraced,

> I call Tiny a coward to his face!
>
> I lose the battle but stoutly declare
>
> He never defeat me fair and square!

CRACKERJACK: Come to the fore and make your charge.

POGO: I only repeat what they know at large,

> That Tiny fight with a mounted stick,
>
> He had a charm, else I woulda lick
>
> In his flank. He could never conquer me
>
> So easy. Obeah save him from my poui.

TINY: You lie!

POGO: Is true!

JOE: Gentlemen, please,

> Don't start a quarrel.

TINY: I could make you bow

> To me anytime. Come, square off now!

POGO: Crow, little cock! This poui chastise

> Warriors who measure twice your size.
>
> Ti Bomina and the great Moscobee,
>
> Myler, renowned for agility,
>
> Johnny Oak, the only human ram,
>
> And Jules Tiepin of the iron arm,

Mungo the dentist, able to pick
Out a troublesome tooth with a single flick,
Fisherman Brush, the Tobago find,
And Fitzie Bainwright who fight even blind!
What you know about stick, Mr Hurry-come-up!
I rule the ring when you was a pup
Still wetting your pants. Now I getting down,
And hope to relinquish a spotless crown,
But instead we have a shadow-king,
Not you, is the obeahman ruling!

SEVERAL: Pogo talk true
Between me and you ...
Is the obeahman
Make the champion ...

CRACKERJACK: Pogo had a great and glorious past,
All stick-man regret he fight his last,
But Tiny Satan record is clear,
I for one hail him as a warrior
Without parallel in the entire village.
Now, true or not, what you allege
Lacking proof. So I say, let's proceed.

[*The men agree vociferously.*]

TINY: No! No crown! Somebody will bleed
For the insult I suffer. I will fight any man
Today or tomorrow with the poui he bring,
Let him cross with me and prove who is king.
Hear me now! I address one and all,
And cast my weapon into the hall,
Pick it up who dare to challenge me,
I will pay for your hole in the cemetery.

[*A silence.*]

POGO: Where all the sons of the brave and bold
To meet this challenge? Must the old
War-horse take to the field again?

TINY: I will plant a statue over their grave!

LILY: Not a man in the crowd! Nobody so brave!

            Where the heroes gone? Here is a chance

            For the crown open to all combatants,

            You will let it pass? Who ain't satisfy

            To live unknown and unknown to die?

            Only the man who put fame above

            Everything deserve a woman's love.

[BRISCOE *steps forward and picks up the poui-stick. The crowd are astonished, then burst out laughing.*]

SEVERAL: Briscoe making joke …

            He is only smoke …

            Give him a cheer

            For clearing the air …

THE MEN: One-two-three

            He's a lion, let him roar-ar-ar!

CRACKERJACK: Briscoe, we appreciate your courage.

[*Laughter and clapping.*]

            But we can't allow suicide in the village.

[*More laughter.*]

            So put down the poui. Drink up and let's go!

BRISCOE: I accept the challenge. Who can say no?

POGO: Take the advice of an old veteran,

            Stick ain't make for every man.

BRISCOE: I will try my luck inside the tent.

POGO: I should never start-up this argument.

            I like a brave man, not a simpleton.

INEZ: Don't be a fool, man, drop the weapon.

BRISCOE: Set a date for the fight and make it soon.

JOE: Briscoe, be reasonable. What tragedy!

BRISCOE: If Tiny wouldn't fight, he must bow to me.

TINY: Bow to you! The man is a lunatic!

BRISCOE: Either you fight or break your stick.

CRACKERJACK: Listen, Briscoe, you don't know to fight.

BRISCOE: I take up the challenge and demand my right.

CRACKERJACK: Tiny, you will have to cross with him.

TINY: The man ain't serious, is a crazy whim.

INEZ: Briscoe, for the last time, put down the poui.

BRISCOE: Never! Until the promise to fight me.

TINY: Is your funeral.

CRACKERJACK: Briscoe –

LILY: Why all you carrying on!
            Briscoe have as much right to the crown
            As anybody. Don't hesitate,
            If he want to do battle, set the date!

INEZ: You, Lily, you is the cause of this!
            You never content until somebody risking
            Limb and life to satisfy you!

LILY: Me? Don't couple me in your to-do!

TINY: Stop the chatter and I hear my decision.
            Since he force me to it, I will take Briscoe on.
            Crackers, set the day.

CRACKERJACK: Bear witness that I
            Cast a strong vote against this trial.
            Two days ahead, as the hands on the dial
            Come to attention, the bugle will blow.

JOE: Senors, senoritas, please clear the store,
            This business will lead to heavy sorrow.

[*The saloon begins to empty noisily.*]

SEVERAL: Excitement for so …
            More trouble and woe …
            A day to recall
            When you grow old …

OTHERS: Briscoe gone crazy
            To tangle with Tiny …
            Is only to prove
            The power of his love …

[*The villagers pass out, leaving* COOLIE *and* PELOO *behind. They move downstage and a traverse curtain falls behind them to permit a scene change during the following action. The location is now a street in the village.*]

COOLIE: So we take a chance, what we have to lose?

PELOO: I say I don't like it. You think Diable Papa

        Will handle two men who fight one another?

COOLIE: All we do is find him a customer

        And draw commission, so much a head.

        That simple enough. What it is you dread?

PELOO: An angry stick-man.

COOLIE: Commit that worry

        To Diable Papa.

PELOO: I know what a poui

        Taste like. It ain't nice.

COOLIE: Talk logically.

        Briscoe get a charm, he pay big for it,

        You and me both collect a profit –

PELOO [*cutting in*]:   Enough to get me a new pair of shoes

        I hope, my foot on the ground.

COOLIE: You confusing

        The issue. All right. Say he enter the ring

        And face Tiny … what the hell I was saying?

PELOO: I always tell you too much logic

        Ain't good for the brain.

COOLIE: Listen, Briscoe need magic

        To beat Tiny and we can supply it.

        Why you holding back? Send him to the hut

        Of the obeahman and get our commission.

PELOO: I wouldn't do it, but I need a soft

        Pair of shoes.

COOLIE: Don't forget my half

        Of the cut.

[COOLIE *leaves.* PELOO *hovers to one side as* BRISCOE *and* TINY *enter.*]

TINY: I bear you no grudge!

BRISCOE: Nor I to you!

TINY: Then why put me in this callaloo?

I don't want to hurt you. First thing the village
Will say is I like too much advantage,
Or call me a coward if I refuse
To fight, and traitor if I should lose.

BRISCOE: I sorry to put you in such distress.

TINY: How much to get me out of the mess?

BRISCOE: I intend to fight and must caution you
That I mean to win.

TINY: You really going through
With your craziness?

[BRISCOE *nods*.]

On your head be it.
I give you a sporting chance to quit.

[TINY *leaves. Old* PELOO *sidles up to* BRISCOE.]

PELOO: He frighten, eh? I hear him offer
To buy you off. The stars in your favour
For I know exactly how to make sure
When you enter the ring, though an amateur,
You will stop Tiny.

BRISCOE: Give me the tip.

PELOO: A tip for a tip!

[BRISCOE *gives him a coin*.]

You must take a trip
Tomorrow at dawn beyond the river
To visit the obeahman.

BRISCOE: Diable Papa?

PELOO: Yes. Tiny using a regular stick,
He can't touch you if you have magic.

BRISCOE: True … but I don't too like the idea
Of mixing with obeah.

PELOO: Is nothing to fear.
Everybody these days takes a little dose
To help them along.

BRISCOE: What about cost?

PELOO: Relative, depending on what you need,

          Et cetera. Don't worry, it won't exceed

          What you can afford. Put coin in your pocket.

BRISCOE: Thanks for the tip. I will think of it.

PELOO: When you succeed, remember old Peloo!

[*He goes out.* INEZ *enters quickly.*]

INEZ: I was looking high and low for you!

BRISCOE: Don't bother say it, my mind is set.

INEZ: I will talk while I drawing breath

          To make you see reason. Is naked death

          You face in the ring. Why challenge Tiny?

          What possess you? Petite Belle Lily

          Got you tie-up under a spell

          Till you can't decipher heaven from hell.

          Go to Diable Papa, pay him well

          To get release from her witchery.

BRISCOE: Stop your raving and listen to me.

          Early tomorrow, crack of the dawn,

          I will go and visit the obeahman

          To charm my poui, preserve my body,

          And save me from all true enemies.

INEZ: Briscoe, you set my heart at ease.

          You want me come with you?

BRISCOE: No, I can manage.

INEZ: All right. Take care and bolster your courage

          To meet Diable Papa. Be wise and wily.

          Now come on home and forget Lily.

BRISCOE: Go ahead. I follow presently.

[INEZ *leaves.* LILY *and* ALICE *cross the stage giggling.* BRISCOE *is angry with himself but cannot help loving* LILY. *He sings of his love.*]

BRISCOE [*singing*]: Who is this lovely girl, Petite Belle,

          Who is this precious pearl of my life, Petite Belle.

          I cannot eat by day, come the night,

Cannot sleep, what a plight,

Only live by the light of her eyes.

[*Chorus*]

I love Petite Belle,

Petite Belle Lily,

I love Petite Belle.

I offer everything, Petite Belle,

A brooch, a diamond ring for a smile,

Petite Belle,

I cannot think of bliss more than this,

Just a kiss, on my knees

Be my wife, take my life it is yours.

And if there is a chance, Petite Belle,

Of tasting of romance in your arms, Petite Belle,

I'll fight the greatest champion ever seen,

Mow him down, win the crown,

Or I'll die for my queen, Petite Belle.

[*The lights dim out. The traverse curtain is raised and the setting for the following scene is revealed.*]

Scene 2

A room in the dwelling-house of DIABLE PAPA, *obeahman, in the woods some distance from the village.*

The house is a wooden hut made of rough-hewn lumber. D. PAPA receives his clients in an untidy and sparsely-furnished room to the front of the house. There are two doors: one leads to the front garden beyond which is a footpath that runs down to the village through the woods. The other door, usually kept open and draped with a curtain, leads to the interior of the house. A hinged window opens on to the garden.

AT CURTAIN

Early morning, before daybreak. Faint drum-beats and chanting afar off. The room is empty. A single flickering candle makes it seem alive with moving shadows. BRISCOE *crosses the stage furtively and knocks at the door.*

BRISCOE: Diable Papa-a-a! Diable Papa-o-o-h!

[*Knocks a second time.*]

Diable Papa-a-a! Diable Papa-o-o-h!

[*Knocks a third time.*]

[D. PAPA *enters from the inner room. About 60 years old, a mulatto with a withered, emaciated casing, he presents at once a repulsive and strangely magnetic figure. His hair is long and matted, his beard fuzzy, his eyes red and bulging, and his fingernails untrimmed. He wears now an old blue shirt, black trousers and wooden clogs for slippers. He hitches up his pants with an old tie, unhangs a black gown from a nail in the wall and puts it on, extracts a money-box from the trunk and places it on a table beside the throne chair. Only then does he unbolt the window and door. Then he returns to sit in the chair and calls in a loud voice.*]

D. PAPA: Man, beast or devil! Enter

    The above of your master, Diable Papa!

[BRISCOE *enters cautiously carrying his poui. He looks about nervously trying to accustom his eyes to the semi-darkness of the room.*]

BRISCOE: Morning, morning, Diable Papa,

    I come seeking your kind favour.

    Hey, where you be? I can't too well

    See you in the dark. You and the shadows

    Make one.

D. PAPA: You too impatienate.

    Three time you assault my door. Knit

    Yourself together, man, and name your name.

BRISCOE: I is Tim Briscoe, blade for blade,

    Old Peloo point me here. He say

    Of all science-men it have today

    You alone is lord and master.

D. PAPA: You come singly?

BRISCOE: Me one.

D. PAPA: Then gather

    Your courage and declare your story.

BRISCOE: Papa, I beg you help me out.

D. PAPA: State systematically in exact terminology

    What business you come about.

BRISCOE: Yes. I going tell you from the start –

D. PAPA: Take time, boy, take time. No cart

    Before horse in this establishment.

    You walk with money?

BRISCOE: I ain't so ignorant!

Peloo say, 'Put coin in your pocket',

So I bring you every penny I got.

[*He hands* D. PAPA *a bag of money.*]

D. PAPA: How much here?

BRISCOE: Twenty-three dollars plus.

D. PAPA: Is all? Huh. Some presumptuous

Body want to make me a mook,

Or you ain't half as smart as you look.

BRISCOE: The money ain't enough, Diable Papa?

D. PAPA: As you trade word with me, no matter

Is two minutes or twenty, your purse

Got to be much fatter.

BRISCOE: How much more so?

D. PAPA: A cool fifty.

BRISCOE: Fifty dollars?

D. PAPA: Flat.

BRISCOE: Alas! Since I born and bred

I never see that size of money yet.

You can't give me an ease-up, Diable Papa?

D. PAPA: Me fee is my fee, pardner. Don't fret

With me. Easing-up is dead against

My policy. Who next outside?

BRISCOE: Papa, you can't send me away empty,

I in the grip of adversity,

Help me, I beg you, help me, do,

I will make good recompense to you.

D. PAPA: I see you on the verge of desperation.

Unload your trouble and, promising nothing,

I will consider some concession.

BRISCOE: You won't regret it. Whenever you need

A friend, call on Briscoe.

D. PAPA: Well, proceed.

BRISCOE: The truth is: I loving terrible bad –

D. PAPA: Who?

BRISCOE: Who else but Petite Belle Lily,

                The little sister of Alice Sugar,

                You know her?

D. PAPA: Is a tragedy.

BRISCOE: Yes. For she always play hard to get.

                But in spite of her flirtatiousness,

                I feel she have a likeness for me,

                So one day I put the question flat

                And this is the way she answer: 'Boy,

                You ain't no hero. When you destroy

                A champion stick-man, then you'll prove

                Man enough to get my love.'

                But, Papa, sad to relate, I promise

                The old lady dying to take care of Inez

                And give up stick, and from then to this

                I ain't touch a poui, so I kinda rusty.

                Then last night her spirit come and say:

                'My son, if there is no other way

                To right your life, take your poui in hand

                And prove to the world that you're a man.'

                So now I determine to enter the ring

                And me and me alone must reign as king.

D. PAPA: Briscoe, Briscoe, you stupid, yes.

                Take my advice, drop this foolishness.

                Courage is good but wisdom better

                And the naked fact of the matter

                Is, you lacking experience. I bet

                You never clash with a tiger yet.

                Go home, take a bath, cool down the heat –

                I have some cooling bush here – and forget

                Lily –

BRISCOE: Papa, you can never know

                What I suffer loving that woman so,

Day turn to night and night turn day,
And all my life just wasting away.

D. PAPA: All right, all right, you don't have need
To carry on so. I take your word.
You love Lily bad. The question now is
What you going do?

BRISCOE: I banking on you
To make me a champion stick-player.

D. PAPA: Maybe, maybe. I have to consider
All angles. Tell me, for instance, who
Is the warrior you fighting?

BRISCOE: Well, a fellow name Roocoo.

D. PAPA: Who Roocoo is that?

BRISCOE: He newly come here
From the city. I have to begin somewhere.

D. PAPA: That sound feasible. Next thing, how soon
You want this stick mount?

BRISCOE: Now self. I fighting tomorrow noon.

D. PAPA: Tomorrow you say?

BRISCOE: As the sun top the sky.

D. PAPA: And is now you come?
You think mounting a weapon is easy-cai,
But is highly complicated and critical.
You have the French-creole, the old-time Spanish,
And the African ritual.

BRISCOE: Papa, believe, I ain't too fussy,
Just give me a short-cut ceremony.

D. PAPA: Then again, something else. I must mention it:
Maljo! Supposing you have a blight
And you loose a chopper on your enemy,
Is you self the blow will cripple oui!

BRISCOE: What that! Jeezu-web! Look trouble!
This obeah business have terrible
Complication. You ain't 'fraid it, Papa?

D. PAPA: Fear is a deceitful counsellor.

              But come back to you. Your predicament

              Is serious. You need thorough treatment

              And that is the sum of the argument.

              How much more money you tote?

BRISCOE: I done give you my last copper, under oath.

D. PAPA: Don't believe it, Briscoe, that you could teach

              Your grandfather to suck egg. I know each

              And every trick in the bag. If you

              Interested in your future, better or worse,

              Empty all the pockets you have in your clothes.

BRISCOE [*searching his clothes and discovering more money*]:

              Ay, ay, I find a vagrant two-dollar note

              I never know was there. And see here

              Is the five-spot I lost three days aback.

              Lady luck smile on me. I better search the tuck

              Of my pants – Lord! A couple there too!

              Here, Diable Papa, take it, is all for you.

[*He hands* D. PAPA *the rest of the money which he had hidden about his person.* D. PAPA *puts the money in his box.*]

D. PAPA: Now, before I commence to charm your poui,

              I have to rid you of all jumbie.

              Where is my medium? Minee! Come gal!

[MINEE WOOPSA *enters immediately she is called: A thin, long-faced Negro girl in her middle teens, she is completely devoted to* D. PAPA *who is the only relation she has and upon whom she looks as a foster father. She half-believes, half-acts the part of medium in his enterprise, speaks with a clipped, mechanical tone of voice, and is dressed now in a white gown which reaches to her ankles, a black head-tie and white canvas shoes.*]

MINEE: Yes?

D. PAPA: Prepare for the Untying Ritual.

[MINEE *nods and exits to make ready.* BRISCOE *follows her to the doorway and turns to* D. PAPA.]

BRISCOE: Is Minee Woopsa working here?

D. PAPA: Yes … and don't let your eyes pass there.

BRISCOE: She want to resemble Soucouyant Jane
           Who, of a sudden, abandon life
           One day after you and she was in strife.
           So the people say.

D. PAPA: You come here to gossip?

BRISCOE: Is the first time that story cross my lip.

D. PAPA: Keep it so and improve your chance of living.
           A wise man heed a timely warning.

BRISCOE: That's right, for you know how you come,
           But who to know how and when you going?

D. PAPA: Remove your shirt and shoes.

BRISCOE: You think it will work, Diable Papa,
           You could make me a champion warrior?

D. PAPA: Obviously you have never heard
           About my reputation. Well, in a word,
           When it come to war, whether stick, knife or gun,
           Is magic assist every single one
           Of the world conquerors. The mighty Caesar
           Employ it and also Alexander
           Who men call great, lion of the East,
           Genghis Khan and Nero, the beast,
           Hannibal – I don't mean the calypsonian –
           And that famous general, Napoleon,
           All seek refuge in the impregnable art
           Which I practise, so you see I had a part
           In their victories since my blood draw
           From the line of witch-doctors who follow war.
           So banish your fear, have faith, mister,
           After God and the devil, is Diable Papa.

BRISCOE: Jeeze-and-age! Papa, I must agree
           You open up my ideas of history.
           I always wonder how come you rate
           So high, but I see that you passing great.
           In fact

[*Lowering his voice.*]

You and the Mister Upstairs is one,

But I think you have the slight edge on him.

D. PAPA: Wisdom respect nobody. Who

Would expect her to look with favour on you?

But come, time is money. Minee, you ready?

MINEE: All ready.

[MINEE *sprinkles salt in a circle on the floor. She places* BRISCOE *within the circle and gives him a lighted candle.* D. PAPA *puts a hand on* BRISCOE's *head and chants.*]

D. PAPA: Wherever thou art, O turbulent,

Powerful and rebellious agent,

O Bandara, symbol of evil and destroyer

Of all spells and charms, I thee conjure.

Rid Briscoe of all evil shades,

Ties and stumbling-blocks placed in his way,

Break the bolts of the gates of Limbo,

Power of Dark, O Entities of Hades,

I implore aid, cure and protection for Briscoe.

[*To* BRISCOE]

Now turn seven times round the candle,

And mind you turn right to left as I sprinkle

You spasmodically with Untying Powder.

BRISCOE: What going happen if I turn left to right?

D. PAPA: You get riddled with blight.

BRISCOE: You better show me my left hand, yes,

I ain't taking no chance with this business.

[MINEE *guides him. He staggers against the wall.*]

Look, Diable Papa, I begin to feel giddy.

D. PAPA: The Untying Ritual not complete. Kneel

Facing east. Minee, the Balm of Healing.

[MINEE *hands* D. PAPA *a bottle. He pours some of the contents in his palm and anoints* BRISCOE's *head, face, neck and arms, while chanting.*]

Even as these cleansing waters purify

Your body, I do urge and compel

Astaroth … who stands for the darkest evil,

Prince of Lucifer, High Priest of Hell,

Release the last remnant of bewitchness from

This accursed and forsaken man.

Protect him against demagnetizing elements,

Poisonous thoughts and the spells of agents
in wickedness.

[MINEE *has been swaying and moaning as in a trance and now begins to
speak in unknown tongues.*]

MINEE: O dumba, kno a bumba, a hobo lo ba,

We bo a, Ashooborac bo yea,

Ashooborac bo yea, tawoo tawoo, tawa,

Tawoo tawa, Damballa.

[*Then chanting*]

Ogun Batalla yea, Ogun Batalla yo yo,

Ogun Batalla yea, Ogun Batalla sho sho,

Ray kay doana, ray kay sassa,

Ray kay doana, ray kay wawara

Ray kay Damballa.

[*During the chanting,* D. PAPA *pounds his fists into* BRISCOE's *back to
drive out the evil spirits.*]

BRISCOE: O Lord! My back breaking in two.

D. PAPA: Powers of Light and Power of Darkness,

Combination of Beings Evil and Divine,

I call for destruction for the last time

Of the knot tied against Briscoe. O befriend

Him, Alpha and Omega, Alpha and Omega,

Alpha and Omega, the beginning and the end.

BRISCOE: Whoy-oy-oy! I glad that done.

D. PAPA: Go behind the screen and strip yourself,

Prepare your body for the final wetting.

BRISCOE: More to come still? Is a full course I getting!

D. PAPA: It is a necessary aftermath

> To wash the blight away in a bath
> Of triple power.

[*He stops and listens intently, then addresses* MINEE.]

> I hear like a cagey
> Footstep outside. See who it be.
> If a client, let him take a breeze
> Till I ready for him.

[MINEE *goes to the door.*]

BRISCOE: Your ears like a razor,
Diable Papa, I didn't hear nothing.

D. PAPA: It don't concern you. Take these bottles
And use according to the labels.
Inside there!

[*He hands* BRISCOE *three bottles of coloured liquid, and the latter retires into the other room.* D. PAPA *turns to* MINEE.]

> Who it is?

MINEE [*whispering*]: Old Peloo.

D. PAPA: What he want here?

PELOO [*shuffling in*]: I come to see you.
I send a customer name of Briscoe.

D. PAPA: He inside now. Keep your voice-box low.

PELOO: Well, to be short, I come for my cut.

D. PAPA: I ain't collect my full quota yet.

PELOO: Is your look-out. Hand up my commission.

D. PAPA: What happen you harbour a suspicion
About my honesty?

PELOO: Don't make me laugh.
Give me what's mine.

D. PAPA: You could get a half.

PELOO: You joking!

D. PAPA: Down, keep it down, I say. Minee,
Go back there and keep Briscoe company
Till we settle this business. Now, Peloo,
A generous half is enough for you.

PELOO: Like fish!

D. PAPA: Three-quarters?

PELOO: You looking for rumpus?

D. PAPA: You is nothing but a cantankerous
          Old man. Anyhow, I will re-consider,
          I like a satisfied customer.

PELOO: It small enough. Why for you want
          To take off some?

D. PAPA: Done the argument.

[*He fetches the money and brings it back to* PELOO.]

          You know anything about this new
          Fellow from town who they call Roocoo?

PELOO: Which Roocoo that?

D. PAPA: The man Brisco fighting.

PELOO: You mean Tiny Satan.

D. PAPA: What fool thing you saying?

PELOO: He fighting the champion, Tiny Satan.

[D. PAPA *pulls the notes away from* PELOO.]

D. PAPA: And you expect Briscoe to beat that man?
          You foolie the fifth, you send him here
          To put me in trouble and blight my career
          With this mamapoule stick-man! Go! Leave quick!
          Else I lace your skin with the poui-stick!

[*He takes up the poui and charges at* PELOO *who exits rapidly.* D. PAPA *replaces the money in the box with a chuckle and turns to the inner room.*]

          What the hell they doing in there so long!
          Minee, send Briscoe where he belong
          Out in the open! Quick-sharp now!

[BRISCOE *runs out joyfully throwing up his hands in the air.*]

BRISCOE: I young and strong!
          Hoorah, horray! The blight wash away!
          I never feel more light in my life,
          I feel like a new-born babe, I feel like a lord!

D. PAPA: You is a new man, I have banished your sorrow,
          Walk straight and prepare for victory tomorrow.

BRISCOE: I strong like a bull and light as a feather,
I feel like a champion stick-fighter.

[*He begins to chant and shadow-play with his poui.* D. PAPA *dodges out of his way.*]

Rain can't wet me, when I have my poui in my hand,
Rain can't wet me, I advancing on the foe like a roaring lion.
Poui! Poui!

D. PAPA: Look, nuh, pardner, this ain't no tent.
Stop gallivanting about like an elephant.
If you finish dressing, leave, and call back
For your stick this evening.

BRISCOE: What o'clock?

D. PAPA: As the sun eye shut – or shutting.
Remember is a rush job you getting.

BRISCOE: I have faith in you, Papa, I ain't fretting
Well, I going now and will see you later.

D. PAPA: Walk good. And let everyman remember
His debts and debtors.

[BRISCOE *leaves.* D. PAPA *bursts out laughing.*]

Ha-ha! Minee! See my cross today,
This idiot come to cuffufle my brain!
Minee, I say!

MINEE [*entering*]: You call me again?

D. PAPA: Who you think Briscoe fighting tomorrow?

MINEE: I don't know. Some novice?

D. PAPA: Novice? Hear sorrow.
He tell me a new-comer name Roocoo,
But I get the full story from old Peloo,
Briscoe fighting Tiny.

MINEE: Tiny Satan?

D. PAPA: He self.

MINEE: You mean Tiny, the champion?

D. PAPA: Don't aggravate me in the extreme!
If I say Tiny Satan, is Tiny I mean,
The one they call Terror, the king stick-man –

MINEE:	But why?
D. PAPA:	How the hell I know why? I is a magician?
MINEE:	And you charm Tiny stick regular,
	Why you take Briscoe as a customer?
D. PAPA:	My policy is to take all clients
	Provided they come with good suppliance,
	And Briscoe was loaded.
MINEE:	You think he can win?
D. PAPA:	Who, Briscoe? When a rooster begin
	To grow teeth. The man is a blowhard,
	All the stick he know is in his backyard,
	He out to win Petite Belle from the Terror,
	But what he will get is blue murder tomorrow.
MINEE:	Call off the fight then.
D. PAPA:	That is damnfool talk.
MINEE:	Tell Briscoe the charm ain't have time to work,
	Cook-up something for Tiny. Tell him you learn
	The spirits displease with the way events turn,
	That the fight too advantageous. I beg you stop
	The fight –
D. PAPA:	And let everything drop!
	You coonoomoonoo! When you ever hear
	Diable Papa give way to womanish fear?
	Rather come let us devise a plan
	How to exploit the situation
	Cause we in it already. I say, let all
	Men beware! I out to make a big haul.
MINEE:	Take my advice. Last night I dream
	Terrible things. A great trembling seem
	To rack the bosom of earth, spirits
	Crack open the doors of their clay pits
	To roam the land like a disease
	Taking revenge on their enemies.
	Nothing we do could turn the tide

	Of destruction, no place to run and hide.
	I wake in a fever. Outside the window
	A lizard was croaking a mournful solo,
	Is a clear warning. The old people say:
	One day, one day, congotay.
D. PAPA:	Perhaps the time come for me to retire,
	Best go when you reach the height of your power,
	For when the fall come is a different story,
	But I mean to go out in a blaze of glory
	And I ain't done yet. We'll pass the word
	I supporting the challenger and pick up a load.
MINEE:	You mean double-cross Briscoe?
D. PAPA:	Is part of the game.
MINEE:	If you let him face Tiny he sure get maim.
D. PAPA:	That is his look-out.
MINEE:	But is treachery!
D. PAPA:	Mistress, you growing out of your shoes,
	To stand up to my face and give me abuse!
	This is my payment for taking you in,
	A castaway of dubious origin.
	Who ask your approval? The business in hand
	Could make us a fortune carefully planned.
MINEE:	But what about Briscoe?
D. PAPA:	He is small matter,
	A speck on the glass you brush off to see better.
	Come, no more argument, time to make ready,
	Take a message to my sidemen, Peloo and Coolie,
	Right away, tell them put out the rumour
	Briscoe will win, being my customer,
	But they must back Tiny on the sly
	With the money I send. We going sky-high,
	This is the job we been waiting for,
	After this we don't have to work any more,
	As long as they live, people will remember
	The reign of the obeahman, Diable Papa.

[*He bursts into song, waving the poui-stick in the air.* MINEE *sings a counter-melody to each verse.*]

[*singing*]: Ole, the time is here

For the greatest triumph of my career,

I will prove my power this very hour,

My fortune waiting to burst and flower,

Ole, the time is here

For the greatest triumph of my career.

MINEE [*singing*]: One day, one day, congotay.

Trouble come when you least expect,

Turn your back and it's on your neck,

Round the corner it lie in wait,

Don't take that turn or you meet your fate.

D. PAPA [*singing*]: Ole, the time is come

To blow the trumpet and beat the drum,

I will charm the foe, gather in his dough,

Hop a sailing ship and away I'll go,

Ole, the time is come

To blow the trumpet and beat the drum.

MINEE [*singing*]: One day, one day, congotay.

Some go with a glorious shout

And some a whisper don't pass their mouth,

Everybody have their own time,

One day for you and one day is mine.

D. PAPA [*singing*]: Ole, the time arrive

To suck the honey from out the hive,

I will make a haul, you will hear men bawl,

And my name will reign as the Rogue of All.

Ole, the time arrive

To suck the honey from out the hive.

MINEE [*singing*]: One day, one day, congotay.

Make sure better than cock-sure, yes,

So you better be sure of your success.

Heed the warning my dreams reveal,

If you won't hear you bound to feel.

D. PAPA *and* MINEE [*singing*]: Ole, the time is here

For the greatest triumph of my career,

One day, one day, congotay.

Ole, the time is come

To blow the trumpet and beat the drum,

One day, one day, congotay.

Ole, the time arrive

To suck the honey from out the hive.

One day, one day, congotay.

Act Two
Scene 1

PORTAGEE JOE's *store as in Act One, Scene 1. The rostrum and crown have been pushed to one side.*

AT CURTAIN

Late afternoon of the same day. The saloon is deserted but for SWIFTY, *the bartender, dozing behind the bar. Huddled in a corner on the covered boardwalk are* COOLIE *and* PELOO, *waiting nervously.*

PELOO: What time you make it?

COOLIE: Setting up for night.

        Soon the men will come down to discuss the fight.

        Minee better reach quick.

PELOO: What Diable Papa mean

        By the message he send?

COOLIE: Some ingenious scheme

        Back of his mind.

PELOO: I hope this time we haul

        In a pile, because the percentage is small.

        If I can't buy candle for my pain and cramp,

        Why involve myself with such a born scamp?

COOLIE: Relax! You getting too jittery

        Nowadays. Take a pill and calm your body.

PELOO: Sometimes I think if I was younger

        I would make a bolt with half the plunder

        We collect for Diable Papa.

COOLIE: Crazy talk!

        He would after you like a chicken-hawk

        Trailing a young fowl and, believe me, brother,

        When he catch you, they wouldn't find a feather.

PELOO: Diable Papa growing more and more bold,

        My one regret is I getting so old

        I won't be around to enjoy his fate

        When the village set out to retaliate.

COOLIE: You sour today. You ain't feeling well?

PELOO: Is my rheumatism giving me hell.

[MINEE *enters quickly and crosses to the two men. She wears a cloth bonnet on her head, plain cotton dress, and carries a large shopping basket with a lid.*]

PELOO: Now, Minee, what is the latest act
Your master want us perform? Whose pocket
To ransack, what new villainy
Will stuff his greed and vanity?

COOLIE: Don't take him on. He ain't feeling good.
What is the ballad?

MINEE: I bring word
That Briscoe fighting with a mount stick
And the stars promise he will put out the wick
Of the champion.

PELOO: The village would never buy it!

MINEE: Say, moreover,
That Tiny Satan fall from favour
With the obeahman.

COOLIE: Well, we could try it!
Logically, the stranger the tale
You tell, the faster to make a sale.
Leave it to me. I will get the men
To back Briscoe against the champion,
When they believe they on to a secret
All their money will flow in our pocket
You with me, Peloo?

PELOO: Here we sit like three
Crows waiting to pounce on a corpse.
Minee, I think you better take off.

COOLIE: But not too far; make a half-tack
And when the men reach, you could pass back
Casual-like, to bear out the story.

PELOO: They sooner believe you than Coolie or me.

MINEE: I will leave you now, hoping you succeed.

           I have to go and collect some weed

           And will come back later. To speak true,

           I don't like the business, but what to do?

           Who could stop when Diable Papa set his heart

           On any endeavour?

PELOO: Before you depart,

           Where the money to spark the betting?

[*She opens the basket and extracts two small clothbags of money which she hands to the men.*]

MINEE: Take this for a start. If you want more

           Go up to the hut, but always make sure

           The stake is a good one. Now I gone.

[MINEE *leaves.* COOLIE *and* PELOO *stroll inside the shop and sit at a table in a conspicuous spot.*]

COOLIE: Swifty! Bring a bottle!

[*To* PELOO *softly*]

           The plan is all right,

           You know how the village like a stick-fight,

           Once they hear that the challenger

           Carrying a charm, look for big wager.

[SWIFTY *brings a bottle and glasses. The two men pour drinks.*]

PELOO: If only we could bamboozle Joe

           As well to go all out on Briscoe.

COOLIE: Work on Inez. The Portagee can

           Never say no to a pretty woman.

[JOE *enters from the back of the store. He is cooling himself with an enormous straw fan.*]

JOE: Hallo, senors, you are the only two

           Sensible men. What else to do

           On so warm an evening, eh?

COOLIE: Hey, Joe take a pew.

           Is your grandpapa pushing the heat?

PELOO: Cool off with a young one.

[*He pours a drink for* JOE.]

	Come, swallow it neat.
JOE:	You know I don't touch the liquor at all.

Come, swallow it neat.

JOE: You know I don't touch the liquor at all.
I so much feel the heat I would drink the whole stall
One time – and my business go pouff!
Thank you all the same …

COOLIE: You drink well enough.

JOE: Not on business. Swifty show you the new rum
From Barbados? The first shipment just come,
So delicious, it make you forget your sorrow,
I keep for special customers of El Toro.

COOLIE: The liquor is good but we sure pay for it.
You don't forget business for even a minute?

JOE: When a man poor, what else you can do?

PELOO: You like to cry poor, but that's only flash,
Everybody know your safe pack-up with cash.
What you going do with all that money?

COOLIE: You can't take it where you going, Portagee,
Why not relax and enjoy a good spree?

JOE: Seven years last December since I come
To this island. I work hard and put by a sum
Regular to return home some day –

COOLIE: You love creole too much, Joe, to go away.

[INEZ *enters from the back-store with a few lighted lanterns which she proceeds to hang up over the door-ways.*]

INEZ: How you do, Coolie, and old Peloo?

PELOO: Not sharp as you.

COOLIE: I waiting for your answer,
My offer still stand anything you ready.

INEZ: You will have to ask my one and only
And he is a jealous Portagee.

[*She hugs* JOE *and caresses his hair.*]

PELOO: Joe, watch yourself. She putting the wool
Over your eyes.

JOE: Inez is very faithful.

[*From offstage comes a chorus of men singing. They are working up their spirits towards an all-night revel in preparation for the stick-fighting contest on the morrow. JOE knows that these drinking bouts invariably lead to brawling. He will close up shop earlier than usual to avoid a skirmish on his premises.*]

CHORUS OF MEN [*singing off*]:

> One-two-three, for the young girls so deceiving,
>
> Four-five-six, they will always leave you grieving,
>
> Run away, run away, go now,
>
> If you stay they will leave you anyhow.
>
> Four-five-six, for the young girls so exciting,
>
> Seven-eight-nine, that a kiss is dynamiting,
>
> Run away, run away, go now,
>
> If you stay they will leave you anyhow.
>
> Seven-eight-nine, for the young girls full of fire,
>
> Ten-eleven-twelve, they will laugh when you retire,
>
> Run away, run away, go now,
>
> If you stay they will leave you anyhow.

[*The following dialogue onstage overlaps with the singing off until the men enter.*]

JOE: The men coming down for their evening carouse,

Hear them singing. Inez, we will shut up house

Early before trouble start tonight.

They get too excited over a fight.

INEZ: As you say, Joe.

COOLIE: Inez, how come you look

So cool, and Briscoe name write in the Book

Of the Dead already. Like you don't care

What happen to your brother?

INEZ: You had better prepare

For a big surprise!

PELOO: Ha! That's a good crack!

JOE: Imagine, Inez want me to back

Briscoe against Tiny, swearing she know

Positive the Terror will bow tomorrow.

All day she behind me to risk my money.

INEZ: Is no risk! If you frighten lend it to me,
I will pay back with interest.

COOLIE: I hear a zeppo
About Briscoe myself and ready to go
All out on him, once I get confirmation.

JOE: Well, you all crazy is my conclusion.

[*Now the men are in sight chipping down the road singing.* HANNIBAL *leads the chorus on his cuatro. Others are* CRACKERJACK, POGO, CUTAWAY *and* DAGGER.]

CHORUS OF MEN [*singing*]:
One-two-three, for the young girls so deceiving,
Four-five-six, but we cannot help believing,
They will never fool us now,
So we stay and love them anyhow.

[*The men gather round a table.*]

CRACKERJACK: Drinks for the crowd! Portagee, pass the ball!

JOE: Right away … Swiftly!

SWIFTY: Coming right down the hall!

[*He appears serving two bottles of rum, glasses and a mug of water.* COOLIE *stands on a chair waving two notes in his hand.*]

COOLIE: Listen here, fellows! I talking serious.
The fight tomorrow bound to be a ferocious
Battle. I offering bet to your throat.

CRACKERJACK: Coolie, stop the racket and pocket your note.
Drink up, boys, we come here for pleasure.

COOLIE: Wait, Crackers! Ten dollars say Tiny will measure
Briscoe coffin tomorrow, for twenty he stop
Him in the first clash, and if you 'fraid to drop
A couple-few dollars, remember I giving
Two-to-one odds. Come, boys, make your living.

CRACKERJACK: Me bet on Briscoe! You drunk or mad!
He's the unluckiest fellow in Trinidad
Today.

PELOO: All the same you mustn't forget
This stick-game have a lot of upset.
I tired see champion fighters get maul.

COOLIE: So nobody in the crowd like Briscoe at all!

INEZ: I will bet on him!

JOE: Inez, get back in the store.

[*She retires reluctantly.*]

COOLIE: The lady have sense or perhaps she know more

            Than me or you. All right, fellows, give odds

            And I take Briscoe in front your tin gods.

CRACKERJACK: Coolie, you drunk, man. Come off the chair!

COOLIE: What a set of cowards I drinking with here!

            Nobody have guts to bet on the bout!

[*This taunt arouses the men who bring out their money and offer to bet* COOLIE.]

CRACKERJACK: Look, fifty on Tiny. Come, match your mouth!

DAGGER: I'll take anything!

POGO: Thirty-five, level bet.

CUTAWAY: On Tiny Satan the sky is the limit!

COOLIE [*laughs and sits down*]: You all is my friend. Hide your coppers
            away,

            Otherwise I would make you paupers today.

            But take warning – Briscoe chance plenty good,

            You can never be sure when wood meet wood,

            The secret will out when the time come to play,

            The might will fall … 'fire-arm-de-fey!'

SEVERAL [*booing*]: You talk through your hat …

            I never hear that …

            Briscoe beat Tiny …

            You will lose your money …

PELOO: Is so I get beat, being too cock-sure,

            I mistime a chopper and land on the floor,

            As I was off-balance, the blow descend

            On my coconut, and that was the end.

            People say Wajanks was better than me,

            But I tell you he win a fluke victory.

[JOE *strolls over to confront* COOLIE.]

JOE: Coolie, you make me little bit curious
              Seeing you repeat what Inez tell us.
              Now Briscoe is her family, so I understand
              She would want him to beat the champion,
              But you have more sense, you know it can't happen,
              Yet you say he will win. What is your reason?

COOLIE: Forget it, Portagee, I make mischief.

JOE: Is no joke. Inez tell me she know positive.

COOLIE: Why not ask her, then?

JOE: She wouldn't say nothing.

COOLIE: I don't know either.

JOE: You hiding something.

SEVERAL: Give us the secret …
              Come on, man, spill it …
              We is all friend together
              Through dry and wet weather …

CRACKERJACK: Coolie, if you know something on the fight,
              Is your duty to tell the boys, otherwise right
              Now we better part company.

  [*The men agree noisily.*]

COOLIE: All right, all right, stop elbowing me.
              This is the leggo. I get a wire –
              But don't ask me from who – that Briscoe hire
              Diable Papa to help him lick the champion.

JOE: Bunkum! That is all superstition!

  [*He turns away but remains within earshot.*]

HANNIBAL: It really sound queer, seeing that Diable Papa
              Keep Tiny as a regular customer.
              How come he working against him now?

PELOO: You didn't hear he and Tiny had row
              After the last fight? They change hard word.

POGO: Oh, yes?

JOE: Senors, please, all that is absurd!
              You can't believe in such stupidness.

POGO: Oh, no? Every man-jack in the crowd
          Have experience with obeah that he ain't proud
          Of. Is a power in the land so don't fool your fat,
          If Diable Papa with Briscoe, I backing him flat.

[*Spirited agreement from the men.*]

CRACKERJACK: Portagee Joe, like you don't agree
          With the feelings of the majority,
          Is a simple way to show your disfavour,
          Put money on the champion, we like the contender.

PELOO: Crackers, Joe ain't a better man
          But if you give odds, I will take you on.

POGO: We want Joe to depend his opinion.

HANNIBAL: Yes, Joe, here is a sporting chance
          To prove your stand against ignorance.

COOLIE: Don't bother with Joe, I know where we could
          Get heavy odds backing Briscoe wood.

CUTAWAY: Let Joe call the hand, since he want to buck
          The general belief, let him try his luck.

JOE: Senors, today you put me in a vise.
          Very well, listen to what Joe decide.
          You all is my friend, you buy from the store,
          I try to make you happy in El Toro,
          But on this one thing we don't see together:
          Obeah is nonsense!

[*A roar of disagreement from the men.*]

          Diable Papa a deceiver!
          A moment, please, gentlemen, don't upset
          Yourself, I will prove it opening a bet
          Right here and now, every penny on Tiny.
          All who like Briscoe, come, bring your money.

[*A moment of hesitation as the men wait on each other to move forward first.*]

          What, nobody betting? Where the talkers gone?

DAGGER: Joe, we have only Coolie's word to go on,
          We need more than that to place a bet.

JOE: Well, who frighten now? Gentlemen, when you settle

Your doubts, come and knock on my door.

[*He strolls away inside the shop.*]

CRACKERJACK: You all make me shame, not a man in the crowd.

POGO: What about you? You was bragging more loud

Than anybody.

CUTAWAY: We have to make certain

Diable Papa really working for Briscoe.

HANNIBAL: Look! Minee Woopsa coming in person,

Let's tackle her, men, she bound to know!

[*The men rise and stroll off nonchalantly as if the whole manoeuvre were prearranged. They take up lounging positions on either side of the street. HANNIBAL plucks at his cuatro. MINEE enters on her way home, carrying the basket which contains herbs she has been out gathering for the obeahman. The men slowly converge upon her, forming a cordon that effectively blocks her exit. Fearing an assault, MINEE runs into the shop and the men surround her closely.*]

CRACKERJACK: Minee, we don't intend you no harm,

But the boys have a question. We know Papa charming

One of the fighters for battle tomorrow.

Tell us who it is? Tiny Satan or Briscoe?

MINEE: I don't rightly know, but early this morning,

Briscoe visit the obeahman without warning.

POGO: Visit him! We want to know truly

If Diable Papa assure him victory.

MINEE: I can't swear to that. Now let me go, please,

I have to reach back home with these.

CRACKERJACK: What you have in the basket?

[*He lifts the lid and peers inside.*]

MINEE: Bush …

POGO: What kind?

MINEE: Go on peeping and see if you don't get blind.

This bush collect for Diable Papa's medicine.

COOLIE [*making reassuring signs to* MINEE]: What he use to make

stick-man invincible?

	You have in the basket?
MINEE:	I don't know what you mean.
POGO:	Don't believe her, men, she famous for lying. [*With bravado, he drags a piece of bush from the basket.*] What this name?
MINEE:	Gully-root.
POGO:	And this?
MINEE:	Cacaput.
DAGGER:	What it good for?
MINEE:	A bad lock-jaw.
CRACKERJACK:	Name this!
MINEE:	Coreillie.
CUTAWAY:	And this?
MINEE:	Jijiree.
HANNIBAL:	Tell us what it cure?
MINEE:	Epilepsy.

[*They move into the song. The men take turns at putting questions and* MINEE *answers.*]

THE MEN [*singing*]: See here …

MINEE [*singing*]: Bois Canoe …

THE MEN [*singing*]: This piece …

MINEE [*singing*]: Callaloo …

I show you whatever I can.

THE MEN [*singing*]: But you still ain't call
The greatest of all.

MINEE [*spoken*]: What bush is that?

THE MEN [*singing*]: Is *Man Better Man*!

MINEE [*singing*]: I show you chenette,
I give you serette.

THE MEN [*singing*]: The bush we want,
You don't name yet.

MINEE [*singing*]: This ease your pain,
This clear out your brain.

THE MEN [*singing*]: Show us what make
A stick-man reign.

MINEE [*singing*]: Zebafam used right,

        Give you second-sight,

        Gru-gru boeuf and dry tan-tan.

THE MEN [*singing*]: But you still ain't name

        The bush of fame.

MINEE [*spoken*]: What bush is that?

THE MEN [*singing*]: Is *Man Better Man*!

MINEE [*singing*]: Chataigne bud,

        Clean out the blood.

THE MEN [*singing*]: Is no damn good

        For a fighting wood.

MINEE [*singing*]: Topee-tambeau

        Make your hair grow.

THE MEN [*singing*]: But it can't slow down

        A crippling blow.

MINEE [*singing*]: Vettivier make you gay

        And a sprig of pomseetay

        Keep you looking spick-and-span.

THE MEN [*singing*]: Only show us the weed

        That a stick-man need.

MINEE [*spoken*]: What bush is that?

THE MEN [*singing*]: Is *Man Better Man*!

JOE [*entering*]: Closing time, senors, please to leave quiet,

        Don't do anything to start up a riot

        Before the contest tomorrow. Minee here?

        What you want, child?

CRACKERJACK: She was teaching us obeah!

    [*Laughter from the men.*]

        Minee, you can't leave till you settle

        The question. Give us a tip on the battle.

MINEE: This is my advice. Take it or leave:

        The stick-man who triumph tomorrow evening

        Is …

[COOLIE *encourages her to say* 'BRISCOE' *but she cannot bring herself to it.*]

Sure to cause a big sensation

For Diable Papa backing him. Now I gone.

[*She leaves quickly as the men argue her enigmatic statement among themselves.*]

JOE: Gentlemen, please! I am closing the shop

Right now. Swifty, start to lock up.

CRACKERJACK: Portagee Joe, the boys all agree

That Briscoe is the man for we,

So bring your cash, we ready to bet.

INEZ [*coming forward*]: Joe, don't bet on Tiny. You will only regret.

JOE: Don't interfere. Bring pencil and paper.

My friends, I try if maybe I can

Expose Diable Papa as a bogus-man,

And I hope tomorrow make everybody wiser.

POGO: Cut out the blag, Mr Philosophizer.

JOE: Come up to the counter, one by one.

[*The men line up and put their money on the counter. JOE checks the respective amounts and INEZ makes a note of the sum and hands each man a receipt. Simultaneously with this action, COOLIE and PELOO converse in their corner of the room.*]

PELOO: You outsmart yourself! Joe will win the money!

COOLIE: Cool down. I form a new strategy.

JOE: Crackerjack, forty. Pogo, thirty-four.

INEZ: Don't do it, Joe.

JOE: Mistress, you keep the score.

A hundred from Dagger.

PELOO: It better be good. Well, what it is?

COOLIE: I making a bold proposal to Inez.

JOE: Cutaway?

CUTAWAY: You giving odds?

JOE: Nothing doing.

CUTAWAY: I'm light today,

Only fifty-and-six.

PELOO: You think she will bite?

COOLIE: Listen to her panic!

INEZ: Joe, listen to me!

JOE: Cutaway, fifty-six. You will make me angry!

COOLIE: Tonight self, when the place get quiet,

            I will broach Inez to reverse the bet.

JOE: How much, Hannibal?

HANNIBAL: Funds kinda low,

            But I'll take twelve dollars on the cuatro.

JOE: Hannibal, twelve. Now for Coolie.

INEZ: Joe, darling!

COOLIE: I want only odds.

JOE: No. Very sorry.

            Last man is Peloo.

PELOO: I taking an out

            Because my mind still running in doubt.

            I hope tomorrow wouldn't be too late

            To try my luck?

JOE: El Toro open at eight,

            And now, senors, time to say goodnight,

            And good luck, everybody, on the fight.

THE MEN: Goodnight, Joe …

            Tomorrow we'll know

            Who luck smile on

            And who get the frown …

[*They leave together singing the reprise.*]

            One-two-three, for the young girls so deceiving,

            Four-five-six, they will always leave you grieving,

            Run away, run away, go now,

            If you stay they will leave you anyhow.

JOE: Swifty, leave if you finish locking.

SWIFTY: Yes, Mr Joe. Goodnight!

[JOE *takes the money to the back of the store to deposit it in his strong-box.* SWIFTY *leaves.* INEZ *removes her apron.* COOLIE *sneaks back inside the shop and whispers to* INEZ.]

COOLIE: Inez, if you sure your brother going win

	Tomorrow, Joe make a mistake betting
	Against him and will lose every penny.
INEZ:	Is true. He is a stubborn Portagee.
	You have a plan how we could master
	The situation and avoid disaster?
COOLIE:	It ain't fully ripen in my mind.
	I have an idea if we could find
	Somebody to go all out on Tiny –
INEZ:	We could alter the bet; but Joe keeps his money
	In the safe … I would have … in the next village
	You think you could draw people to engage
	In a brave gamble?
COOLIE:	I willing to try
	If you cut me in. But time flying
	Fast.
INEZ:	I will have to get the key
	To the safe tonight and bring you the money.
COOLIE:	A rich fortune waiting for you and me,
	Girl. The Four Roads people don't know
	'Bout the charm and all that.
INEZ:	But supposing that Joe
	Find the money all gone?
COOLIE:	We only borrowing
	It for a night. He will thank you tomorrow.
INEZ:	All right. I will try and get the key.
COOLIE:	Remember, half the profit you rake
	In is mine, for the trouble I take.
INEZ:	Whatever you say. Go now and conceal
	Yourself outside till I bring the money.
	I will protect Joe and his property.

[COOLIE *leaves.* INEZ, *alone, fetches her handbag and shawl and spruces up herself.* JOE *returns.* INEZ *pretends to be leaving the store.*]

JOE:	You not going already?
INEZ:	Yes, Joe.

JOE: It is yet early,
          You could stay and keep me company.

INEZ: If you want.

JOE: I sorry to bet against your brother,
          But the men give me no option. Now another
          Thought begin to harass my mind. Supposing
          Briscoe meet his fate in the ring?

INEZ: Don't talk about it. I want an inkling
          Of something.

JOE: Yes?

[*He comes close and caresses her hair.*]

INEZ: Where I stand with you.

JOE: You vex?

INEZ: Oh, no!

[*He bends down to kiss her. She resists.*]

          But I like to provide
          For the future and I can't quite decide
          If you coming or going.

JOE: Only you I love.

INEZ: So you say everytime, but without proof.
          Perhaps you take me for all the others,
          But no, Mister Man, I have too many offers.

JOE: You mean Coolie, that rascal. I hear him today.
          What he want?

INEZ: Same as you, and he willing to pay
          For it too.

JOE: But you tell him Joe have first choice.
          That's my girl. Come, a little caress …

INEZ: No, Joe. [*But her actions belie her words.*]

JOE: Why for this contrariness?

INEZ: You can't expect it to be otherwise
          When lately you ain't treating me nice.

JOE: I give you run of all my affairs,
          What more you want?

INEZ:	You don't trust me
	To go to the safe or handle the key.
JOE:	Is not important.

[*He tries again to kiss her.*]

INEZ:	It is to me,
	To prove your love you must give me the key.
JOE:	All right, I promise to give you tomorrow.
INEZ:	Tonight.
JOE:	Then later.
INEZ:	Now, give me now.
JOE:	Oh, such a tormentor
	You are, Inez. Come, a little peck.
INEZ:	First show me the key.
JOE:	See it here round my neck!

[*With a sudden tug, INEZ breaks the string holding the key and very deliberately, she slips it into her bosom. JOE watches with fascination. INEZ stands before him in an attitude of daring and invitation. JOE accepts the challenge. He reaches forward slowly, ostensibly to retrieve the key, but is soon enveloped in mounds of flesh.*]

Scene 2

The stick-playing arena is a bamboo shelter with a thatched roof (commonly called a 'tent') situated in an open lot of land in the village. Plaited palm fronds surround the lower half of the walls of the enclosure whose upper portion is open so that passers-by may stand outside and view the contest. Within the shelter, benches are placed around the sides for the patrons, while the central area, referred to as the 'ring', is left free for the combatants. Singers and drummers occupy one end of the shelter. A raised dais along another side accommodates the more privileged spectators. Two stools opposite each other are for the fighters.

AT CURTAIN

A bugle sounds twice to announce the holding of the contest. This is followed by male voices offstage chanting a stick-fighting chorus. Presently a group of four men dance on, attired in gay stick-fighter's costume: multi-coloured satin shirts and breeches, adorned with kerchiefs and spangles, stockings and alpargatas. They carry poui-sticks. The men are CRACKERJACK, POGO, CUTAWAY and DAGGER, with HANNIBAL, the calypsonian, in attendance. They have all come to witness the fight, rigged out in their own colours, but being stick-men they pass the time sparring with each other.

This introductory scene may be played before a traverse curtain to facilitate a change of setting from the store to the 'tent'.

CUTAWAY: I sound my challenge. Who feel he is king,

               Let him throw a token into the ring.

CRACKERJACK: You tired living?

CUTAWAY: Match that!

[*He pulls a ring off his finger and tosses it on the ground.*]

POGO: Count me in.

[*He places a jewel next to the ring.*]

CRACKERJACK: All right, you ask for it, Mister Mouth,

               We will see who is hero to take them out.

DAGGER: Make it four-square. Now, fellows, beware!

[*Four pieces of jewellery are on the ground. The contestants form a ring around the stakes and begin the play. Each one tries to snatch up a bauble while giving and/or parrying blows with his stick. HANNIBAL, on the cuatro, leads the chorus. The play continues for a few rounds and is interrupted by the entrance of LILY, ALICE, SWIFTY, COOLIE, PELOO and other villagers.*]

[*At this time the traverse curtain rises to reveal the whole stick-playing arena.*]

LILY: What going on here?

CRACKERJACK: Ah, Petite Belle Lily!

               In all creation the sweetest filly!

DAGGER: Not to mention her sister, rosy Alice Sugar!

SEVERAL: Morning, Lily.

               Alice Sugar …

               My, what a daisy …

               Try and pick her …

LILY: Who in charge?

CRACKERJACK: At your service, lady!

LILY: Crackers, you never to service me!

CUTAWAY: Lily, you look sweeter than honey.

DAGGER: Don't let that fool you, she sting like a bee.

LILY: How come you know, Dagger? You get bite?

DAGGER: When I went bathing by you last night!

Two blue crab nip me as I jump in the water.

ALICE: Because you went where you shouldn't oughter.

LILY: Enough! Crackerjack, everything set?

CRACKERJACK: The poui ready to make strife,

The bloodhole waiting to take life,

Only I don't see the players yet.

ALICE: Who you backing, Rimbeau?

CUTAWAY: Briscoe for the grade,

Though the Terror is a hard man to invade.

SWIFTY: If Briscoe win it will cause a riot!

PELOO: Swifty, keep your young tail quiet!

CUTAWAY: So tell us, Lily, what would happen

If Briscoe nail the great Tiny Satan

With a lucky blow?

ALICE: What? Briscoe topple

The Terror? Poor man, he going get cripple.

CUTAWAY: I speaking to Lily. Suppose Briscoe take

The crown this morning. You will give him a break?

LILY: That is my business. What you better learn

Fast is no break for you where I concern.

CUTAWAY: You 'fraid me, you hear 'bout my reputation!

LILY: Cutaway, your spouting need insulation,

You too soft for me, boy.

[*Guffaws from the men.*]

Crackers, you really think he can win?

CRACKERJACK: Who, Briscoe? Most of the boys betting

On him.

LILY: Is true?

CRACKERJACK: He got youth and power.

COOLIE: And beside he fighting to win you over.

HANNIBAL: Briscoe love Petite Belle too bad.

Love riding him till it send him mad.

CUTAWAY: Lily, like you promise him a favour!

LILY: Who want a novice for a lover?

And still the fooly haunting my door

Bringing me presents and flowers galore,

Though I tell him is no sense going on

He worship the ground I walk upon.

ALICE: We only like men who could pelt stick good.

CRACKERJACK: In all directions, eh, Alice? You like wood

That break down all opposition, I hear.

ALICE: You know the correct thing, Crackers, dear.

[*Loud guffaws from the men.* JOE *enters hurriedly.*]

JOE: I hear the summons and haste to the tent,

Senors, senoritas, before the big event

Come off, because I have a proposal

To make that the fight is too criminal

And I beg you stop it.

SEVERAL: Joe talking rot ...

He up to some plot ...

Briscoe send him or Tiny

To thief people money?

JOE: You don't understand.

Is my conscience! Last night you demand

I back my charge against the obeahman;

Later my conscience say is a mistake

Because something bigger than obeah at stake

And that is a life –

DAGGER: Joe, it don't ring true.

Try your guile at something new

To convince the boys your real intention

Is to save Briscoe.

PELOO: Joe making ruction

About nothing at all. Is not the first time

A stick-man face death before his prime.

Remember the killer, Conjo Jack? When him

And me clash, it was blue lightning.

I brake the first charge, but pardner, the second

Bore my defence like it come from a gun.
I didn't know what hit me, ten seconds I freeze,
Then like a soft popsicle I fall on my knees.
I know then my time to retire had come –

JOE: Lily, you prepare for this martyrdom?
If you have heart, don't let Briscoe do it.

LILY: How it concern me?

JOE: Is an open secret
You is the instigator of the bout.
Give Briscoe the cue and he will back out.

SEVERAL: The fight must go on …
Everybody want fun …
Briscoe got a charm
He won't come to no harm …

JOE: Whatever happen, Lily, most of the blame
Fall on you.

LILY: Hear this meddler! Man, you ain't shame
To expose your ignorance! Briscoe looking fame,
He is man enough and must do as he choose.

JOE: He fighting for you, Lily, win or lose
Everything is for you, we know that well,
And you sending the young man straight to hell
To show off your pride.

LILY: You damn Portagee!
Your face like a chew-up piece of cane-peeling.
Eh, eh, but you men listen to this rank
Abuse, and nobody lick in his flank?

DAGGER: Lily talking sense. If Briscoe want glory
He must face the same risk as anybody.

CRACKERJACK: Beside, a heap of us share the opinion
That Briscoe will be the next champion.

SEVERAL: That's my contention …
He will eat up Satan …
Briscoe will be hero
Today and tomorrow …

[JOE *throws up his hands in despair and sits down moodily, alone, to one side of the tent.*]

COOLIE: I find it have too much argumentation,

High time to call an intermission.

Pass the rum while we waiting and, Hannibal,

Give us a number that's topical.

CRACKERJACK: Sing the ruso about Petite Belle!

ALICE: I don't like that calypso at all.

It shameful. Hannibal, choose another.

LILY: I like it. Hannibal, sweetheart,

Give us the chorus. Come, make a start!

Is calypso! What all you frighten for?

I enjoy it everytime more and more.

[*She begins to sing the chorus.*]

Petite Belle Lily. Petite Belle Lily,

[*Others join in.*]

L'homme camisole, l'homme sans camisole,

Tout monde casserer bamberole.

HANNIBAL [*singing*]: Petite Belle is a real enticer,

She got the goods and she got them nicer,

Every man in the place just dying to taste

A little piece of Petite Belle waist.

CHORUS [*singing*]: Petite Belle Lily, Petite Belle Lily,

L'homme camisole, l'homme sans camisole,

Tout monde casserer bamberole.

HANNIBAL [*singing*]: The way she move is something fantastic.

She got extension really elastic

She will send you up high like a bird in the sky,

Poor man if you cannot fly.

[LILY *cuts into the song with her own improvised verses.*]

LILY [*singing*]: There's nothing in the world finer than man,

And it's woman job to serve him, best as she can,

But my heart will only care,

For someone beyond compare,

I have no use for the fellow who also ran.

HANNIBAL [*singing*]: I accustom loving women in galore,

As a calypsonian I never keep score,

But since Petite Belle kiss me

I finish with Esme,

Iris, Jane and Dorothy.

LILY [*singing*]: Some women set their heart on silver and gold,

The highest bidder takes them to his fold,

But whether you're rich or poor,

That's not what I'm asking for,

My idol is the man who is fearless and bold.

HANNIBAL [*singing*]: Red as a rose and sweeter than honey,

Men offer her their life and their money,

When she cast round her spell,

They fight stick like hell

For a night with sweet Petite Belle.

LILY [*singing*]: Some sing of love but that's mere flattery,

Gems and jewels I scorn as trumpery,

For the true paragon of men,

Will dare to the lion's den,

That's the only man who ever will conquer me.

[*The calypso puts the whole arena in a gay, boisterous mood. Rum flows freely and there is much laughter and horseplay. During the singing of the last chorus, however, D. PAPA, accompanied by MINEE, suddenly comes in. The singing stops raggedly and all present stare with discomfort at the obeahman.*]

D. PAPA: I know why the gathering stand amaze,

Is not customary for me these days

To leave my abode and indulge the common

Amusements of the village. But I make exception

Today, because of the great commotion

Over the fight. Who in charge of the tent?

CRACKERJACK: Me, Crackerjack.

D. PAPA: I hope you don't resent

My company?

CRACKERJACK: No, Diable Papa. We glad to have you.

D. PAPA: And my medium, Minee?

CRACKERJACK: She could stay too.

D. PAPA: Good, good. I like to know where I stand
               And who I stand with. So my next proposition
               Is a roll call. You have no objection?

CRACKERJACK: Is all right by me. The women begin.

THE COMPANY [*naming themselves*]: Petite Belle Lilly …
               and Alice Sugar …
               Cutaway Rimbeau … and Dagger Da Silva …
               Crackerjack … Old Peloo … and Coolie …
               Pogo over here … with young Swifty …
               Here with the cuatro is Hannibal …

D. PAPA: Pleased to meet you, one and all.
               Somebody in the house don't call their name.
               Is because they too proud? Perhaps they claim
               The right to choose between friend and foe?
               Let him declare now which way he go!

   [*No response from* JOE.]

CRACKERJACK: The silent one is Portagee Joe
               Who this morning come to try and prevent
               The fight, saying Briscoe is no opponent
               For Tiny. He ain't in a talking mood.

HANNIBAL: Joe pit himself 'gainst the multitude
               Who believe that you, Papa, control the power
               To swing the fight one way or the other.
               Discover for him now, so all will know,
               The next champion bound to be Tim Briscoe.

JOE [*springs up to face* D. PAPA]: Say it if you dare!

   [D. PAPA *flashes him a look of hatred, then breaks into a sardonic
   chuckle and speaks in a purring, menacing tone of voice.*]

D. PAPA: You want me to read
               The future give you, Mister Joe? Then proceed
               According to the rules. First, I must examine
               You carefully in order to determine

	How much blight you have, and also my fee.
	Or perhaps you expecting my service free?
JOE:	Name your price here and now!
D. PAPA:	As everyone know
	My business don't run as a poppyshow,
	but in the seclusion of my room
	I deal in secrets beyond the tomb.
JOE:	Secrets! Bah!
D. PAPA:	All who want proof of my magical art,
	Come to my den in the woods apart.
JOE:	I say it behind you, now to your face,
	Diable Papa is a fake! And is a disgrace
	The way people swallow your trickery –
D. PAPA:	Hold, foreigner, hold your tongue! Life is short!
JOE:	Fraud!
D. PAPA:	Take warning, Presumption! You can't abort
	What lay in the belly of time. Now hear!
	Three days' grace, and the fourth – beware!
JOE:	I done say my piece, so make your play,
	The village will come to their sense one day.
	As to the fight, my heart go out
	To Briscoe, walking into the lion's mouth.
	Whatever happen, he can count on me
	To see him through this catastrophe.
	Well, I leave you now to enjoy your war,
	Whoever want me come to the store.

[JOE *stomps out angrily. There is a hush as the villagers remain aghast at the open defiance of the obeahman.* D. PAPA *senses the first signs of doubt in his power.*]

D. PAPA:	Cross him off the list of the living, Minee,
	This spell the end of one fool Portagee,
	Three days he have, then wish he was dead,
	For the vengeance of Moko will fall on his head.
	Back to the fight. Where the contestants?

CRACKERJACK: They ain't reach yet.

D. PAPA: Sound the bugle at once

Is time they begin.

SEVERAL: Make the bugle speak …

We been waiting a week …

Fight like you crazy

For blood and money …

[*The bugle sounds again twice. The crowd waits expectantly.*
BRISCOE *and* INEZ *enter.* BRISCOE *carries his poui-stick.*]

CRACKERJACK: A hail for the brave contender! To Briscoe!

[*General hail.* BRISCOE *ignores this and goes to sit on his stool.*
INEZ *stands beside him.*]

PELOO: Take your call now, boy. When your blood flow

In the hole later on, nobody will cry.

CUTAWAY: Petite Belle, wish your lover-boy luck with his try.

LILY: I have one lover and he don't need luck.

DAGGER: But Briscoe showing so much pluck

You must give him a little encouragement.

CRACKERJACK: Don't let Lily throw you off the scent,

We know she love Briscoe.

LILY: My man ain't reach yet.

HANNIBAL [*to* BRISCOE]: What happen, friend, you in a cold sweat?

INEZ: Keep your head, Briscoe, don't listen to them.

POGO: Watch Tiny good, watch for finger-tricks.

PELOO: Watching alone can't ward off the licks.

DAGGER: Finesse to the left, is his weakest side.

COOLIE: Don't forget, Briscoe, keep your eyes open wide

So you know when the time come to run and hide.

ALICE: Inez, I hope a doctor coming?

INEZ: Why? You expecting Tiny to want him?

CUTAWAY: We don't want a doctor, call a priest,

Briscoe determine for murder at least.

What you say, pardner?

HANNIBAL: Briscoe keeping quiet.

	Come on, man, take a drink and chat
	With the boys. It ain't a funeral!
SWIFTY:	He saying his prayers to build-up morale.
BRISCOE:	Is time Tiny reach!
LILY:	Some people want fame
	But ain't prepare for the odds in the game.
INEZ:	If Tiny don't come now we leaving here.
LILY:	The brave challenger beginning to scare.
BRISCOE:	Who is Tiny to keep people waiting like this!
LILY:	Tiny is champion, that's who he is!
BRISCOE	[*rises and goes over to musicians*]: You choose the calinda
	music yet?
LILY:	Tiny say 'Thousand' is his favourite.

[*She begins to chant the stick-fighting chorus which* TINY *has chosen.*]

Thousand – ten thousand to bar me one!

Bring on a hundred stick-man.

Ten thousand to bar me one.

BRISCOE: To hell with Tiny! You will sing 'Battalion'.

INEZ [*chanting*]: Me alone, me alone

Me alone like a man

I will face hell battalion,

Only me alone.

[*Now partisans of the two fighters join in the choruses and the crowd grows restless and belligerent.*]

CRACKERJACK: All right, all right, take it easy,

Cool down, I say, we ain't quite ready,

You can't hear! Stop singing! Come bet I blister

Somebody with this poui! Where the hell Tiny is!

SWIFTY: Tiny coming! Tiny coming!

CRACKERJACK: Take your places one time.

It late already. I don't have to prime

You how to behave. Any interference

And the body will feel the weight of my patience.

[*The spectators take up their positions.* TINY *enters to a lukewarm reception.* LILY *runs to him and kisses him ostentatiously before the crowd. Whistles and cat-calls. The two fighters come forward and face each other across the ring.*]

CRACKERJACK: Anybody want to ask any question?

Anybody want to change their weapon?

BRISCOE: I will keep my poui.

TINY: Any one will do me.

[CRACKERJACK *hands him a poui-stick.*]

CRACKERJACK: Everybody satisfy? No objection?

All right then. Start the calinda!

Is 'Girl in the Coffee' I choose for this war.

STICK-FIGHTING CHORUS: That girl in the coffee, that girl in the cocoa,

Doo-doo, tell me why you singing so for …

That girl in the coffee, why you singing so for.

I know your labour ain't so nice

So tell me, why you singing so for …

That girl in the coffee, why you singing so for.

Is I alone, is I alone,

So tell me, why you singing so for …

That girl in the coffee, why you singing so for.

I know you like to dance the bongo,

Why you singing so for …

That girl in the coffee, why you singing so for.

[*A lone voice begins the chant and others take up the refrain. The drums follow and the bamboo-beaters. Everyone is singing, beating and swaying rhythmically with the music as the two combatants measure distance and the fight begins.*]

[BRISCOE *puts up the battle of his life. He moves quickly to attack, surprising the champion, who retreats and has to defend himself against some vicious slashes. Then* TINY *loses his footing, falls on one knee, and* BRISCOE *moves in for the kill, but the little giant spins neatly out of danger and with an upward flick of the wrist he deals* BRISCOE *a nasty whack across his body. The challenger loses his nerve and caution.* TINY *feints skilfully,* BRISCOE *shifts his guard and leaves an opening which the Terror bores through with a chopper.*]

[BRISCOE *crumbles before the stunned spectators. Then* COOLIE *and* PELOO *begin cheering the champion. The crowd joins in, lifts* TINY

shoulder-high and carries him out of the tent to celebrate at El Toro.
LILY *looks down at the fallen* BRISCOE *with pity and admiration before following the crowd off.*]

[INEZ, *in tears, runs to help her brother, bathing his head with a wet towel.* D. PAPA *sits impassively.* MINEE *tugs at his sleeve, urging him to leave the tent, but he waves her off and presently addresses* BRISCOE *in an attempt to explain his defeat.*]

D. PAPA: Briscoe, *mon ami*, too sad, too sad.

You is the worst stick-fighter in Trinidad.

Remember, I warn what the outcome would be

If, wilful, you determine to have Lily.

Let the experience make you wise,

Take profit from your morning exercise.

INEZ: You have the brass, Diable Papa, to remain

Behind and laugh at Briscoe in pain!

Your heart is a stone, to stand and mock

A man you turn into a laughing-stock.

D. PAPA: What you saying! Briscoe take me for joke!

He come to my yard early morning, woke

Me out of my slumber to charm his stick,

Not sufficient, I must do it quick-quick,

Though it take seven days to mount a poui

And on top of the bargain he short-pay me.

INEZ: You ain't no good! Your magic spoil!

Portagee Joe did the right thing to soil

Up your reputation in front the tent,

Now nobody would trust you with a cent!

D. PAPA: Don't talk like an idiot, child. Is a piece

Of luck for Briscoe that he get release

From blight; if I didn't purify him

Tiny woulda tear him limb from limb!

The courage he show was part of my plan,

Briscoe suffer defeat, but fight like a man.

MINEE: Let us go, Papa!

D. PAPA: So Briscoe, friend,

All things work for best in the end,

Next time when you come, give me good notice,

And beware of the sin of avarice!

[D. PAPA *moves to the doorway, preceded by* MINEE *who edges forward at a safe distance from* BRISCOE. *The stick-man, now recovered from his wound, attacks the obeahman. Swearing profusely, he seizes a poui and charges at D.* PAPA, *who backs away, but* BRISCOE *gets between him and the door. He moves grimly towards the obeahman, murder in his eyes.* D. PAPA *realizes that his life is in danger and he tries to talk his way out.*]

BRISCOE: Diable Papa! Ça c'est slau saqui buho!

D. PAPA: Hey, Briscoe! You idiot! Take time, mister!

What, you gone mad! Hold! I would blister

You with blight! Blight! You hit me! Remember,

Your life in my hands, I am Diable Papa!

[BRISCOE *hammers a poui at him and D.* PAPA, *showing surprising agility, twists out of the way. The obeahman begins to mumble his magic words and to gesticulate, while he twists and turns like a toreador before an enraged bull.* BRISCOE *corners him again and gets in a glancing blow.* INEZ *tries to reason with her brother, but he pushes her off and closes with the obeahman once more. This time the blow lands home and D.* PAPA *shrieks with pain.* INEZ *rushes outside for help.*]

INEZ: Murder! Murder! Briscoe gone mad!

He going kill Diable Papa, he beating him bad!

Murder! Murder!

[*Inside the tent,* BRISCOE *lands another blow and now* MINEE *goes into action. She grabs a stout poui and attacks* BRISCOE *from behind. For the second time the stick-man drops to the ground.* MINEE, *crying out in terror, discards the stick and cowers away in a corner of the tent. A babble of voices off announces the return of the spectators. D.* PAPA, *always the opportunist, retrieves his wand and, chanting the unknown tongues, begins to make weird passes over the prostrate figure of* BRISCOE. *The crowd, led by* INEZ *re-enter. They pull up short in surprise and fear at the spectacle before them.*]

D. PAPA [*chanting over* BRISCOE]: Damballa, Shango, Ogun, o-way!

Ashooborac, bo-yea, bo-yea!

Damballa, Shango, Ogun, o-way!

Ashooborac, bo-yea, bo-yea!

Ashooborac, bo-yea, Damballa!

INEZ: Alas! Diable Papa destroy him. Oh!

    He throw a spirit on poor Briscoe!

SEVERAL [*backing away and crossing themselves*]:

    Diable Papa blight him …

    He do it to spite him …

    Briscoe finish for true …

    Look what love can do …

D. PAPA [*addressing crowd*]:

    Bring your sackcloth and ashes! Woe

    Betide the man who become my foe.

    Briscoe assault me, now witness his fate,

    He measure the ground before me prostrate,

    This is the payment for all who try

    To rise against me and my power defy.

[LILY *enters and pushes her way through the crowd. Pity and affection for the unfortunate challenger overcome her. She drags* D. PAPA *away and kneels before* BRISCOE, *bathing his head, nestling it in her arms.*]

LILY: Shift yourself! Make way! Is me, Lily,

    Come to view this new tragedy!

    O God, Diable Papa, you hooligan!

    What again you will do to the man!

    Poor Briscoe, he suffer all for me …

D. PAPA: To one and all I say, Remember,

    Après Bon Dieu épi Diable, c'est Diable Papa!

    Minee, come!

[*He stalks out followed by* MINEE. JOE *enters.*]

JOE: Bring him to my room back of the store,

    Somebody ride in to town for a doctor.

LILY: I will nurse him myself. He love too strong,

    I never believe it and treat him wrong.

[*She sings softly.*]

    Men sing of love but that's mere flattery,

    Gems and jewels I scorn as trumpery,

    For the true paragon of men,

Will dare to the lion's den,

That's the only man who ever will conquer me.

THE CROWD [*singing sadly as they move in to stand around*
BRISCOE]: *Petite Belle Lily, Petite Belle Lily,*

L'homme camisole, l'homme sans camisole,

Tout monde casserent bamberole.

Act Three

Scene 1

'El Toro' store, several hours later.

The excitement caused by the fight and its unexpected sequel has subsided and the villagers are beset with feelings of guilt over BRISCOE who now lies, apparently seriously ill, in JOE's room at the back of the store.

AT CURTAIN

The company are discovered in the saloon in a mood of apprehensive waiting. Absent are HANNIBAL, COOLIE and PELOO, while LILY is in the room off attending to the sick BRISCOE. The men sit at tables silently, toying with drinks. INEZ and ALICE sit on either side of the door leading to the sick room. JOE stands at the counter, SWIFTY dozes behind the bar.

HANNIBAL enters and crosses to JOE to deliver up his cuatro which he has lost. JOE waves him off and he joins the men at a table.

JOE: I hope everybody well satisfy,

The only thing left is for Briscoe to die.

Though you feel sorry now, is kinda late,

Sorry alone can't less the weight

Of guilt each and everyone carry,

It will haunt us while we have memory.

CRACKERJACK: Inez, go and find out the news.

INEZ: How much time I tell you, Lily refuse

To let anyone in.

ALICE: Only cooing and clucking

Like a mother hen over a sick chicken.

TINY: So with all women, it take a tragedy

To penetrate their mentality.

DAGGER: You didn't ought to hit him so hard!

TINY: What fool thing you talking! I had to guard

Myself when the man unleash his attack

As if the devil was riding his back,

Believe me, fellows, I never intend

To damage Briscoe, he was my friend.

POGO: The friend of us all!

INEZ: But Diable Papa cast a bad spell over him.

POGO: Poor Briscoe! His chance to recover is slim!

Obeah ain't so easy to overthrow.

ALICE: Lily trying all the science she know.

JOE: I think we should send to town for a doctor.

ALICE: Yes, get Cassirip, he is a concoctor

Of note. People called him the white magician.

JOE: I refer to a qualified physician!

[LILY *enters from the sick room. She carries a tray with medicines, dishes, etc. The men crowd around her.*]

SEVERAL: Give us the news

Of the brave loser …

We longing to know

The fate of Briscoe …

INEZ: Lily, ease my heart. How is Briscoe?

LILY: Lingering on in the land of limbo.

I bandage his head and the bleeding stop,

I rub him down and the fever drop,

I use potions, bush and prayers as well,

But nothing I do can't break the spell

That settle on him like a heavy mist.

INEZ: He give no sign that his body resisting

The magic?

LILY: Only now and again

When I hold him close a passionate moan

Come from his lips as if my presence

Stir his spirit to break out from the trance,

But soon he will fall back quiet and cold,

Content to remain half-dead to the world.

ALICE: Is the obeah fasten strong on him.

INEZ: Poor Briscoe, his future looking dim.

JOE: Lily, why not send for a doctor?

ALICE: Contact Cassirip, the old sorcerer.

LILY: First, pass me another bottle of rum,

I will rub him again.

SWIFTY: What become

            Of the first one you had. It finish already?

            Somebody in there must be on a spree.

JOE: Shut that, young fellow! You too insolent!

            Hand me the bottle.

   [*To* LILY, *giving her the bottle of rum.*]

            This is ninety-six per cent

            Proof liquor, so apply it with care.

CRACKERJACK: Lily, if you want a bright idea

            Give Briscoe a little to warm up the body,

            And burn two candles over the bed.

INEZ: You use the aloes plaster on his head?

CUTAWAY: I have some snake-oil hideaway in my room.

ALICE: Don't forget, Lily, to turn the broom

            Upside down and scatter salt on the floor.

DAGGER: The old people say put a cross on the door

            And a circle round the bed to keep away spirits.

LILY: I do all that already. My poor wits

            Explore every piece of science in the book.

            Briscoe time come if this don't work.

   [*She returns to the sick room. A pause.*]

JOE: No! I can't stomach this mockery

            While a man's life in jeopardy.

            Swifty, saddle the horse, Inez, take command,

            I going for the best doctor in the land.

SWIFTY: That will cost plenty money.

   [*He goes outside.*]

JOE: If only I can

            Save Briscoe it will ease my shame.

HANNIBAL: Needless to say, we all feel the same.

JOE: Before I leave, senors, permit me to say

            One more word. After what happen today

            I have no conscience to keep the money

            That I win through this catastrophe,

Therefore I decide – not to buy your favour –
But because blood on it, to redeliver
Every man his bet.

INEZ: Joe, you can't do it!

JOE: Why not?

CRACKERJACK: She mean the proposal ain't fit
With the rules of the game.

INEZ: Yes, that's right!

JOE: Pardon me, I never mean to slight
Anybody, but how you expect me to keep
This money in my house? How I can sleep
Sound knowing what trouble it cost? Inez,
Open the strong-box, you have the keys.

INEZ: Joe, please –

JOE: No more. I won't listen!

INEZ: O God! Oh!

THE MEN: What happen? What happen?

INEZ: Forgive me, please, Joe!

JOE: Forgive you? For what?

INEZ: I take the cash – we only borrow
It really – Coolie say – where Coolie? – tomorrow
Everything will be – O God! – now we lost –
You hear? Lost the money – what a cross!

JOE: Compose yourself, girl, and say what happen.

SWIFTY [entering]: The horse rearing to go. What happen?
He dead?

ALICE: Inez, what new trouble lay ahead?

THE MEN: What happen? What happen?

[INEZ *begins to relate the story in a chant, singing so softly that the men pick up her words and pass them along until the whole company are echoing her in growing concern and despair over this new misadventure.*]

INEZ [*singing*]: After you leave me,

THE OTHERS [*singing*]: What?
After he leave her,

INEZ [*singing*]:	Last night when you leave me,
THE OTHERS [*singing*]:	Last night when he leave her,
INEZ [*singing*]:	I take all the money,
THE OTHERS [*singing*]:	She take all the money,
INEZ [*singing*]:	And I give it to Coolie.
JOE [*spoken*]:	You take all my money?
INEZ [*singing*]:	Every cent of the money,
THE OTHERS [*singing*]:	Every cent, every penny,
INEZ [*singing*]:	And I give it to Coolie!
THE OTHERS [*singing*]:	She give it to Coolie!
	To Coolie! To Coolie!
	Oh-oh-oh-oh!
JOE [*spoken*]:	Why you give it to Coolie?
INEZ [*singing*]:	Coolie come and he tell me,
THE OTHERS [*singing*]:	What Coolie tell you?
INEZ [*singing*]:	He tell me truly,
THE OTHERS [*singing*]:	Truly? Truly?
INEZ [*singing*]:	Joe will lose all the money,
THE OTHERS [*singing*]:	Lost all the money?
INEZ [*singing*]:	If he put it on Tiny,
THE OTHERS [*singing*]:	Oh, no! Oh, no!
INEZ [*singing*]:	So I give it to Coolie,
THE OTHERS [*singing*]:	She give it to Coolie,
INEZ [*singing*]:	Call Coolie, call Coolie.
THE OTHERS [*singing*]:	To Coolie! To Coolie!
	Every cent, every penny!
	Oh-oh-oh-oh!
JOE [*spoken*]:	What he do with the money?
INEZ [*singing*]:	Coolie take all the money,
THE OTHERS [*singing*]:	Coolie gone with our money,
INEZ [*singing*]:	To Four Roads Valley,
THE OTHERS [*singing*]:	Down in the valley,
INEZ [*singing*]:	That's what he tell me,
THE OTHERS [*singing*]:	Say so, say so,

INEZ [*singing*]:	To bet against Tiny,
THE OTHERS [*singing*]:	Didn't go, didn't go,
INEZ [*singing*]:	So I give it to Coolie,
THE OTHERS [*singing*]:	She gave it to Coolie,
INEZ [*singing*]:	Every penny to Coolie,
THE OTHERS [*singing*]:	To Coolie! To Coolie!
	She give all the money,
	Oh-oh-oh-oh!
INEZ [*spoken*]:	Where Coolie is now?
THE OTHERS [*spoken*]:	Coolie gone! Coolie gone!
INEZ [*singing*]:	Oh!
THE OTHERS [*singing*]:	Oh!
JOE [*wailing*]:	Oh!

[LILY *re-enters the room.*]

LILY: You better postpone your weep and wail
         A little, for Briscoe stamina failing
         Fast and you will need water to cry.
         Joe, darling. I beg you, please hurry
         And bring the doctor.

SWIFTY: Joe lose every penny!

SEVERAL: Inez give it away.
         She fall a prey
         To a smart manoeuvre
         From a born trickster …

JOE: I believe the world and his wife gone crazy!
         Inez, what possess you to take all my money
         And reverse my bet on Tiny Satan?

INEZ: Briscoe consult the obeahman
         Who promise to make him the champion.

ALICE: You sure of that?

INEZ: I tell him to go.

JOE: You, Inez?

INEZ: Forgive me, please, Joe.

JOE: All I had put by, you mean everything
         You throw away.

INEZ: Except the gold tie-pin
Your mother send you.

JOE: Everything down the drain?
And you, Inez, who I hope would remain
With me permanent, you give me this blow?

INEZ: I make a big mistake. Ask pardon, Joe.

CUTAWAY: Wait a minute, men! It look like a plot
From morning to thief every penny we got.
Is not Coolie first tell us Briscoe will win?

POGO: And Peloo back him up most genuine!

JOE: And neither one come in on the betting.

CRACKERJACK: They ain't here!

DAGGER: Where they went?

HANNIBAL: They stand condemn being the only absent
Ones in the crowd.

POGO: We'll peel their skin!

CRACKERJACK: And finish the havoc they begin!

JOE: A moment, please, senors, listen to me.
You thirst for revenge, but think carefully,
Who is the faker behind the fraud?
If Peloo is mouthpiece, who give the word?
Coolie perform it, who make the plan?
Who is the chief culprit?

THE MEN: The obeahman!

[*Carried away by the discovery of the plot, the men instinctively shout their latent mistrust of* D. PAPA. *But immediately they realize that they are up against no ordinary enemy. They break away uneasily.*]

ALICE: Why you hesitate? What you waiting for?
Here is provocation to warrant war
And rebellion! Grab your poui in hand
And drive the traitor off the face of the land!

[*No action from the men.*]

INEZ: Why the delay? Everybody have cause
Enough to make this reckoning yours!

CRACKERJACK: But Diable Papa is a treacherous villain
      Who walk with all kind of mysterious weapon
      About him.

LILY: While you prate and prattle
      Your friend inside losing the battle
      Of his life. Joe, the doctor coming?

JOE: Swifty, the horse! I will go for him
      Right away, hoping my influence
      Will count for enough dollars and cents
      To bring him back. Meanwhile, senors,
      We need that money. You know what to do.
      Is high time you paddle your own canoe.

[*He goes out quickly.*]

LILY: Now, who going root out the ring-leader,
      The blood-sucker, arch-deceiver,
      Diable Papa? He bamboozle all of us here
      And laughing his head off from ear to ear.
      Who going root him out?

[*She moves into a warrior song.*]

[*singing*]: Who is the villain!

THE OTHERS [*singing*]: *Diable Papa!*
      The bogus magician!
      Diable Papa!
      Who we must destroy!
      Diable Papa!
      Drive out the island!
      Diable Papa!

THE MEN [*singing*]: Clear the way, make your play,
      The brave alone will survive today.

THE COMPANY [*singing*]: War and rebellion, war and rebellion,
      War and rebellion, we fighting for freedom!

ALICE [*singing*]: Who is the faker!

> *Diable Papa!*
>
> A born mischief-maker!
>
> *Diable Papa!*
>
> Who we must destroy!
>
> *Diable Papa!*
>
> Now and forever!
>
> *Diable Papa!*

THE MEN [*singing*]: Clear the way, make your play,

> The brave alone will survive today.

THE COMPANY [*singing*]: War and rebellion, war and rebellion,

> War and rebellion, we fighting for freedom!

TINY [*singing*]: Who thief high and low!

> *Diable Papa!*
>
> Make us pappyshow!
>
> *Diable Papa!*
>
> Who we must destroy!
>
> *Diable Papa!*
>
> With a mighty blow!
>
> *Diable Papa!*

THE MEN [*singing*]: Clear the way, make your play,

> The brave alone will survive today.

THE COMPANY [*singing*]: War and rebellion, war and rebellion,

> War and rebellion, we fighting for freedom!

INEZ [*singing*]: Who bring misery!

> *Diable Papa!*
>
> Who keep us in slavery!
>
> *Diable Papa!*
>
> Who we must destroy!
>
> *Diable Papa!*
>
> In a raging fury!
>
> *Diable Papa!*

THE MEN [*singing*]: Clear the way, make your play,

> The brave alone will survive today.

THE COMPANY [*singing*]: War and rebellion, war and rebellion,

War and rebellion, we fighting for freedom!

TINY: All who agree we march and invade

The enemy, show their hand.

[*Hands go up slowly and come down quickly. Only* INEZ *keeps her hand high.*]

Well, that rule out.

LILY: Because you stick-men only have mouth!

You 'fraid, all 'fraid, like cat 'fraid water,

Craven like sheep of an old bush-doctor

Who got you like putty-mix in his hand,

Ready to twist you which way he demand,

And not a soul to stand up and fight!

You will die as you live – a bunch of white-

Livered cowards crawling into your grave!

TINY: Stop your abuse! Tiny Satan is brave

As any man living. I will face any mortal!

DAGGER: And me!

POGO: Me too!

CRACKERJACK: That goes for all!

HANNIBAL: But Diable Papa ain't no common trickster,

Not poui and blade but ingenious magic

Is what he fight with, the charm and spell,

And who want to clash with a demon from hell?

LILY: Then Diable Papa really is the king

Of all stick-men, and he rule the ring.

[*She picks up the crown.*]

Why we keep the crown? Now glory is past,

The last great warrior breathing his last!

If he die, I pray God that his spirit

Make every one of you pay dead for it!

[*The door leading to the sick-room opens slowly and* BRISCOE *enters in night-gown with his head swathed in bandages.*]

SWIFTY: Is Briscoe spirit! He done dead for true!

THE COMPANY [*crossing themselves*]: Is Briscoe spirit

Paying a visit …

To reckon with all

Who cause his downfall …

[BRISCOE's *eyes glance round the room and come to rest on* TINY. *He moves a step forward.*]

BRISCOE [*whispering*]: Tiny …

TINY [*kneeling before* BRISCOE]: Ask pardon, Briscoe, for

knocking you down,

I only do it to defend my crown,

So help me, God, I never intend

To kill you dead, you was my friend.

THE MEN [*kneeling*]: The friend of us all!

BRISCOE: Inez …?

INEZ [*kneeling*]: Spare me, Briscoe, spare and forgive

Your one and only close relative,

Though is me send you to the obeahman,

As God above, I had good intentions.

LILY [*kneeling*]: And me, Lily, cause-principal

Of the sudden tragedy that befall,

A bed of sorrow will end my days,

For I love you, Briscoe, now and always.

[BRISCOE *turns his gaze on* ALICE *who is the only one left standing. She suddenly realizes this and falls to her knees in terror.*]

ALICE: And spare me too!

THE COMPANY: Spare us! Spare us!

[BRISCOE *takes stock of the situation. For the first time in his life he enjoys undisputed power. If only his luck would hold long enough. He comes to a decision and, stiffening himself, moves to the outside door. The prostrate company half-rise as he is about to leave the store. BRISCOE, making sure he is still in command, wheels about and stops them with a gesture. They all bow again and remain in the position as he struts jauntily out.*]

[*The traverse curtains falls and* COOLIE *and* PELOO *enter downstage arguing.*]

COOLIE: All right, you ain't satisfy with the cut!
          Why you didn't say so? Why wait till he shut
          The door-mouth behind you to cry and complain
          In my ears?

PELOO: Because you shoulda retain
          A good price of the loot for you and me,
          Instead you hand over all the money
          To Diable Papa – from Joe, from the men,
          Everything we collect you give to him,
          And what we get back? Hardly enough
          To buy eucalyptus drops for my cough!

COOLIE: I tell you already. When you about
          To thief from Diable Papa, count me out.
          I don't want no quarrel with black magic
          You observe how his obeah turn the trick
          On Briscoe?

PELOO: True, and now he lay dying.

COOLIE: Well, what the hell you signifying
          Like an old woman for?

PELOO: My bunions burning,
          When that happen, is a sure warning
          Trouble ahead. You going to the village?

COOLIE: Just as well we take anchorage
          Out here in the woods, close by Diable Papa,
          In case anything happen.

PELOO: But the cold air and damp
          Ain't good for my old bones and cramps.

[COOLIE *spreads his jacket on the ground and they sit, clearly unnerved. A silence.*]

PELOO: Anything like what? What could happen?

COOLIE: I will pose you all angles within reason.
          First to begin, if Briscoe recover –
          I hate to say it – your tail in hot water.

PELOO: Why me?

COOLIE: Is you send him to Diable Papa,

            I tell you no. Then again, if not,

            Two things could happen, his mind could blot

            Out and he wouldn't remember nothing.

PELOO: What is the third chance in your reasoning?

COOLIE: He could kick the bucket.

PELOO: I feeling sick.

    [COOLIE *hands him a flask of rum. He helps himself generously.*]

COOLIE: Don't upset yourself.

PELOO: Damn you and your logic!

COOLIE: Relax! Ghosts only walk by night

            And we have a good hour of fading light.

            Come amuse yourself. I have some dice

            In my back-pocket. Bet you half-dollar

            I nick before you.

PELOO: Jack up the figure.

COOLIE: For a round dollar watch the ivory roll!

    [*He rolls the dice.*]

PELOO: Two single ace! A dead man poll!

COOLIE: Come again, my luck kinda frivolous

            Today. Sebby-lebby, now!

    [*He rolls the dice.*]

PELOO: They with us

            Still! Two singletons unseparable

            Stand for a whole heap of trouble!

COOLIE [*desperately*]: Last time! Come, angels, break the spell,

            Some fours and treys …

    [*He throws again.*]

PELOO: Devils in hell!

            Three times you throw a double dummy!

    [BRISCOE *enters quietly at the other side of the stage and watches the play. He chuckles.*]

PELOO: Look, Briscoe ghost! Lord have mercy!

            He come for revenge!

COOLIE:	Don't look on me,
	Is Peloo send you to charm your poui!
PELOO:	But Coolie thief Portagee Joe money!
COOLIE:	You lie!
PELOO:	Is true!
COOLIE:	Briscoe, spare me and take old Peloo,
	He near dead already.

[BRISCOE *moves forward slowly. The two men gather their last bit of courage and run for the lives.* BRISCOE *collects the money they have left behind and moves on as the traverse curtain lifts to reveal the obeahman's hut.*]

Scene 2

DIABLE PAPA's *house as in Act One, Scene 2. It is late afternoon of the same day.*

AT CURTAIN

D. PAPA *sits at a low table with his winnings before him, counting them over and over, checking the amounts in a rough ledger, actually gloating over his success. The old trunk is open and contains not only money, but also small valuables and deeds which he has from time to time extracted by roguery from the villagers.*

MINEE *stands at the window, peering out through the half-opened shutter.*

D. PAPA:	Ha-ha-ha! Minee, cast your eyesight
	On the spoils we pick up after the fight.
	I set my bait, when I spring the trap
	See the fortune that tumble into my lap!
	Ha-ha-ha! I prove myself smarter
	Than the whole damn village lump together.
	Come from the window, girl. What need
	To stand there moping when you can feed
	Your eyes with all this?
MINEE:	The things that I see
	Overcast my mind with tragedy.
D. PAPA:	Then drink some bush. I climbing to the top
	And the devil himself can't call a stop.
MINEE:	You forget Portagee Joe. He will defy
	You to the end.

D. PAPA:	So he have a stroke and die,
	Or else, say, one morning he forget
	To wake up and so pay back the debt
	Every man owe his mother.
MINEE:	You mean to kill Joe!
D. PAPA:	Only once.
MINEE:	No! No! You musn't do it,
	You pushing your luck to the outer limit.
D. PAPA:	I tell you I holding the upper-hand!
	I must let a fool Portagee stand
	In my way? That is rank foolishness.
	Joe will perish for his meddlesomeness …

[MINEE *tries to interrupt him.*]

	And petticoat morals ain't going influence
	My decision neither, so save-up your defence
	For St Peter.
MINEE:	This is what I was dreading,
	I will not follow the path you treading.
D. PAPA:	You mean to desert me?
MINEE:	You force me to go.
D. PAPA:	Where to?
MINEE:	First to warn Portagee Joe.
D. PAPA:	But everything here is yours, Minee!
MINEE:	Be quiet and listen while I impart
	The signs and omens that suddenly start
	To harass me since this business begin.
	Yesterday when I was out gathering
	In the field, a bush start to shake,
	Coil-up underneath was a coral snake.
D. PAPA:	A dangerous sign!
MINEE:	Coming home I stumble
	On a tomb-stone and hear voice grumbling
	Under the ground.
D. PAPA:	A call from the grave!

MINEE: Take time, don't flinch, more to come. I save
The worst for last. In the tent when I hit
Briscoe, I swear that I see his spirit
Rise off the ground and point at me,
Then it disappear laughing with glee.

D. PAPA: Why you keep silent and let me proceed
So far in the business?

MINEE: You wouldn't take heed
No matter how I caution and plead,
Now you must stop before whatever brewing
Come to a boil and cause your undoing.

D. PAPA: It look like the right time to take a trip.

MINEE: Papa, you can't give fate the slip.

D. PAPA: Then what to do? The omens appear
To surround and threaten you everywhere.

MINEE: Is why I decide now that running away
Will only postpone the evil day.
No, Diable Papa, is one chance only
Open to us, we must give back the money
In person and make a full confession.

D. PAPA: What! You crazy to make that suggestion!
They would pin me up in the market-place
For all and sundry to laugh in my face,
Call me fraud, snake-in-the-grass,
And children to pull at me as I pass?
Never! I will stay and face up to it,
Whether beast, devil or avenging spirit!

[*A thundering knock at the front door.* D. PAPA *and* MINEE *freeze.*]

D. PAPA [*whispering*]: Take a look, see who is the knocker.

MINEE [*whispering*]: You go. It might be a customer.

[*They wait indecisively. The knocking is repeated.* D. PAPA *gets a stout poui, unbars the door, and steps back ready to do battle, calling in a voice that has lost its arrogance.*]

D. PAPA: Don't spend your strength on the old door,

Come inside and let your courage roar!

[COOLIE *and* PELOO *rush in. Exhaustion and fear have temporarily paralysed their vocal organs. They pantomime to* D. PAPA *and* MINEE *making odd guttural sounds.*]

D. PAPA: When you finish babble and squeak,

Explain, if you still have tongue to speak.

COOLIE: He coming …

PELOO: To get you …

COOLIE: He out …

PELOO: To upset you …

D. PAPA *and* MINEE: Who? Who?

COOLIE: We want protection …

PELOO: In this affliction …

D. PAPA: But who after you?

COOLIE: Quick, start up a charm …

PELOO: To keep us from harm …

D. PAPA: What frighten you so?

COOLIE *and* PELOO: The ghost of Briscoe!

D. PAPA *and* MINEE: Briscoe ghost!

[*The two men begin forcibly to dress* D. PAPA *in his magic robes.*]

COOLIE: He meet us in the wood,

Ten foot tall and covered in blood!

PELOO: A fat piece of poui in either hand,

And his footstep cover a chain of land!

D. PAPA: Minee, start packing! We changing address.

MINEE: I done pack already. You going to confess

To the village?

D. PAPA: No, we will head for the river.

COOLIE: We jump from the frying-pan into the fire!

You all running away?

D. PAPA: A change for the health.

PELOO: Where your magic gone?

D. PAPA: I have enough wealth

And decide to retire.

PELOO: Running wouldn't help
           If Briscoe spirit after a scalp.

D. PAPA: Shut that talk! I run from no man!

MINEE: Let us go and make a full confession!

COOLIE: Peloo, whatever happen, we got to stick
           With them.

PELOO: But don't look for too much gymnastic
           From my old bones.

D. PAPA: Everything ready?
           You have the money-box safe, Minee?
           And the jewels too? Peloo and Coolie,
           Brace yourself and follow me.

[D. PAPA *leads the procession to the front door. He opens it and stiffens. A low chuckle is heard off. With as much dignity as his fear will allow,* D. PAPA *makes a right-about turn and retreats quickly through the back with the others in his train.*]

D. PAPA: We will try the back door.

[*The hut is empty.* BRISCOE *enters calmly and walks through in unruffled pursuit of the four fugitives as the traverse curtain falls and the quartet appear downstage.*]

[D. PAPA *is in front,* COOLIE *follows, then* PELOO, *and finally* MINEE *struggles along carrying a basket of clothes and dragging the trunk after her.*]

PELOO: Take half-time let me catch my breath!

COOLIE: The only thing catching today is death!

PELOO: My cramp coming back, the going too rough.

COOLIE: As if being haunted ain't enough
           He must catch cramp!

PELOO: I beg you take a rest.

D. PAPA: Look, Peloo, this ain't no time to jest,
           We got to keep going.

PELOO: What you want me to do?

COOLIE: Of all the idiots to be saddled with you.
           You would like a doctor, I suppose?

PELOO: Give me respect! Until my eyes close
           And they pack me away, give me my due!
           I have twice your years!

COOLIE: And twice stupid too!

            What you say, Papa, we pushing on?

D. PAPA: That is the obvious solution,

            My motto is: devil take the hindmost!

COOLIE: And the devil today mean Briscoe ghost!

MINEE: He is your friend, you will leave him to die?

COOLIE: Is his funeral. Peloo, boy, goodbye,

            Was nice knowing you. You coming, Minee?

MINEE: I will stay and keep him company.

D. PAPA: Don't be an idiot! We got to keep going!

MINEE: Where to?

D. PAPA: The river-boat and then start rowing

            For life and money.

MINEE: I staying here.

COOLIE: Save yourself, girl. Peloo favour a pair

            Of old shoes ready for the dust-bin.

D. PAPA: This delay is the first sign of ruin.

MINEE: What human ever outsmart a ghost?

            Try all we can, the game done lost.

            Briscoe biding time and leading us on

            To a final reckoning and retribution.

D. PAPA: More reason to hurry, let us begone,

            Give me the money-box, I will take charge.

MINEE: No! It going with me to the village.

COOLIE: She off her mind! Hand over the loot

            And we better divide it here to boot.

            By rights a quarter belong to me.

            And as Peloo near dead, share it in three.

D. PAPA: Like fish! Not a farthing there is yours!

COOLIE [*showing his poui*]: I have a lawyer to plead my cause,

            Don't make him vex!

D. PAPA: Get out my sight

            Or prepare to suffer a crippling blight!

COOLIE: Stop fooling yourself! Your magic is fake!

            One-third of the spoils for the risk I take.

D. PAPA [*squaring off*]: I will sing that chorus over your wake!

   [*They go at each other furiously.*]

PELOO: Minee, stand close. You safe with me,

           Nobody ain't touching you or the money.

   [BRISCOE *enters quietly and watches the fight. He chuckles.*]

           God almighty! The ghost come again!

   [*The fugitives scatter in all directions.* BRISCOE *strolls off laughing. Shrieks and cries off, topped by* BRISCOE's *laughter. Then one by one the four miscreants re-enter.*]

PELOO [*entering*]: Wherever I turn the spirit appear

           Before me, well, let them bury me here,

           I ain't running no more.

MINEE [*entering*]:   He laughing still!

           He will keep on haunting us until

           We give up to the village.

PELOO: Then let us go.

COOLIE [*entering*]: Every place I look I seeing Briscoe.

           What to do to get rid of this spirit?

D. PAPA [*entering*]: Every tree, every shadow is a counterfeit

           Of this ghost.

   [*He shouts at the woods.*]

           Hell and brimstone!

           Briscoe, you done dead! Leave us alone!

COOLIE: You will only incite him to attack.

   [*Gentle laughter off. They huddle together.*]

PELOO: Braix for yourself, he coming back!

COOLIE: I see something moving over this side.

MINEE: A shadow here too!

D. PAPA: The spirit divide-up

           Himself to bamboozle us. Look here!

PELOO: No, no, over there!

COOLIE: He's everywhere!

   [*The laughter grows and dies away.*]

MINEE: He gone!

PELOO: Taking every piece of courage
            I ever had. Now is back to the village
            For me. I want a place to rest,
            Whether cell or tomb the Lord know best.

MINEE: I will come with you hoping to appease
            The spirit, and win a little ease.

D. PAPA: It look like the two of you gone mad!
            What you say, Coolie?

COOLIE: Believe me, I had
            Enough of this business and ready to quit
            If it will send this god-damn spirit
            Back to the grave. You must come too,
            Is only a total confession will do.

D. PAPA: I going on alone. Hand me the money.

MINEE: Never!

D. PAPA: Give me my share!

COOLIE: Over my body.
            You coming back with us or I swear
            They carry one of us out of here.

PELOO: You responsible for the callaloo
            That we in, Diable Papa. You must come too.

MINEE: Let the four of us go and surrender,
            Ask pardon and give back all the plunder,
            If the villagers do their uttermost,
            Is better than tangling with a ghost.

D. PAPA: I see is hopeless to make resistance.
            Lead on to my shame and submittance.

[*They move off,* PELOO *in front, followed by* COOLIE, *then* D. PAPA *and* MINEE *carrying basket and trunk.* PELOO *starts a hymn to bolster their flagging spirits and keep away the ghost.*]

THE FOUR [*singing*]: How beautiful Heaven must be,
            Sweet home of the happy and free,
            A haven of rest for the weary,
            How beautiful Heaven must be.

[*As they exit on one side of the stage,* BRISCOE *enters from the other side and crosses after them. The traverse curtain rises to disclose the store once again.*]

Scene 3

'El Toro' store. Evening of the same day.

AT CURTAIN

The villagers whom BRISCOE *left in the store are still there, seated and in silence, at a conspicuous distance from the door of the sick-room.* SWIFTY *moves around refilling glasses. He knocks over a bottle. The sudden clatter causes the company to spring to their feet. They sit again with relief.*

CRACKERJACK: What we waiting for?

DAGGER: I have no place to go.

CUTAWAY: Nor me.

POGO: Me neither.

HANNIBAL: I would like most
To find out what happening.

ALICE: We sure was a ghost
Who walk out of here?

LILY: You could see right through
The clothes he was wearing!

INEZ: You think I wouldn't know
The ghost of my brother?

POGO: If it ain't Briscoe
Who else it could be?

ALICE: I only ask whether
We sure was a spirit?

POGO: You choose a devil
Of a time to ask it.

SWIFTY: He leave the store without making a sound
And I notice his foot never tread the ground!

CRACKERJACK: If you doubt, Alice, take a peep
In the sick-room, see if he only sleeping
Or dead for true.

HANNIBAL: Yes, Alice, thief
A cagey look and bring us relief.

ALICE: I willing to do it, in company
With somebody else. Who going with me?

CRACKERJACK: Death is one caller I don't welcome.

DAGGER: Nor me.

CUTAWAY: Me neither.

HANNIBAL: It ain't no fun
　　　　　　To tamper with the corpse of a man
　　　　　　Who have reason to form an objection.

ALICE: Tiny Satan, you call yourself king
　　　　　Stick-man, let both of us go in.

TINY: I resign one time if to keep the crown
　　　　Mean molesting a ghost, I put it down
　　　　Diligently, and you all could elect
　　　　A new champion who favour the prospect.

LILY: Fame is a beggar and none in the land
　　　　Willing to stretch out a helping hand.

INEZ: Let's all go together!

THE COMPANY: Agreed!

　　[*They prepare to make the attempt.*]

SWIFTY: Who so bold
　　　　　To be first man across the threshold?

　　[*This thought stops the men and they sit again dejectedly.*]

CRACKERJACK: Is no sense fooling about any more,
　　　　　　We have to wait till the spirit return
　　　　　　To the body before this session adjourn.

SEVERAL: You talk real smart ...
　　　　　Straight from the heart ...
　　　　　Nobody so brave
　　　　　To dig their own grave ...

　　[*JOE enters.*]

JOE: Coming back from the city, the news overtake
　　　　Me, riding hard, that Briscoe forsake
　　　　Life for good. This is a sorry end,
　　　　The village lose a sturdy friend.

LILY: Briscoe gone, but his spirit alive
　　　　Patrolling the country to contrive

	A fearsome fate for his enemies
	After which his soul will rest in peace.
JOE:	Spirit alive! Explain what you mean.
CUTAWAY:	He stroll out of here, calm and serene
	As if going for a cool promenade!
SWIFTY:	And as the sun hit him, he start to fade!
JOE:	This is damn nonsense! You went in the room?
INEZ:	Don't go in there! You will meet your doom!
JOE:	Superstition is a rope round the neck
	Of the village, choking your intellect.
	Loose me, Inez, I intend to enter
	That room –

[*He stops as singing is heard off. The villagers look up in amazement as* MINEE, COOLIE, PELOO *and* D. PAPA *enter, the latter dragging the trunk after him. They stand shoulder to shoulder before the company.*]

THE FOUR:	We come to surrender
	And return back all we thief and plunder.
PELOO:	I was the old fool of a spy.
COOLIE:	I join with him, the devil know why.
D. PAPA:	I was the head trickster terrifying
	The village with spirits that never exist.
MINEE:	I, frighten Friday, was one who assist
	In all and commit the chiefest fault
	When, to save Diable Papa, I assault
	Briscoe in the tent and cause his death.
THE FOUR:	Then a real spirit come, fully enrage
	And hunt us down all over the village
	Till we decide on open confession,
	And beg forgiveness for our transgression.
SEVERAL:	Diable Papa is a faker …
	A rank mischief-maker …
	A quack obeahman …
	A bogus magician …
JOE:	Your reign is over, time to vamoose,
	I know your chickens would come home to roost.

SEVERAL: Banish the villains

Out of the island …

Make them pay double

For all the trouble …

OTHERS: An eye for an eye …

A tooth for a tooth …

It write down plain

In the Book of Truth …

SWIFTY [*approaching* D. PAPA]: So Papa, you don't really have magic?

Let me see you charm this poui-stick.

[SWIFTY *pokes* D. PAPA *in the ribs with his stick. The villagers laugh derisively.* SWIFTY *pokes* COOLIE *and* PELOO. *More laughter.* SWIFTY *returns to taunt* D. PAPA *but the obeahman in a rage snatches away the poui and slaps him down.*]

D. PAPA: Enough is enough! No force-ripe pup

Will ever brag that he ramfle up

Diable Papa. If the time come to go

I will leave in style, not a poppyshow.

Let the village gibe and jeer as they will,

I am the great Diable Papa still.

[*He stalks off in the stunned silence that follows his outburst.* PELOO *nudges* COOLIE *and the two agents creep out after their leader, leaving* MINEE *behind. The villagers now go into action and begin to harass the two accomplices. As they converge upon them outside, a low chuckle is heard. The men retreat into the store followed by* BRISCOE *who passes into the sick-room, giving* JOE *an apprehensive glance.*]

SEVERAL: The spirit come back …

He finish ransack

The traitors nest …

Now he will rest …

JOE: Spirit, my eye! I going to find out

What all this rigmarole is about.

Crackers, deal with Minee.

[*He goes into the room. The others crowd round the door.* CRACKERJACK *crosses to* MINEE.]

CRACKERJACK: Minee, you don't belong to that crew
          Of rascals, so you can choose whether you
          Will stay in the village and suffer revile
          Or follow Diable Papa into exile.

MINEE: I will go with him.

CRACKERJACK: Then depart now
          And don't darken the face of the village nohow
          Again. You bear a heavy cross, girl,
          Being born on the wrong side of the world.

[MINEE *leaves. After a moment* BRISCOE *emerges from the inner room, dressed normally, looking slightly dazed.* JOE *follows.*]

LILY: Is Briscoe self! He ain't really dead!

JOE: I find him faking sleep on the bed.

SEVERAL: Briscoe alive …!
          How come he revive …?
          Is a miracle
          We cannot unravel …?

INEZ: Briscoe, you come back among the living?

HANNIBAL: The occasion call for a bright thanksgiving.

ALICE: I had a feeling he wasn't a spirit.

SWIFTY: Me too! Somehow he didn't look right!

CRACKERJACK: Briscoe, we glad you ain't dead for true,
          But you have a deal of explaining to do.

SEVERAL: Tell the mystery …
          It will make history …
          How you come over
          Old Jordan river …

BRISCOE: I will try and explain best as I can
          But, believe me, I ain't no wonder-man,
          Whatever happen, happen by chance,
          Up to now I ain't sure of the circumstance.
          I know that I wake-up after the fight
          And couldn't get my bearings aright,
          I was lying there in the room alone

With Petite Belle Lilly, who had turned
Into an angel.

[*The crowd jeers at this.*]

Is true! For she even
Had water in her eye. I say I in heaven,
Especially when she start to caress
Me and do all kinds of stupidness.
Well, fellows, if this happen to you,
I ask you as man, what you would do?
So I decide not to break the spell
But stay quiet there, now, and then helping
Myself to a handy bottle of nectar –

JOE: Ninety-six proof Barbados liquor!

BRISCOE: After a while, I begin to feel good,
Ready to battle with all kinda wood,
Then, like a stab, suddenly I remember
That doctor-shop knife, Diable Papa,
How he deceive me. I jump out of bed
With one thought uppermost in my head
To pay him off; when, behold, a host
Of people declare: Briscoe is a ghost!
They carry on so, I could only suppose
Is true, I done dead and haunting my foes.
Well, I make for Diable Papa and Minee
One time, collecting old Peloo and Coolie
On the way. I harass the whole pack
Of them till they didn't know belly from back,
In the end, they decide to come and confess,
I say, Spirit, you do well and deserve a rest,
Go home, let them repose your body …
Next thing, Joe was shaking the life out of me.

CRACKERJACK: The strangest ballad
Told in Trinidad!

ALICE: He clear the land
Of the obeahman!

DAGGER: Death take a licking,

Briscoe is king!

TINY: Half my property go to Briscoe!

HANNIBAL: I will make him immortal in calypso!

THE MEN: One-two-three,

He's a lion, let him roar-ar-ar!

CRACKERJACK: Briscoe, I speak for the whole brood

Of stick-men, you earn our gratitude,

You come from behind and spring to fame

With lion courage, rescuing the game

From obeah, greed and politics,

And you give it back to the poui-sticks.

Therefore is needful we demonstrate

That the village consider you a great

And glorious warrior of renown,

Men, what you say?

THE MEN: Ay! Give him the crown!

The crown, the crown, give Briscoe the crown!

CRACKERJACK: Is the least we could do.

[*He beckons to bring up the rostrum.*]

Now, Briscoe, name,

The fair one who will share your fame.

BRISCOE: Circle the world, you will never find

A creature more loving, tender, kind,

A nurse to the sick, a staff to the weak,

A helper, inspirer, defender, the pick

Of everything lovely, warm, cool,

Soft, smooth, all woman, full

Of hidden delight, by day a sun

And when night come, the gentle moon.

I live and love under her spell

And offer my heart to the one Petite Belle.

CRACKERJACK: Lily, come forward and take your stand

Beside the champion, crown in hand.

> Tim Briscoe, conqueror of the field,
>
> Swift as lightning, sharper than steel,
>
> Wizard of wood, a terror in war,
>
> Brave as a lion whose mighty roar
>
> Spell death and destruction to the enemy,
>
> We crown you king!

[LILY *places the crown on* BRISCOE's *head.* HANNIBAL *leads the company in a victory chorus to the tune of 'Tiny the Champion'.*]

HANNIBAL [*singing*]: Briscoe catch the obeahman,

> Drop him in a frying-pan,
>
> When his bottom get real hot,
>
> Briscoe take 'way all he got.

CHORUS: Who win? Briscoe!

> Tim Briscoe is the hero.

A VOICE [*singing*]: Briscoe walk in the lion mouth,

> When you think he dead, he jump back out.

CHORUS: Who win? Briscoe!

> Tim Briscoe is the hero.

HANNIBAL [*singing*]: Briscoe set the village free,

> Make it safe for you and me,
>
> Briscoe prove the better man,
>
> Briscoe is the champion.

[*The crowd dances off carrying* BRISCOE *aloft.* INEZ *persuades* JOE *to leave the store and join in the merrymaking.*]

[*Curtain*]

CSEC® study guide for *Ti-Jean and His Brothers*

The CSEC English B syllabus

In the current CSEC English B syllabus, there are two examination papers plus a School Based Assessment (Paper 031, which carries 45 marks and a weight of 21 per cent of the total assessment).

Paper 01 is 1 hour 45 minutes long and consists of **three questions**, one from each of the three basic genres: drama, poetry and prose fiction. Each question is made up of between five and seven questions that require **short answers**. All the questions are compulsory. This paper carries 60 marks and a weight of 29 per cent of the total assessment.

Paper 02 is 2 hours 10 minutes long and requires **essay-type answers** to **three questions**, one from each genre: drama, poetry and prose. This paper carries 105 marks and a weight of 50 per cent of the total assessment.

In the drama section, there are two questions, one on each prescribed text. You must therefore answer the essay-type question on *Ti-Jean and His Brothers*, if this is the play you have studied. **Only one essay-type question will be based on this text.**

Practice for Paper 02 questions is provided in **Essay questions** (page 260).

The syllabus insists that drama is a unique literary genre. It includes elements of prose and poetry, but teachers and students should always bear in mind the following:

- Plays are meant to be performed, not read.
- Stage directions are cues to actors and directors.
- We understand character in drama primarily through the interactions onstage.
- Lighting, costumes and stage props help to develop character, themes and atmosphere in a production.

Because *Ti-Jean and His Brothers* is a dramatic work, seeing a live or filmed production is highly rewarding. Reading sections of the play in dramatic form (as if for a radio play) leads to discussions about character development and motivation, tone and the thematic concerns of the playwright, and the use of dramatic devices such as production elements and stage business. The ultimate reward probably comes from staging a production in the class or school, after the play has been thoroughly digested.

See page 246 for a key to some **Dramatic and literary terms** that will be useful in your study of *Ti-Jean and His Brothers*. Brief questions are also included to stimulate your thinking about the play.

Studying the text

A thorough knowledge of the text is essential in preparation for answering questions on *Ti-Jean and His Brothers*. At least three readings are recommended.

On the **first reading** you should become familiar with the plot and the main characters, and get some idea of the setting. You should complete this reading without any reference to notes or criticism or commentary. See **Explanatory words, phrases and notes** (page 250) for explanations of unfamiliar words and phrases.

Following the first reading, you should do some background work (see **Preliminary activities** (page 225).

The **second reading** involves close reading of the text, making notes and observations as you go along. Organize your notes under a series of headings, such as characterization, key themes, structure, dramatic techniques, use of props and other devices. This will help you to develop considerable insight into the play. You can use the **Review questions** (page 256) to focus your thinking, and provide you with practice for the short-answer questions in Paper 01.

Following the second reading, you should read Professor Hill's introduction to this play (pages 4–10), and the sections of this study guide that follow on the author, themes, characters, and dramatic and literary techniques (pages 228–249). See how many of the observations you agree with, or have picked up on your own. Remember as well that you are free to disagree with what critics or observers have said or written, once you can defend your point of view with evidence from the text.

The **third reading** is another fairly close reading, during which you begin to assemble your various perspectives on the play, and prepare to present a position, or defend one, on some aspect of the play as both a literary work and a text for live production.

After this reading, you should look at the **Essay questions** (page 260), which will help you to prepare for Paper 02. Begin by outlining possible answers to the questions listed, as well as to the other questions your teacher provides, or questions you may have seen elsewhere.

Preliminary activities

1 Prepare a short biography of Derek Walcott, highlighting the aspects of his life that recur in his poetry and plays. Attach a list of his plays in chronological order.

2 Explore and discuss the meaning of the following literary and dramatic terms:

    a Allegory

    b Fable

    c Verse drama

    d Morality play

    e The 'fourth wall' in a stage production

    f Folk tradition

    g Dramatic conflict

3 What do you consider to be the importance of the following in a stage production?

    a Music

    b Dance

    c Costuming

    d Set design and décor

    e Sound effects

    f Lighting and other visual effects

4 What are the functions of the following personnel involved in the production of a stage play?

    a Playwright

    b Director

    c Producer

    d Musical director

    e Stage manager

    f Actors

    g Choreographer

5 What do you understand by the following terms?

    a The colonial experience

    b The plantation economy

    c Existential struggle

Discuss the long-term effects on Caribbean life and society as a result of colonial rule.

6 Write brief descriptive notes on the following characters from Caribbean folklore:

   a Papa Bois

   b the Bolom

   c Douen

   d Loup Garoux (*lagahoo*)

   e Soucouyant

7 Is a play designed for production on a stage less effective when only read as a text? Are there any advantages to reading it as a text in addition to seeing a live performance?

8 Choose one instance of a rebellion by enslaved peoples in the Caribbean. What conditions prompted the outbreak? How successful was it, both in the short term and the long term?

9 Music and lyric sheets for *Ti-Jean and His Brothers* exist, and may be available (at a price) through Brenda Hughes at Monkey Mountain Ltd in Trinidad (tel: 1-868-463-7465; email: tisbea@hotmail.com.) A DVD version of a live performance is also available from the same source. If you can obtain one or other of these, this would be invaluable for any planned production, and would also help while studying the play.

10 Attend a local live production. Pay attention to how the production elements (lighting, music, dance, set, costume, etc.) function as part of the performance.

Answering essay questions

Essay-type answers to examination questions on literature texts require that you read the question carefully. You should determine exactly what you are being asked to do, for example, discuss, compare and contrast, explain, outline. A glossary of these words is available at the end of the current syllabus for the CSEC English B examination. Ask your teacher to go through them with you, and ask for further explanation and illustrations if necessary.

Answering a literature question is like preparing a legal argument. The argument is sounder and more convincing when you can cite evidence to support the point you are making. Evidence is generally one of the following:

- An event or set of events in the text
- What a character says or does
- What a character says about another character or something else

Be aware, however, that what a character says about another character or something else can often tell us more about the character speaking than the character or event they are speaking about.

Evidence should always be complementary, that is, one piece of evidence should support another. Evidence that contradicts other evidence, or contradicts your argument, will damage your answer.

Direct quotation is not absolutely necessary, so there is no need to learn long quotations from the text. You can paraphrase what a character says, or describe what a character does, or an event that takes place.

Pay special attention to the cues given in the stage directions about props and locations. These give information about how the playwright wants the audience to respond to a scene, character or particular action. You can cite these in your answers.

Derek Walcott

Derek Walcott was born on 23 January 1930 in Castries, St Lucia. His father, Warwick, a self-taught painter, died in 1931. Walcott, therefore, was raised primarily by his mother Alix, a schoolteacher who also took up sewing to help raise her three children. Of mixed ethnic heritage, Walcott was also Methodist by faith. This made for complications living in St Lucia, a predominantly Catholic island with a strong French cultural background, particularly as he went to a leading Catholic school on the island. St Lucia also boasted of a rich heritage of folklore that had amalgamated West African and European traditions.

Walcott's enthusiasm for poetry and painting was evident from an early age. His interest in painting was nurtured by fellow St Lucians Harold Simmons and Garth St Omer; he published his first collection of poems, *25 Poems,* in 1949, with financial assistance from his mother. As a student at the University of the West Indies' Mona campus, 1950–54, he also developed an interest in drama. While still a student there, he wrote and directed his earliest plays, including *The Sea at Dauphin*, set in St Lucia, and *Henri Christophe,* based on historical events in Haiti.

Walcott moved to Trinidad in 1958, and founded the Trinidad Theatre Workshop. This was initially a repertory company, performing a cycle of plays by various authors, but soon became almost exclusively a vehicle for Walcott's own growing body of dramatic work, with parts tailored for specific members of the company. Walcott's association with Beryl McBurnie, founder of the Little Carib Dance Company, gave him a vision of a truly West Indian theatre, and *Ti-Jean and His Brothers,* originally written as a simple folk fable in 1958, was soon expanded to include dance and music in a highly popular 1970 version.

Walcott's accomplishments in poetry and drama over the years have been internationally celebrated. His poetic output includes *In a Green Night* (1962), *The Castaway and other Poems* (1965), the autobiographical *Another Life* (1973), *The Fortunate Traveller* (1982) and *Omeros* (1989). His works for theatre include *Dream on Monkey Mountain* (published 1970), *The Joker of Seville* (published 1978), *Pantomime* (published 1980) and *The Odyssey: A Stage Version* (published 1993).

His prolific output was managed against a backdrop of lecturing and professorships at universities, staging or overseeing productions of his work internationally, and giving readings of his work.

Walcott's contribution to arts and letters, society, and West Indian and world culture has been recognized regionally and internationally, most significantly by the Nobel Prize for Literature in 1992, and by the following awards, among others:

- 1972: Order of the British Empire (OBE)
- 1981: MacArthur Foundation for Genius
- 1988: Queen's Gold Medal for Poetry
- 1992: Order of the Caribbean Community (OCC)
- 2011: OCM Bocas Prize for Caribbean Literature
- 2016: Knight Commander of the Order of St Lucia (KCSL)

Derek Walcott died in March 2017.

Themes

Good versus evil

At its simplest level, *Ti-Jean and His Brothers* can be read, like many folktales from many cultures, as an allegory about good and evil. It draws as well on the morality plays popular in medieval Europe, in which good and evil were in constant battle for human souls, which religious doctrine saw as inherently weak. In these plays, a central character or series of characters embark on a journey where their faith is severely tested. The protagonist is usually a composite character, who was called Everyman in the fifteenth-century play of the same name from which the term derives. While on a journey, the protagonist is set upon by the Devil in a variety of forms, usually the seven deadly sins, or as a composite of sins known as the Vice.

In this light, we can see the three brothers as a single composite character, which accounts for their names all being Jean, or John. Each brother has a unique attribute that alone cannot withstand temptation but when they are joined together, they wield formidable strength ('Here's a bundle of sticks that/ Old wisdom has forgotten. Together they are strong,/Apart, they are all rotten' page 67). Their antagonist is also a composite character, Old Man (Papa Bois), Planter and Devil, armed with a bagful of tricks and powerful enforcers (his band of assistant devils) to back him up.

As a shapeshifter who 'can hide in several features' (page 34), the Devil undoes the first two brothers by playing on what they consider their great strengths. Gros Jean boasts, 'I have nothing, I 'fraid, man, beast or beast-man' (page 36), so he is worn down by menial, repetitive tasks and by being called names which deny his individuality and manhood. Mi-Jean assumes intellectual and scholarly airs, but is bested when these are exposed as shallow and pretentious. Both brothers are victims of pride; they are also victims of desiring material things: wealth, property and fame.

The Devil's great asset is his understanding of human weaknesses, and his ability to exploit them. He is also prepared to renege on his word: 'He who would with the devil play fair,/Weaves the net of his own despair.' (page 63). Punishment for those he entraps is presented in the traditional colours of Hell: 'springs of sulphur, where the damned souls are cooking' (page 55), and where the only refreshment cocktail is 'brimstone with a saltpetre chaser' (page 59).

The forces of good arrayed against the Devil are primarily the Mother and the forest creatures, but survival also depends on belief in and love of God, and a healthy blend of 'Instinct', 'Conscience' and 'plain sense' (page 51). The forest creatures are themselves powerless against the Devil, and flee from him whenever he approaches, but their knowledge and their indirect assistance reward Ti-Jean, the only brother to respect them and heed their advice. The Bird can therefore help expose the Old Man (page 55), and the Frog urges Ti-Jean to sing in harmony with Nature and God to help ward off the Devil (page 65).

Ti-Jean is the character through whom the idea of goodness is expressed in specifically Christian terms. The absolute belief of the Mother in God's concern for man's welfare ('Wait, and God will send us something.' (page 28) is transmitted also to Ti-Jean. 'You have told me yourself … our life is God's own.' (page 50) he tells her, and he repeats this credo to the Old Man: 'Whatever God made, we must consider blessed.' (page 54). 'I'm as scared as Christ.' (page 63) he tells the Devil under threat, and what he sings at the urging of the Frog at his moment of greatest desperation is a mini-prayer of acceptance (pages 65–66).

The Mother is the most potent symbol of good in the play. She is identified with light (page 27), 'white light' (page 63) and 'the golden/Light of the sun' (page 65), which emphasize her function both as the light to guide her sons as well as the light of God and goodness that must be invoked against the Devil. As the intercessor (one who pleads on behalf of others), she is clearly being associated with the Mother of Jesus, who is ascribed this role in the Christian, especially Catholic, tradition. She is also the universal Earth Mother of traditional folklore who nurtures and protects all humanity.

The Mother is also presented as the embodiment of that most divine grace, selfless love. It is that discernible quality in her that makes the otherwise hostile Bolom momentarily reach out to her. She is called a 'creature of gentleness', in whose otherwise wretched hovel 'Love keeps the house warm' (page 31). For the Bolom, she is the opposite of the woman who 'hated my birth' (page 31). Even from beyond the grave, she reaches out to protect her youngest son (page 65). It is the quality of the bond between son and mother that eventually touches the Devil and leads him to spare Ti-Jean.

It is useful to remember, however, that the playwright does not suggest that Ti-Jean's escape means that the victory of good over evil is inevitable. The play ends on a somewhat ambiguous note. 'We shall meet again, Ti-Jean.' says the Devil on departing, 'The features will change, but the fight is still on.' (page 67). The Devil has also suggested the ambiguous nature of good and evil earlier in the play: 'Yet we were one light once up there, the old man [God] and I, till even today some can't tell us apart.' (page 60), and reminds us that he once sat in Heaven at God's right hand.

Even the choice of the Bolom to be human may prove to be a double-edged sword, as Ti-Jean warns: be careful of what you ask for. In this ambiguity, therefore, Ti-Jean is forever cast in folklore as a vigilant protector of human safety, the Moon that offers some light in the dark of night, needed 'to lighten the doubt of all travellers through the shadowy wood of life' (page 67). As the Frog says in the Prologue, 'God put him in that height/To be the sun's right hand/And light the evil dark' (page 24).

Resistance and rebellion

Ti-Jean and His Brothers is also an allegory about resistance and rebellion in West Indian life. It draws on the shared history of the Caribbean as a place where enslaved peoples and indentured labourers were brought, and where the burden of that history and the colonial system that it imposed critically limited the potential of these people and their descendants. Slavery, the plantation system, indenture and the colonial structures and social systems that dominated Caribbean history for over 400 years created ways of seeing and thinking about the world that are still evident today.

In broad terms, the Planter/Devil is identified with the white ruling class of pre- and post-emancipation societies. As colonial master, the Planter controls all means of production, and worries about his 'eighty-five per cent of the profit' (page 38): 'It might rain, people may be stealing from me now. The market is unsteady this year.' (page 40). While others starve, he however 'is eating/From plates painted golden' (page 28) and lives in 'a hell of a big white house' (page 38).

In his world view, all on his plantation, whether free or not, are little more than means to an end, and without identity or significance. 'Can't tell one face from the next out here', he complains (page 39). Calling Gros Jean by a litany of incorrect names denies him any individuality; 'we people in charge of industry forget that you people aren't machines', the Planter tells him (page 40).

It is difficult to escape the innuendoes in the script which suggest that some of the Planter/Devil's attitude has its basis in a sense of racial and social superiority. His skin is 'Powdery as leprosy' (page 27); the Old Man cautions Gros Jean about 'the white planter' who will 'work you like the devil' (page 36), and Gros Jean himself complains about being overworked by the 'damn white man' (page 37). Even the Mother challenges the Bolom in the Prologue: 'What does your white master/The Devil want from us?' (page 31).

Because the Planter/Devil also controls the education system, and dominates social life in the territories, the colonial establishment throws up people like Mi-Jean who mimic his affectations and thus become objects of parody. The Planter/Devil mocks Mi-Jean's pretensions to be like he is: 'Descendant of the ape, how eloquent you have become! How assured in logic! How marvellous in invention! And yet, poor shaving monkey, the animal in you is still in evidence', (page 49). He explodes in anger at Ti-Jean when he realizes he has been outwitted by someone he considers inferior: 'I've been watching you, you little nowhere nigger!' (page 63), a reprise on an earlier comment made about Gros Jean's ambition: 'Other people want what I have, Charley, and other people have more. Can't help myself, Joe, it's some sort of disease and it spreads right down to the common man.' (page 39).

The Planter's life relies on keeping others poor and dependent. Their existence reads like a compendium of relentless and mind-numbing activity on the plantation, whether sugar, tobacco or cotton: counting leaves on the canestalks, catching fireflies or chasing a capricious goat. Walcott deliberately makes these activities tedious and pointless to suggest that life in the service of the plantation and colonial society is a life devoid of quality or meaning.

He goes further, in the character of the unborn Bolom, to suggest that generations of Caribbean people have been denied the opportunity to fulfil themselves and their potentialities, 'a child which was strangled/Who never saw the earth light …Twisted out of shape,/Deformed past recognition.' (page 31). It is symbolic that the Bolom should want so much to be alive, to become 'man', regardless of the warnings offered by the Mother and Ti-Jean.

We may therefore read *Ti-Jean and His Brothers* as a sequence of attempts to resist a political, social and economic system that has historically limited Caribbean man. Some have interpreted the episodes involving the three brothers in the context of plantation slavery. In this view, Gros Jean's 'rebellion' is that of the resentful 'field slave', with little else to call on but his own brawn. Mi-Jean is aligned with the 'house slave' ('come up to the house, check and polish the silver, rearrange my library', (page 46) who tries to come to terms with his situation by absurdly aping his master. Ti-Jean, in this interpretation, is cast along the lines of a Toussaint L'Ouverture, choosing 'rank disobedience' (page 61) and invoking the ancestral spirits in his cause.

Another interpretation looks to the events of more recent historical times, and sees the efforts of the brothers as that of Caribbean people trying to come to terms with a legacy of enslavement, exploitation and diminishment under colonial rule. This view interprets Gros Jean's desires to control the economic means of production as characteristic of the mass labour movement and unrest that swept across the Caribbean in the 1930s. Mi-Jean echoes the middle classes of the early and mid-twentieth century, many of whose mantra was to come to terms with the ruling classes (speak, hear and see no evil). Like their former masters, success seemed to lie in entering the merchant trade (hence the reference to 'rich captain', (page 42) or taking up law or similar professions.

One senses in the characterization of Mi-Jean an added barb aimed at the lawyer-politicians of the post-Second World War era who, in the opinion of many, failed to provide visionary leadership when it was so urgently needed. Ti-Jean, in this reading of the play, embodies the spirit of the nationalist movements of the 1960s, the radicalism of the American Black Power movement (which had many people of West Indian origin in its leadership), and the resurgence of racial consciousness and the value placed on inherited traditions throughout the region.

Ti-Jean's success, we can argue, derives from his willingness to use all avenues at his disposal, including attacking the very heart of the system by uniting the masses behind his cause, using his native wit and intelligence instead of playing strictly by the book, and invoking the religious and cultural traditions represented by his Mother and the forest creatures. The Bolom, for whom Ti-Jean requests life, becomes symbolic of a new if challenging promise for Caribbean people, Ti-Jean's 'little brother' (page 67), setting off on a journey of self-discovery under the protection of the man in the moon.

Coping with life's challenges

Ti-Jean and His Brothers raises the question of how we cope with life's challenges, and whether we can ever successfully manoeuvre our way through or around them. Life, in a sense, is like the dark, mysterious forest through which the brothers must pass, and there is no guarantee that we will emerge safely.

These challenges exist at a number of levels. The most basic level involves coping with social and economic circumstances. The poverty and hardship the family faces are emphasized throughout the Prologue. 'Oh that was poverty, bird!' exclaims the Frog (page 25), after our attention has been drawn in the stage directions to the 'empty bowl' (page 24) suggesting this. 'One time again it have nothing to eat,' Gros Jean complains (page 27); 'God forget where he put us'. (page 28). This is not a universal condition, however, since others like the Planter eat with silver forks off golden plates.

For the deprived, such wealth and power have enormous appeal. When the Old Man tells Gros Jean that what counts in this world is money and power, the eldest brother doesn't only want wealth, he wants it in the quickest way possible. Mi-Jean, for whom physical work is too hard, dreams of being first a rich sea captain then a successful lawyer. But power and knowledge, the script indicates, are not enough in themselves. 'Power is knowledge, knowledge is power, and the Devil devours them on the hour!' exclaims the Old Man (page 50), referring to the deceased elder brothers. Without the 'wit', or intelligence to unite and guide them that Ti-Jean exhibits, power and knowledge have limited value.

At another level, the play provokes questions about the value of life itself. Existence is shown at times to be a finite and often difficult thing, and death is always lurking. The Mother tells the Bolom that it might be better 'Never to be born,/To the horror of this life/Crowded with shadows,/Never to have known/ That the sun will go out,/The green leaf rust' (page 30). The sense that all life is finite and fragile, and that death hovers over everything, recurs time and again during the play. The Mother is reluctant to let her third son surrender to 'the blind jaws/Of the carnivorous grave' (page 50) and even the Devil intones mockingly in semi-intoxication, 'Oh, I lack heart to enjoy the brevity of the world!' (page 60). Flesh, as the Old Man says, is decidedly 'deciduous' (page 37).

Yet interestingly, the Devil himself yearns to abandon immortality; 'He is dying to be human.' (page 32), says the Bolom, giving an ironic twist to the narrative. The Bolom itself wishes to be human, despite the early warning of the Mother, and the final injunction by Ti-Jean: 'Don't blame me when you are suffering,/When you lose everything,/And when the time come/ To put two gold coins/On your eyes.' (page 66). Ti-Jean himself says that he thinks 'nothing dies' (page 54). Like its central character, the play seems to be ambivalent on the question of whether human life is meaningful, leaving both him and the audience no less clear on 'the tangled opinions of this life' (page 67).

Other themes

Appearance versus reality

There are several warnings in the play that things should not be taken at face value. 'The Devil can hide in several features', the Mother warns Gros Jean (page 34), and the forest creatures tell Ti-Jean to 'Beware of an old man whose name is worldly wisdom.' (page 52). The Devil/Planter/Old Man is the best example of this uncertain reality, the play being scripted in such a fashion that they are barely distinguishable from each other.

Celebrating West Indian culture and tradition

The use of West Indian colonial history as the background to the story, the inclusion of folk elements like the Bolom, Papa Bois and the storytelling structure, and the extensive use of indigenous music and dance give this play a strong Caribbean flavour. Deliberately choosing to use a mix of dialect, French patois, standard French and standard English idiom also suggests the multicultural heritage of the islands.

The virtue of common sense

Ti-Jean has neither the arm of iron of his eldest brother, nor the bookishness of Mi-Jean, but he accomplishes what they cannot by listening (to his Mother and the forest creatures), testing what he sees or is told, and applying his own intuition and inventiveness to solving the tasks given. Common sense guides him as well to forge strategic alliances (with the forest creatures and the field hands) and to call for help from external sources (the spirits of his brothers, his Mother and God) when everything else fails.

Characters
The family

The family of three, under the protection of a mother figure, appears regularly in folklore. The number three also has religious and mystical properties in many cultures. The journey that each son must make, through a dark and threatening forest, is essentially a journey of self-discovery, and the older sons usually fail as a result of flaws in their characters. It is the third son, seemingly less well equipped for the challenges ahead, who eventually triumphs over adversity.

The Mother

In this play, the Mother lives in isolation and poverty. Despite the deprivations of her life, she maintains a strong core of religious belief, and a conviction that when all else fails, God will provide. She schools her children in this tradition. She is associated with images of light, and parallels both the Virgin Mary of Catholic tradition and the Earth Mother of African and Asian cultures by acting as an intercessor with the divine on behalf of her children. As Earth or Universal Mother, her maternal instincts make the Bolom, otherwise hostile, warm to her.

She is positioned in the play as the Devil's antithesis, though he himself sees her as the victim of a misplaced religious fervour, a 'poor withered fool who thinks it's holy to be poor, who scraped her knees to the knuckle praying to an old beard that's been deaf since noise began' (page 62). Two of her three sons die, and so does she; the Devil loses nothing and attempts to abandon the agreement he has made via the Bolom in the Prologue.

Gros Jean

As has been suggested by a few commentators on the play, Gros Jean echoes elements of a limited kind of resistance to enslavement and colonial rule. He is aspirational, seeing a future in which he could be in charge of his own destiny: 'Because I come from that mountain forest, don't mean I can't come like you, or because I black. One day this could be mine!' (page 39).

He boasts of an arm of iron and a sharp axe, but he ironically keeps the latter rust free by not using it when he should (page 27). This may imply an inability to effectively employ all resources at his disposal. He is unable to cope when the Planter handicaps his strength by giving him repetitive tasks that call for brain rather than brawn.

Following the traditional structure of the fable, his is a journey for material rather than spiritual success. He disregards the advice of both his mother and the forest creatures, even the ironic guidance of the Old Man/Papa Bois, whom he knocks over and threatens with violence. 'With your arm of iron, the first thing to kill is wisdom?' (page 36) says the Old Man ironically. His approach to life is captured, perhaps mocked, by the martial music that is his accompaniment in the stage directions.

Mi-Jean

Would-be lawyer and wealthy sea captain, Mi-Jean's props are a net of behaviours and ambitions in which he has seemingly entangled himself, and a book, to which he is intellectually enslaved and out of which he expects to find all answers. Mi-Jean fits, as we have seen, into several interpretations of the enslaved or oppressed who seek liberation by internalizing as best as they can the world view of the dominant class, into which they will never be accepted.

'Please know your place' (page 41), he admonishes the forest creatures, echoing the superior attitude the Planter displayed to his elder brother, and foreshadowing the similar putdown he will himself experience. Such individuals, it is suggested, become not only absurd in themselves, but cannot compete in a contest for which they have neither the expertise nor the experience.

Like Gros Jean, Mi-Jean ignores any opportunity for advice from either the forest creatures or the Old Man ('I don't need none, but will listen'. (page 43). He pays for the lack of perception brought about by his own vanity, claiming that the Old Man cannot be the Devil 'Since he would never expose/His identity so early' (page 44). His debate with the Devil, phrased in quasi-intellectual mumbo-jumbo, is among the play's funniest moments.

Ti-Jean

The titular hero of the play says little in the Prologue and is entirely absent in Acts One and Two. The youngest brother, small in stature, weak of arm and lacking book learning, he ventures into the contest with the Planter/Devil, however, with assets of his own. These include: a firm belief in the power of love as espoused and passed on by his mother and her religious faith; the folk hero's natural sympathy and identification with the forest creatures, and a willingness to listen to them; an innate sense of scepticism about the behaviour and intentions of those he meets on his journey; and an understanding that emancipation from a superior force will only result from utilizing all the resources at his disposal.

He is prepared to call on his fellow field workers to join the resistance, and invoke the strength and intervention of his brothers, his Mother and God when all else fails. He shares with the Anansi figure of African and West Indian folktales, the *picaro* of popular Spanish culture and the monkey of Hindu and Buddhist folklore, a strong strain of inventiveness, common sense and street smarts. Identified by critics as perhaps referencing Toussaint L'Ouverture, or more contemporary challenges to the legacy of colonialism, he is responsible for earning the Bolom life, and the hope of new beginnings.

The Devil

Like the three brothers, the Devil is also a composite character, partially modelled on the Vice of European morality plays, a character whose task it is to lure unsuspecting or ill-prepared humans to Hell. In *Ti-Jean and His Brothers*, the Devil wears two convenient masks, first that of Papa Bois, the Old Man of the Forest, drawn from African and West Indian folklore, then that of the Planter, oppressive symbol of a history of enslavement and diminished humanity.

Papa Bois

The use of the Papa Bois figure confirms Walcott's intention to give his play regional relevance. Papa Bois is usually seen depicted as a reclusive forest character, protector of fauna and flora, but a threat to those who work or dwell in the forest. His cloven hoof yet human features indicate his mixed parentage, half human and half divine, like his counterpart Pan in Greek mythology.

Papa Bois is the first of the three incarnations each brother meets on his journey; for each he offers enigmatic advice, like the Oracle of Greek tradition. Gros Jean is told in ironic terms, 'He'll work you like the devil, but that's what you want' (page 36). He is disregarded by Mi-Jean. He duels philosophically with Ti-Jean for a brief moment, but morphs quickly into the Devil at Ti-Jean's insistence once his secret is discovered.

The Planter

The Planter represents the economic control wielded on the estates and under colonial rule. As the encounter with Gros Jean suggests, even after emancipation, and possibly political independence, key control remains in the hands of industrialists and capitalists. We have, the script hints, substituted one form of servitude for another.

The Planter hears and resents Gros Jean's desire to be like him in social and economic terms. His attitude to Gros Jean also has roots in a sense of racial and social superiority, and this is emphasized further when Mi-Jean attempts to match wits with him on what he considers an intellectual level. 'Your brother was a sort of politician, but you're a thinker.' (page 48), says the Planter mockingly.

The Devil

Stripped of his Papa Bois and Planter masks, Walcott's Devil is presented not as a one-dimensional bad guy, but as one who has internal dramatic conflict over his sense of lost prominence as God's former 'bright, starry lieutenant' (page 62), and the curse of immortality, provoking a latent desire to be human.

Walcott endows his Devil with a caustic sense of humour, occasionally self-directed, which makes his exchanges with the three brothers some of the playwright's funniest work. He disarms Gros Jean in a show of false camaraderie (pages 38–40); as the Planter, he ties Mi-Jean up into intellectual knots. There is a hilarious interlude when the intoxicated Devil momentarily ruminates on the tragic dimension of his existence and his fall from grace, then dismisses it: 'Oh, to hell with that! You lose a job, you lose a job' (page 60), which is followed by his growing realization that Ti-Jean has turned the tables against him (pages 61–63).

The Devil, we are reminded from time to time, however, is also an ominous presence, heralded in the Prologue by the Bolom as he who 'Has done all that is evil/Butchered thousands in war,/Whispered his diseases/In the ears of great statesmen' (page 32), or revealed to Ti-Jean in all his frightening glory (page 56). There is an ongoing subtext that God and the Devil are like opposite sides of the same coin. This 'is like looking/At the blinding gaze of God', exclaims Ti-Jean on seeing the Devil's face (page 56). This plays to the proposition that knowledge of good requires knowledge of evil; in Ti-Jean's words, 'To know evil early, life will be simpler.' (page 53).

The Devil's yearning to be human gives the play an interesting ironic tone. Having presented human life as little more than an inevitable journey of suffering to decay and death, the instigator of much of that suffering desires to experience it: 'O Christ, how weary it is to be immortal.' (page 60). Part of mortality involves the experience of love, which is no longer his. 'Oh, nobody loves me,' he complains. 'I had the only love of God once … but I lost that' (page 60). There is, it would appear, an ironic downside to being forever imprisoned in the role of evil tormentor.

The critic Paul Breslin has suggested that in this brief moment the Devil represents the former colonial powers eager to grant their former colonies political independence in the face of civil unrest, diminishing profits and cumbersome administrative requirements. If so, his parting words seem prophetic: 'The features will change, but the fight is still on.' (page 67). Will one master be replaced by another, who is even more deceptive and dangerous?

The Bolom

The Bolom, or spirit of an unborn child, is a creature of West African and Caribbean folklore. Presented in the play initially as an emissary of the Devil, it responds instinctively to the love inherent in the Mother, recognizing her as a 'creature of gentleness' (page 31) whose house is kept warm by that love. Like the Devil, the Bolom too feels the urge to be mortal, and is rewarded with this status as a result of Ti-Jean's success.

The Bolom's symbolic value in the drama is that of the many enslaved or indentured generations who have laboured in the plantation system, and who have yet to be truly 'emancipated' from the internalized consequences of colonialism. That freedom is the fragile promise offered by the birth it is granted.

The forest creatures

Collectively, the forest creatures echo the functions of the Greek chorus, keeping the audience informed about things not visible onstage, providing insight into character motivation and plot development, commenting critically on the action being played out, and at times interacting with the characters onstage. Like the allegorical creatures of fable, they are endowed with the power to communicate with each other and with humans. They are benevolent to people like Ti-Jean who treat them respectfully and recognize their individuality. They are powerless against Papa Bois and the Devil, and are afraid of them, but their insider knowledge assists Ti-Jean on his journey.

The Frog is the most individualized of the creature chorus, being the primary storyteller who both opens and closes the action of the play. He is the one at whom Gros Jean aims a kick, Mi-Jean insults, and whose appearance briefly frightens the Devil (page 60).

The Cricket, Bird and Firefly provide the reprise in the tell-and-respond storytelling format employed the creatures.

Dramatic and literary techniques
Structure

Ti-Jean and His Brothers is divided into a conventional three-act structure, preceded by a prologue drawn from Greek classical drama. This Prologue introduces all the main characters, outlines the principal plot device, establishes the various locations for the action to follow, and provides context (for example, explaining the significance of the Ti-Jean story in folklore). In this Prologue, the forest creatures who narrate the action are also given individual speaking parts, and are allowed to intervene in the main action on occasion. Furthermore, the Prologue emphasizes the key roles that music, song and dance will play in the production.

The Prologue establishes many of the elements of West Indian folklore that will be incorporated within the play. The opening spoken couplets, employing a series of puns, remind us of the opening salutation of an oral folktale. The setting and characters are unmistakeably West Indian in presentation, if not in origin, and the tale itself draws on St Lucian folklore to tell the story of a challenge between the Devil and three sons. The invasion of the stage by the band of devils draws on street theatre in the Caribbean, in particular the traditional Devil mas of the Trinidad Carnival. The use of French patois, alongside dialect and standard English, anchors the play's West Indian setting.

Each of the following three Acts follows a parallel dramatic spine:

- A farewell to the Mother and home (by implication only in Act Two)
- A meeting with the forest creatures
- An encounter with Papa Bois, the traditional Old Man of the Forest
- A climactic encounter with the Devil
- A denouement, or resolution, of the action (more prolonged in Act Three)

Spectacle

Spectacle is one of Aristotle's six Elements of Drama in classical Greek theatre (the others being plot, theme, characters, dialogue and rhythm). It is defined as all of the aspects of scenery, costuming and special effects, such as lighting and sound in a stage production, and their contribution to the overall presentation. Modern theatre has replaced 'spectacle' with an alternative term, 'convention', which refers to all of the techniques used by a playwright and director to create a desired effect.

The impact of spectacle is appreciated only by seeing a live or filmed production. In classroom study, the impact of spectacle is easily lost, suggested only by cues in the stage directions, if any, or what is embedded in the dialogue or onstage action.

Set and set design

The stage directions before the Prologue relate to the set: a hut on a remote mountain, vaguely illuminated within, overlooks a forest, which itself fringes a plantation. Only in the imagination, however, does the action onstage take place in these locations; the actual playing area becomes an abstract representation of the three spaces. A set design for this play, depending on available resources, could range from the elaborate and detailed to the stark and restricted.

Lighting

Detailed cues for lighting are provided. Light is used to symbolize character or condition (for example, blue for the Bolom). The references to evening and early dawn can be created by lighting, and there are invitations to creative light design when the devil band invades the stage (page 26), when the Devil first exposes his true self to Ti-Jean (page 55) and when explosions and smoke mark the end of Gros Jean and Mi-Jean (also serving to mask the actors' disappearance from the stage). The offstage burning of the fields and estate house also invites relevant lighting effects.

Sound effects

Sound effects are extensively cued in the script. Some are executed via music or musical instruments (the crashing of cymbals, the chanting of devils) while others, like the bleating of a goat, the sound of thunder or the crying of a child, rely on offstage effects.

Costuming

There are few suggestions in the text to guide costuming except for those relating to the character of the Devil, who is given a cloven hoof, a tail, a sackcloth robe (for Papa Bois), perhaps a Planter's outfit, and two masks used interchangeably in various sequences. The forest creatures depend on costuming of some sort to distinguish them. A costume designer will outfit the family members as prescribed by their poverty-stricken circumstances, except for the axe that Gros Jean wields, and the net and book for Mi-Jean, which are essential to their characterization.

Music, song and dance

Music, song and dance are integral to this version of the Walcott play
(the earlier 1958 version lacked these). Their inclusion resulted from the
playwright's association, while resident in Trinidad, with Beryl McBurnie, folk
dance pioneer and champion, and composer/musician Andre Tanker.

The nature of most of the music employed is suggested by either character or
context. Gros Jean's aggressive outlook is complemented by drums, a military
rhythm and his own marching feet. Each stanza of Mi-Jean's 'The Song of
Silence' is a parody of the 'speak, hear and see no evil' stance he chooses to
adopt as a strategy against the Planter. Ti-Jean's plaintive sung prayer (page 66)
is followed by the call-and-response energy of a communal Baptist spiritual or
a stick-fighting song. Even the Devil has a brief solo in the santimanitay (*sans
humanité*) calypso tradition (page 59).

Dance elements vary from the frenzy of the devil band (page 26) to the
suggested grace of the forest creatures (page 52). Several productions have,
in fact, choreographed all of the movements of the forest creatures onstage,
suggesting distance from human turmoil and a harmony with nature and each
other (pages 35–37).

Language

Walcott's use of language in *Ti-Jean and His Brothers* is particularly striking.
The Devil, for example, is the only character, in his various entities, who
speaks in standard English throughout, either in prose or blank verse (except
for his brief flirtation with calypso); the effect is to emphasize his foreign
origins, especially as a Planter.

The Planter's tone and mannerisms with Gros Jean, however, are those of
a stereotypical American businessman, betrayed by his use of names like Joe,
Charley and Mac, and his repeated insistence on industry, the markets and the
profit imperative. The manner and language set adopted for Mi-Jean appears
closer to that of the patronizing Englishman, via specific vocabulary (bugger,
gaff), referencing Hamlet and Pythagoras (essential knowledge in a classical
British education) and the concealed insult within what appears to be praise:
'You're the kind of chap I like to talk to. Your brother was a sort of politician,
but you're a thinker.' (page 48).

The three brothers, on the other hand, utilize a West Indian dialect, liberally
sprinkled with French patois. Gros Jean's monologue (pages 37–38) is the
best extended example, but it is funny to hear Mi-Jean fumbling to maintain
a pretence of supposedly sophisticated language as the Planter snares him in a
net of words.

Ti-Jean switches effortlessly from dialect to standard English. He also uses lyrical verse, which groups him with the Mother, the forest creatures and the Bolom. This may well indicate the playwright's intention of indicating their singularity as well as a connection with divine or other-worldly forces.

Despite its often serious subject matter, *Ti-Jean and His Brothers* is laced with humour throughout. Some of this is visual, for example, Mi-Jean's futile pursuit of the goat, or Gros Jean's exaggerated marching style. But most of it stems from how language is used. Walcott's love for the pun leads him to play on the sound and meaning of words throughout the text. Some are self-evident, such as Mi-Jean's de bait and debate, or 'It have plenty recipe/But it don't give the source!' (page 43) or Gros Jean's lament at the pain of his futile attempt to catch fireflies: 'one whap with the hand! Thinking was a bunch but was nothing, only stars!' (page 38).

Many of the puns have ironic or satirical intent. 'You have an eye for detail!' (page 43) is the backhanded compliment paid to Mi-Jean who fails to see the Devil's tail in the Old Man. He directs Ti-Jean to find the Devil in 'the springs of sulphur, where the damned souls are cooking' (page 55). Even the Devil gets in, so to speak, on the pun: 'this is no play, son./For here is the Devil' (page 56).

There is irony, we have seen, in the portrayal of the Devil, trapped in the paradox of his purpose in life, namely to destroy man, yet secretly wanting to experience mortal experience and emotion. He is, one may claim, the antithesis of all God represents, yet, as he recognizes, 'It is hard to distinguish us' (page 56). We are reminded, through the Devil, of the dual nature of the world, where often what seems desirous and attractive may well be poisonous.

Dramatic and literary terms

Allegory

In an allegory, characters in a picture, story, poem, play, novel, etc., are used to represent particular ideas or qualities. The intention is to give added layers of meaning to the work. Often, the allegorical dimension focuses on moral, political, religious or social issues. Famous examples of allegory include George Orwell's *Animal Farm* and John Bunyan's *The Pilgrim's Progress*. Modern use of allegory tends to be less explicit than in those two works. *Is the Mother in* Ti-Jean and His Brothers *an allegorical figure? What about the Bolom?*

Blocking

Blocking is the positioning of actors onstage in relation to the set, other characters and the audience during specific scenes. Effective blocking can suggest the dynamic between actors in a scene or exchange. Blocking also serves the practical purpose of ensuring that actors remain visible to the audience, and that critical moments are not lost by being too removed from important focal points. *How would you block the sequence in the Prologue when the Devil and his fiends invade the stage (page 26)?*

Chorus

In Ancient Greek theatre, the chorus was a group of performers not directly involved in the central action, but often used to narrate events, provide continuity over passages of time, and to comment knowingly on events and individuals. They were also involved intermittently in ensemble singing and dancing. Some dramatists later allowed them to be involved in the action at key moments. Aeschylus was the playwright first credited with individualizing members of the chorus, a device Walcott also employs in *Ti-Jean and His Brothers*. *When does the chorus (Cricket, Frog, Firefly, Bird) intervene directly during* Ti-Jean and His Brothers, *and with what consequences?*

Conflict

Conflict is the core of all drama. It is the struggle between opposing forces in a play. These forces may be external, such as between characters, or between opposing points of view. The antagonist (opposing force) need not always be an individual; it may be fate, or circumstances, or sometimes just another point of view. Conflict can also be internal, within characters, when opposing tensions within an individual propel the drama. Some levels of conflict only become apparent when a play is critically examined; sometimes characters in a play are unaware of the conflict within them, which leads to irony. Whether the levels of conflict within a script are successfully resolved, and how this is attempted, often creates what is called the dramatic spine of a work. *Identify the conflict you observe between the Mother and the Devil, and within the Devil, in* Ti-Jean and His Brothers.

Costuming

In a carefully thought-out production, the costumes not only capture some of the essence of a character, but the overall costuming design will work with the set design to complement or enhance the director's interpretation of the script. *What ideas would you have for costuming each of the three brothers and their mother in* Ti-Jean and His Brothers? *With limited resources at your disposal, how would you costume each of the forest creatures?*

Fable

A fable is usually a short fictional work in which animals, creatures and inanimate objects are given human qualities and allowed to speak. The intention of a fable is usually didactic, that is, to illustrate or emphasize some moral lesson. Aesop's fables are the best known example of this genre, but fables are universal and found in most cultures, especially those with rich oral traditions, where they were important teaching tools. *Are we meant to learn any moral lessons from* Ti-Jean and His Brothers?

Irony, satire and parody

While they are commonly employed as literary or linguistic devices even in normal daily conversation, defining and distinguishing between these three can pose some challenges. The intention of irony is to highlight differences between what is said or done, and reality. Its tone can range from deeply tragic to bitingly critical. Satire is a close cousin to irony, but more easily apparent, since it exposes and ridicules follies and vices critically, by making fun of its targets. Parody has a similar intention, and depends heavily on irony and satire for effect, exaggerating appearance, speech, mannerisms and practices. *Who or what is the playwright satirizing in the portrayal of Mi-Jean in this play? Is there any irony implied in the Bolom's desire for human life?*

Line reading

This refers to the way in which an actor delivers a particular line in the script. It is often determined by the director, sometimes in collaboration with the actor. The line reading can help audiences to understand nuances, tone and perspective, and are generally consistent with the director's overall interpretation of the script, or the actor's understanding of his/her character. *Ti-Jean's responses to the Devil in Act Three (pages 61–62) invite a variety of line readings; explore some of them.*

Monologue

A monologue is an extended, unbroken number of lines given to an actor and addressed directly to either the audience or other characters in the play. In an interior monologue, or soliloquy, the character externalizes thoughts and feelings solely for the audience's benefit, and cannot be heard by other characters onstage; a dramatic monologue is usually addressed to other characters. Analyse the effectiveness of Gros Jean's monologue in Act One (pages 37–38) and the Devil's intoxicated soliloquy in Act Three (pages 60–61). *Would you consider any of the songs in* Ti-Jean and His Brothers *to be monologues?*

Prologue

Another theatrical device that traces its history back to classical Greek drama, a prologue also occurs in other literary forms. A prologue opens the narrative by establishing the locale, introducing the main characters and hinting at the principal themes, thereby providing background detail. An epilogue, which is less widely used, brings closure to the work. The function of an epilogue is often replaced by lines spoken by an actor involved in the central proceedings, as we see in *Ti-Jean and His Brothers*. *How effectively does the Prologue achieve its objectives in* Ti-Jean and His Brothers? *To what extent do you think it necessary to the play?*

Set design

An effective set design uses the available stage space to create atmosphere and establish locale. Set designers can work in a highly realistic mode, or can opt for symbolic or abstract sets. The set design is generally complemented by the costume design. *If you were asked to design a set for* Ti-Jean and His Brothers, *what would you need to consider before you make your first sketch?*

Stage

The stage is the physical space where a production is staged. Traditional (or proscenium) stages are 'enclosed' on three sides, with an imaginary fourth wall separating the onstage action from the audience. Some productions attempt greater audience intimacy via use of a thrust stage, which extends from the proscenium into the audience. To further break the fourth wall, an actor sometimes addresses the audience directly.

Greek drama was originally staged in open-air amphitheatres, with semi-concave elevated seating and the staging area in the middle and towards one end. Many modern stage designs, for example, theatres-in-the-round, use variants of this design. Some directors have opted for open-air stages, or have used any available space. *If you were directing a production of* Ti-Jean and His Brothers, *what would be your choice of stage?*

Stage business

The actions and behaviours of characters onstage are generally determined by cues given either explicitly in the stage directions, or implicitly through the dialogue and actions suggested by the dialogue. Stage business can give us clues to a character's personality or state of mind, and also helps explain or emphasize particular lines or moments. Directors also use stage business to keep actors not involved in the central action from appearing embarrassingly wooden on stage. The use of too much stage business, however, can detract from a production. *What kind of stage business might a director assign to the Planter during his conversation with Gros Jean in Act One (pages 38–40)?*

Stage geography

Traditional proscenium stages are divided into four broad areas as considered from the actors' viewpoint: stage right, stage left, downstage (closer to the audience) and upstage (away from the audience).

Stage properties (props)

These include the furniture or bulky objects onstage which are not an integral part of the actual set, the trim or props used to decorate or dress a set and the hand props, or items handled by the actors onstage. Responsibility for their care and attention lies with the property manager. *Identify props that must be used in a production of* Ti-Jean and His Brothers *by each of the following: Gros Jean, Mi-Jean and the Devil /Planter/Papa Bois.*

Explanatory words, phrases and notes
Prologue

page 24 'Greek-croak, Greek-croak'   Walcott puns on the traditional croaking sound of the frog to acknowledge the partial roots of the play in classical Greek drama.

page 24 'Aeschylus me!'   Another Walcott pun ('Excuse me'), also acknowledging Greek drama. Aeschylus (c. 525–455 BCE) was a Greek dramatist credited with introducing the use of multiple, interacting characters within the chorus, rather than having the chorus speak in unison, a pattern Walcott follows in this play.

page 24 'And Ti-Jean in the moon'   The story of the man-in-the-moon who outwitted the Devil is a traditional St Lucian folktale.

page 24 'The cricket cracking a story'   Another pun, this time on the tendency of storytellers in the folk West Indian tradition to end their stories with the words 'crick, crack'.

page 24 'faggots'   Bits of forest branch, etc., used for lighting fires in poorer communities.

page 24 Ti-Jean   'Ti' is the shortened and more intimate use of the French word 'petit', meaning small. The brothers are all called Jean for a dramatic purpose, 'Gros' (big) being the eldest and 'Mi' (from 'demi', middle-sized) the second son in the traditional list of three sons in folklore.

page 24 Papa Bois   The traditional Old Man of the Forest in West Indian, especially Eastern Caribbean, folklore. He is a protector of wildlife and the environment, capable of transforming himself into animal form to lure hunters into the forest and get them lost. Tradition demands that you greet him politely and refrain from staring at his cloven hoof.

page 25 Stage directions: 'Comic quatro, martial'   The quatro (or cuatro) is a four-stringed instrument, a larger version of a ukulele, and of Latin American origin. Note that it accompanies Gros Jean.

page 25 'Old hands dried up like claws'   Note the poetic elements of the language up to the arrival of the Devil onstage. Look for other instances of this throughout the play.

page 26 Arrival of the Devil and his group of fiends   This stage element draws heavily on the Devil bands prominent in traditional Trinidadian Carnival, featuring a King Devil surrounded by lesser imps.

page 26 *The Bolom*   Another aspect of West Indian folklore, with roots in West Africa. The unbaptised soul of a child that wanders lost in the forests is called a 'douen' in Trinidadian folklore. The Bolom is a feature of St Lucian folklore, a miniature individual, brought into being on Good Friday to do the evil work of the person who has summoned him/her. Walcott has united both traditions in this character.

page 29 *'Line the step with fine sand'*, etc.   A superstitious practice meant to ward off evil; also, turning over the hem of the skirt and using the fingers to form a crucifix.

page 31 *'a ball of moving fire'*, etc.   The evil spirits in West Indian folklore are imagined to assume several forms such as this. The 'clothful of skin' is the temporary human form a particular spirit assumes to prey on real humans, which it must shed before daylight.

page 32 Stage directions: *'The Bolom rolls in a blue light'*   The colour blue associated with the Bolom is the colour of twilight, of in-betweenity. Note the colours associated with other characters, such as red with the Devil, white with the Mother.

page 32 *'sovereigns'*   British gold coins used commercially for several hundred years. They were also minted in several other countries, such as Canada, Australia and India.

Act One

page 34 *'Maman'*   French, 'mother'

page 34 *'ça pas tout'*   French, 'that's not all'

page 35 *'Gibier'*   French, 'animal or bird', usually designated as prey for hunters.

page 35 Stage directions: *'cloven'*   Split in two. The cloven hoof, common to animals such as the goat and cow, is also associated with the Devil.

page 35 *'Bonjour'*   French, 'Good day'. *'Bon matin'* is specifically 'good morning'. *'Vieux papa'* is French for 'old father', the polite greeting required when meeting Papa Bois.

page 35 *'chiggers'*   Small bugs belonging to the same family as spiders and ticks. The name of the bug is used to describe an infection of the feet, caused by working barefoot in the fields or in contaminated water.

page 37 *'flesh is deciduous'*   Deciduous trees are trees that lose their leaves annually. 'Deciduous' also means to fall away after a purpose is fulfilled. The Old Man is echoing the Mother's warning to her son that physical strength alone is not enough in the world, and the broader theme in the play that humanity is a frail thing, subject to death.

page 38 '*Shime!*'   Variant of an expression, 'Oh, shims, man!', expressing exasperation. Roughly equivalent to 'for goodness' sake!'

page 39 '*the heights that great men reached*'   The Planter half-quotes the poet Longfellow's 'The Ladder of St Augustine': 'The heights by great men reached and kept/Were not attained by sudden flight,/But they, while their companions slept,/Were toiling upward in the night.' The Planter is mocking Gros Jean.

page 40 '*impatianate*'   A made-up word, punning on 'impatience'.

Act Two

page 41 Stage directions: '*foraging*'   Looking for food

page 41 '*But see my cross, oui, ay-ay!*'   To 'look at one's crosses' is to express surprise. The line means roughly, 'But what kind of strange things am I seeing here?' There is, of course, an intended pun on 'cross', given the onstage reality of Gros Jean's cross in the background.

page 42 '*le philosophe*'   French, 'the thinking man', or 'philosopher'

page 42 '*the jurist*'   The man of the law. Also '*avocat*', French for 'lawyer', and 'litigant', the lawyer who pleads a person's case in court.

page 42 '*whereas, and hereunto affixed*'   Phrases used commonly in legal documents.

page 43 '*tautology*'   Saying the same thing twice, in different ways. Walcott implies that the language of law can often descend into boring repetitiveness.

page 44 '*polarities of belief*'   Two apparently contradictory points of view held at the same time, each existing because of or nourishing the other.

page 44 '*Bon Dieu*'   French, 'My goodness!', literally, 'Good God!'

page 44 '*juck*'   Pronounced (and often spelt) 'jook', meaning to stab with a sharp instrument.

page 45 '*Socrates*'   Greek philosopher and teacher (*c.* 470–399 BCE) who was executed by the Athenian Government for corrupting the minds of youth and not believing in the gods of the state. Execution was via drinking hemlock, a deadly poison.

page 45 '*ruction*'   Violent noise, protests

page 46 '*bugger*'   Pest, or irritant

page 46 'bush lawyer'   Used to describe people who pretend to know about the law without having the required qualification. Also a term of scorn for incompetent lawyers.

page 46 'The goat'   To 'get one's goat' means to arouse someone to anger. In this ironic reversal, the Planter irritates Mi-Jean by ensuring that he does *not* catch the goat. Goats were thought to have a calming effect on racehorses and were put in the horses' stall the night before an important race; competitors sometimes stole the goats to ensure the horse would be upset and lose the race.

page 47 'the Devil comes in through apertures'   An aperture is a small hole. The Devil can exploit the smallest opportunity.

page 47 'Good old Master Speak No Evil'   A reference to the three wise monkeys of the Japanese proverb, 'See no evil, hear no evil, speak no evil', generally depicted pictorially with hands over eyes, ears and mouth respectively. Each verse of Mi-Jean's song praised one of these attributes. In the Western world, however, the proverb and image are often used to describe refusing responsibility, or looking the other way when action is clearly demanded.

page 47 'biped'   Two-legged. 'Capriped' (page 48) means having the legs of a goat.

page 47 'a plethora of cacophony'   A lot of noise. Mi-Jean uses big words to sound intelligent, with the result that he does not sound intelligent. 'Lustiferous', for example, is an invented word which should really be 'lustful'.

page 48 'Which Greek scholar ... animals?'   A reference to the theory popularized by the Greek philosopher Pythagoras, which claims that after death the soul transfers into another body, human or animal, as part of an ongoing process of reincarnation.

page 48 'animadvertently imbue'   'Animadverently' is another invented word that Mi-Jean thinks sounds important and intellectual. To imbue is to invest, or bestow on.

page 48 'pantheist'   In its simplest terms, someone who believes that there is a divine presence in all aspects of created life, human and non-human.

page 48 'apogee'   Literally 'the highest point'. Here, it means the most perfect.

page 49 'Descendant of the ape ... invention!'   The Planter partially echoes Shakespeare's *Hamlet* (Act 2, scene 2): 'What a piece of work is man! How noble in reason, how infinite in faculty!' Hamlet ends by saying that despite his apparent qualities, man is little more than mere dust; the Planter ends by saying man is little more than an animal like the goat.

Act Three

page 50 '*Power is knowledge, knowledge is power*'   The Old Man echoes the assumptions made by Gros Jean and Mi-Jean in the earlier Acts.

page 50 '*a veal-witted young man*'   Veal is the flesh of a young calf. Used here in the sense of 'weak', with an intentional pun on the word.

page 50 '*carnivorous*'   Flesh eating. A reference to the fact that flesh rots after death.

page 52 '*David*' and '*Goliath*'   A reference to David's slaying of the giant Goliath in the Hebrew Old Testament.

page 52 '*Ah, bon matin, compère Crapaud*'   French, 'Ah, good morning, brother Frog'

page 52 '*castanet music*'   Music created by knocking together small, concave bits of ivory, plastic or wood attached to the fingers. Predominantly found in Spanish and Latin American music and dancing.

page 53 '*Bonjour, vieux cor*'   French patois, 'Good day, old father' ('*vieux cor*' is French patois for '*vieux coeur*', meaning 'old heart').

page 57 '*Goat seed*'   The testicles of the goat

page 57 '*eunuch*'   Someone who has been castrated. Modern usage also suggests someone who is useless, or unable to express a personal opinion because of fear.

page 58 '*catechism*'   A brief summary of the important elements of any belief or doctrine.

page 59 '*Ayti?*'   A pun on Ti-Jean's name ('Aye, Ti') as well as on Haiti, the island where the first revolution against colonial rule occurred (1791–1804).

page 59 '*Burn the cane*'   Burning the cane fields was used to destroy pests and dangerous wildlife prior to harvesting. But burning cane fields also became an important part of and symbol for rebelling against enslavement and colonialism in West Indian territories and in West Indian literature. Interestingly, Walcott's Ti-Jean orders two of the three important plantation crops to be burnt: cane and cotton (the other was tobacco).

page 59 '*brimstone with a saltpetre chaser*'   A reference to the act of drinking alcohol, followed by a 'chaser', usually water or some other mixer. Here the alcohol is brimstone, the ancient term for sulphur, chased by saltpetre (potassium nitrate), used in the manufacture of explosive black powder. The inference is that this is what you get to drink in Hell.

page 60 'Fire one!'   The cane fields are being fired. Walcott again uses a drinking analogy: to 'fire one' is to have another drink.

page 60 'When I was the Son of the Morning ... Prince of Light.'   A reference to the biblical origins of the Devil as Lucifer, or the Morning Star, who once sat at God's right hand and is expelled from Heaven for wanting to be greater than God. Once expelled, he changes his name to Satan ('adversary').

page 61 'Show me the way to go home.'   First lines of a popular song about going home tipsy after drinking.

page 61 'the old fellow with the big notebook'   St Peter is often thought of as sitting at the gates of Heaven, assessing souls who wish to enter on the basis of the sins recorded against them in a ledger during their lives.

page 62 'Filambo! Azaz! Cacarat!'   The names of the assistant devils summoned to appear.

page 63 'hackneyed'   An insult, meaning unimportant or boring.

page 63 'two immortalities'   A reference to God and the Devil, both immortal.

page 64 'One moaning from weakness ... doubt.'   The punishments of both Gros Jean and Mi-Jean echo that of the biblical Samson, blinded and condemned to turn a mill wheel.

page 66 'To put two gold coins/On your eyes.'   The Greeks placed coins on the eyes of the dead as payment to Charon, the mythical boatman, who ferried dead souls over the River Styx to the underworld, Hades.

page 67 'creek. Crack.'   Walcott ends the play with another pun, but using the traditional Caribbean folktale sign-off.

Review questions

Prologue

1 How does the Prologue set the scene for all that is to follow later in the play?

2 Ti-Jean has little to say in the Prologue, but a good director would give him lots of stage business so that he doesn't remain unseen and forgotten while others are in the spotlight. What would you have him do:

   a when his older brothers are complaining that he does nothing (page 28)

   b when the Bolom makes its presence felt (page 28)

   c while the Bolom and his Mother are conversing (pages 29–30)?

3 You have been asked to play the role of the Bolom in a stage production, with responsibility for your own costume and onstage actions. Describe and explain your choices.

4 What are the origins of the Bolom? What role(s) does it perform in the Prologue? How do all of the production elements involved (lighting, stage direction, music, offstage noises, dialogue) combine to make the Bolom frightening? Why do you think it seems at times to reach out to the Mother?

5 The Mother is set up as a dramatic foil, or adversary, to the Devil. What are the qualities in the Mother that an actress must emphasize to demonstrate this? What line of dialogue or actions in the Prologue support each characteristic you have identified?

6 Gros Jean has an arm of iron, walks to the accompaniment of martial (military) music and carries an axe, which he is reluctant to get wet. Why do the forest creatures laugh at him?

7 There are several moments in the Prologue that invite the use of stage effects. Identify two or three of these, and the stage effects you would include as a director.

8 Why does the playwright use several forest creatures instead of using a single individual as narrator or a chorus? Are they differentiated from each other in any way? What is their function in the play?

9 What do we learn about the conditions of life experienced by the family from the:

   a stage décor

   b background music

   c comments of the forest creatures

   d comments made by the characters themselves?

Contrast these to the lifestyle and activities of the Devil as described by the:

   a Mother (page 28)

   b Bolom (page 32).

10 Identify elements or moments in the Prologue that show the playwright's familiarity with:

   a Greek playwriting tradition

   b West Indian folklore

   c modern existential theory (which argues that human life is an ongoing struggle, and that we cannot rely on divine assistance to save us).

Act One

1 The focus of Act One is Gros Jean and his journey to his ultimate fate. What do we learn about Gros Jean from:

   a what he says and sings about himself

   b his attitude to and treatment of the forest creatures and the Old Man, prior to his encounter with the Planter?

Are these findings consistent with what we learned from the forest creatures and Gros Jean himself in the Prologue?

2 Gros Jean is easily outwitted by the Planter/Devil. How does Gros Jean's arm of iron help him, if at all? What strategies does the Devil use to annoy Gros Jean and win his wager? What is achieved by constantly addressing him by the wrong name?

3 The playwright identifies the Planter with the Devil. Which two themes of the play are unified by using this dramatic device?

4 On the evidence of this Act, is the Old Man another aspect of the Devil, or a unique character in his own regard? Support your reasoning by referring to the text.

5 Events in this Act take place in three different locations. How would you stage the events in this Act without destroying the continuity of the action?

6 Consider the costuming required for the Old Man, given that the same actor will also play the Planter as well as the Devil. What would be your recommendations as costume designer?

7 Examine Gros Jean's song carefully (page 35). What clues are given in the stage directions as to its rhythm and accompaniment? How would this song be best delivered by the actor playing the role?

8 Read Gros Jean's monologue (pages 37–38) about meeting and working for the Planter. What challenges face an actor in delivering such a long, uninterrupted sequence of lines? How might these challenges be overcome in a live production?

Act Two

1 How does Mi-Jean's treatment of the forest creatures echo that of Gros Jean? Is it consistent with their mother's advice in the Prologue and Act One?

2 Mi-Jean boasts of being a scholar and an aspiring lawyer. Why does Walcott make him a fisherman and equip him with a net as a stage prop?

3 What is Mi-Jean's strategy for dealing with the Planter/Devil's wiles? What causes this strategy to fail?

4 Like Gros Jean, Mi-Jean is also given a song (pages 44–45). How does it reflect his character? Is it ironic in any way, i.e. does it point critically back at Mi-Jean? How should an actor sing this? Should Mi-Jean stand motionless onstage while singing or not?

5 Mi-Jean's attempts to catch the goat make for great visual comedy, or slapstick. What other kinds of humour have you observed in Act Two?

6 Provide further evidence that one of the playwright's intentions in this play is to suggest that human existence is full of struggles and contradictions.

7 It has been argued that Mi-Jean represents a phase in regional history when the colonial subject, with no other known role model, imitates the airs and behaviours of his former masters. What evidence supports this theory?

Act Three

1 This Act begins at dawn, as have the previous two Acts. The action of the play itself begins on the evening before the first day. Is this reminiscent of any major Christian event? There are other groups of three in the play; identify them. Why is the number three so frequently used in religious, mystical and cultural traditions, as well as folklore, literature and drama?

2 How does Ti-Jean's treatment of the forest creatures differ from that of his brothers? What benefits accrue from this approach?

3   Gros Jean roughs up the Old Man, and Mi-Jean's cockiness leads him to both ignore the Old Man's advice and to make incorrect conclusions about him. What are the differences in Ti-Jean's approach?

4   Ti-Jean's mother advises him to use 'Instinct', 'Conscience' and 'plain sense' as he ventures out (page 51). Is there any evidence in this Act that he heeds her advice? What advice did she give to his older brothers, and with what results?

5   'The snake moves from me', the Old Man tells Ti-Jean (page 54). How do you interpret this line?

6   We return, in this Act, to what the Bolom said about the Devil in the Prologue: 'He is dying to be human.' (page 32). Does the Devil betray any inner conflict in this Act? If so, what does he seem to regret most? Does his growing intoxication influence his mood?

7   Identify the various colours associated with certain characters in the play. Suggest imaginative ways in which a lighting director could help the audience relate to the significance of these colours.

8   Ti-Jean represents, partially at least, the power of the Christian tradition in perpetual conflict with the Devil. Identify three occasions in Act Three where this becomes obvious.

9   'For the next dish is man-wit, common sense.' (page 50) says the Old Man as Ti-Jean approaches. On what occasions does Ti-Jean demonstrate that common sense is an integral part of our defences against all evil?

10 The Devil remarks that he and God are sometimes indistinguishable from each other. When does he do so? What point is the playwright making by repeating this line?

11 Given Caribbean history, what significance does the burning of the cane fields and cotton fields acquire? Is there a similar undertone to the castration of the goat?

12 Each of the three songs Ti-Jean is given to sing in this Act occur in different contexts. Given their differing contexts, how would you expect each to be delivered?

13 There are cues for significant onstage spectacle in this Act. Identify three such moments. What does each sequence demand? Would the play be any less effective if these elements were omitted?

Essay questions

1 Walcott has often called *Ti-Jean and His Brothers* his most West Indian play. Account for his opinion.

2 Why does the playwright use French, French patois and local dialect in this play? What advantages and disadvantages does this present?

3 What is the so-called fourth wall in a dramatic production? Identify three occasions in *Ti-Jean and His Brothers* when characters break through this fourth wall. What happens as a result of using this device?

4 What is the function of the Bolom in *Ti-Jean and His Brothers*? What challenges face an actor or director when presenting this character onstage?

5 The play is constructed so that the same actor plays the Old Man/Papa Bois, the Planter and the Devil. Suggest reasons for this.

6 If you interpret *Ti-Jean and His Brothers* as depicting, among other things, resistance and rebellion against colonial rule and oppression, what dimension or historical moment would each brother represent? Why does Ti-Jean succeed, where the others fail?

7 Defend the proposition that *Ti-Jean and His Brothers* is a deceptively simple play that deals with fairly significant ideas.

8 Lighting, music, dance, spectacle and sound effects are essential aspects of this production. Describe three moments in the play when these production elements are especially effective.

9 What are the functions of the forest creatures in this production? Are they distinguishable from each other in any way?

10 Discuss the role of the Mother in *Ti-Jean and His Brothers* with specific reference to her:

   a role as guide and mentor to her children

   b role as dramatic foil to the Devil

   c importance as an agent of intercession in the final Act of the play.